Building the Modern Workplace with SharePoint Online

Solutions with SPFx, Power Automate, Power Apps, Teams, and PVA

Harinarayanan V P

Apress®

Building the Modern Workplace with SharePoint Online: Solutions with SPFx, Power Automate, Power Apps, Teams, and PVA

Harinarayanan V P
Melbourne, VIC, Australia

ISBN-13 (pbk): 978-1-4842-6944-2   ISBN-13 (electronic): 978-1-4842-6945-9
https://doi.org/10.1007/978-1-4842-6945-9

Managing Director, Apress Media LLC: Welmoed Spahr
Acquisitions Editor: Smriti Srivastava
Development Editor: Matthew Moodie
Coordinating Editor: Shrikant Vishwakarma

Cover designed by eStudioCalamar

Cover image designed by Pexels

Distributed to the book trade worldwide by Springer Science+Business Media LLC, 1 New York Plaza, Suite 4600, New York, NY 10004. Phone 1-800-SPRINGER, fax (201) 348-4505, e-mail orders-ny@springer-sbm. com, or visit www.springeronline.com. Apress Media, LLC is a California LLC and the sole member (owner) is Springer Science + Business Media Finance Inc (SSBM Finance Inc). SSBM Finance Inc is a **Delaware** corporation.

For information on translations, please e-mail booktranslations@springernature.com; for reprint, paperback, or audio rights, please e-mail bookpermissions@springernature.com.

Apress titles may be purchased in bulk for academic, corporate, or promotional use. eBook versions and licenses are also available for most titles. For more information, reference our Print and eBook Bulk Sales web page at http://www.apress.com/bulk-sales.

Any source code or other supplementary material referenced by the author in this book is available to readers on GitHub via the book's product page, located at www.apress.com/978-1-4842-6944-2. For more detailed information, please visit http://www.apress.com/source-code.

Printed on acid-free paper

This book is dedicated to the loving memory of my dear friend, Jojo Varghese, who taught me the difference between a CPU and a monitor. Your love, your voice, and your laughter will forever be imprinted in our minds.

Table of Contents

About the Author

Harinarayanan V P is a seasoned SharePoint professional with more than ten years of experience in the design and development of applications using Microsoft 365, SharePoint, Azure, Teams, Power Platform, .NET, and React. He has built SharePoint solutions for various clients across the world. He is a Microsoft Certified Azure Solutions Architect, a Microsoft 365 developer, and a Power Platform developer. He is based in Melbourne, Australia, and works as a SharePoint specialist in the Victorian public sector. His email is harivpau@gmail.com.

About the Technical Reviewer

 **Vijai Anand Ramalingam** is a Microsoft MVP in Office apps and services and an experienced modern workplace architect with deep knowledge of SharePoint and Office 365. He is a blogger, author, and speaker, and has published 1,300 blogs and articles on C# Corner. He currently works as a technology architect at Cognizant Technology Solutions in the United Kingdom. Vijai has worked on Microsoft SharePoint on-site and online, Office 365, and Azure.

Acknowledgments

I must begin by thanking my amazing wife, Divya, for her steady motivation and nurturing support while writing this book. I would like to thank our little daughter, Ithal, for her adorable interruptions throughout the process 😊. I would like to thank my mom for her endless care and support.

Thanks to everyone at Apress for giving me the opportunity to publish my first book. Special thanks to Shrikant Vishwakarma, the coordinating editor, who made my job easy by providing continuous support, and Smriti Srivastava, the acquisitions editor.

I would also like to thank Vijai Anand Ramalingam, the technical reviewer, and Matthew Moodie, the development editor for their excellent suggestions and corrections. Finally, I would like to thank all my wonderful friends and coworkers, who have been an integral part of my SharePoint journey.

Introduction

Offering endless integration capabilities, SharePoint Online is a great choice to build a workplace solution. You might have already decided to use SharePoint Online to develop your modern workplace solution. In this book, I'll try to help you in your decision-making process and guide you in your building process from start to end. We'll go through different areas of development that are possible with SharePoint Online and see how the platform can be used to leverage your needs in building a modern digital workplace.

The chapters are designed to help you convert a set of requirements to the most practical and modern solutions by integrating SharePoint Online with the other Microsoft 365 suite of products. The approach used in this book is mostly focused on requirements, solution design, and development.

The focus of the first chapter is getting you started with the basics of SharePoint Online. Chapter 2 introduces a case study and familiarizes you with different kinds of requirements and suggested approaches. Each chapter from there onward discusses on different solution aspects using different methods and tools.

If you'd like to learn SharePoint Online development from scratch, this book is a great choice. If you'd like to learn about specific customization tools like SharePoint Framework (SPFx), Power Platform, and Teams, this book will take a problem-and-solution approach that will definitely make you proficient in using them.

CHAPTER 1

Getting Started with SharePoint Online

In this chapter, you will learn about the basics of SharePoint Online and how it can meet your needs in building a modern digital workplace. With endless integration capabilities, SharePoint is definitely a great choice for building a workplace solution.

We will start with an introduction to SharePoint and how it has evolved over the years. Next, we will get an overview of the platform's licensing, developer programming, and Admin Center. We will learn about how to add users to Microsoft 365 Admin Center and how to create a site. We will also learn about the templates, lists, list templates, columns, and content types that are available. We will then review the different developer tools and frameworks.

The "Permissions in SharePoint" section covers different permissions and how access is managed. We will receive a quick overview of Document Library and versioning. We will learn about web parts, pages, and how to add web parts to a page. By the end of this chapter, you will be familiar with basic concepts of SharePoint and the different tools it interacts with.

Not Just a "Point" to "Share"

I have encountered a lot of situations where it is assumed that SharePoint is just a place to share your content, much the same as Google Drive. It is not just that.

SharePoint is a collaborative platform where employees of an organization can access, author, publish, share, secure, automate, search their content, and much more. That's right, SharePoint is all about content and its presentation. You can configure it to meet your needs. That is the reason it is one of the most powerful tools for modernizing a workplace.

© Harinarayanan V P 2021
Harinarayanan V P, *Building the Modern Workplace with SharePoint Online*,
https://doi.org/10.1007/978-1-4842-6945-9_1

Quick Catch-up on SharePoint Yesterday and Today

SharePoint started out in 2001 as SharePoint Portal. Following this, the platform was upgraded to SharePoint Server 2003 and SharePoint 2007. SharePoint 2007 brought with it the content management and publishing features. SharePoint 2010 added quite a number of additional features as well as a new user interface. With SharePoint 2013, SharePoint 2016, and SharePoint 2019, the platform continued to evolve as an on-premises solution.

In 2014, Microsoft began offering SharePoint as a cloud service among its 365 suite of products. SharePoint Online does not require you to install anything on your current server, and you can access it from anywhere at any time. Our focus in this book is only on SharePoint Online.

Licensing and Admin Center

Before starting a project using SharePoint Online, you will need to purchase a Microsoft 365 license based on your specific requirements. Different regions have different licensing plans. Individual licenses can be managed from the Microsoft 365 Admin Center (Figure 1-1). Here, you can do such things as configure a license for a user to use premium connectors for Power Apps and Power Automate. I will cover the different licensing requirements in detail as we come upon them.

For the purposes of this chapter, it will be helpful to sign up for a free Microsoft 365 E5 developer subscription at `https://developer.microsoft.com/en-us/microsoft-365/dev-program`. The subscription can be extended for up to a year.

Once you sign up, you'll have access to the Microsoft 365 Admin Center, which you can find at `https://admin.microsoft.com/`.

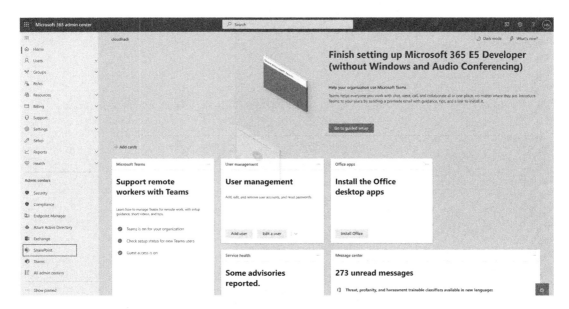

Figure 1-1. *Microsoft 365 Admin Center*

In the Admin Center, subscriptions can be managed from the Billing section, which you can access on the left side of the screen. Individual user licenses and groups can be managed from their respective sections.

You will also see a SharePoint option on the left, as highlighted in Figure 1-1. If you do not see it, click the Show All from the bottom of the left navigation.

Clicking SharePoint will take you to the SharePoint Admin Center, where you manage all your sites, content services, migration, policies, and other such elements, as well as your application programming interface (API) access (Figure 1-2). You can also manage Term store, User profiles, Search, and other features using the More Features option.

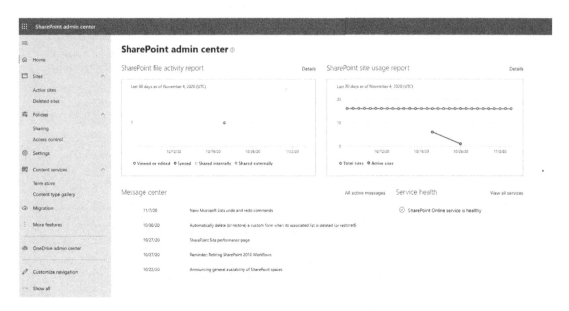

Figure 1-2. *SharePoint admin center*

Users

Before creating your SharePoint site, you will need to create at least one user in the Microsoft 365 Admin Center, as shown in Figure 1-3. Here, you can add a user, remove a user, export a user, add multiple users, reset a password, and set up multifactor authentication.

By selecting a particular user from this page, you can manage their licenses and roles.

Figure 1-3. *User management*

Site

A *site* is a website that contains different items like lists and pages. A site will have a home page. To start a project, you first need to go to SharePoint Admin Center and create a site. To do so, select Active Sites and then click Create, as shown in the Figure 1-4.

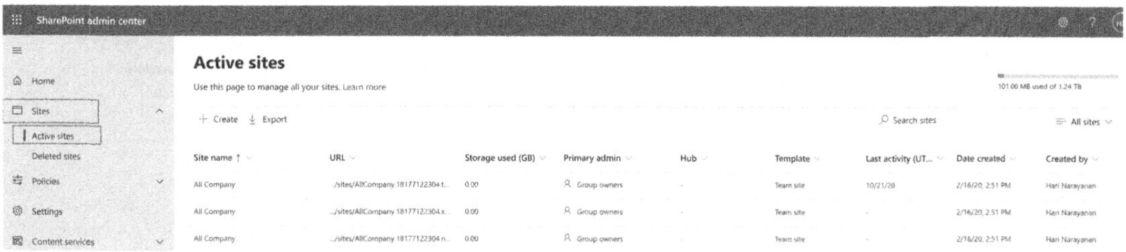

Figure 1-4. *Admin interface for sites*

Doing this will present you with number of templates that you can choose from. But before getting into that, let's have a look at what a site template is.

Site Templates

In SharePoint, site templates are prebuilt definitions for a site. These definitions are designed with specific business needs in mind. You can make use of these templates to create your own SharePoint site and then add in your own customizations after that.

In SharePoint Online, you will mainly come across two types of templates: the Team Site and the Communication Site. A Team Site connects you and your team to the content, information, and apps you rely on every day. You can use a Team Site to store and collaborate on files or to create and manage lists of information. The Communication Site, on the other hand, is a great place to share news, reports, status, and other information in a visually appealing way.

How do you choose between using a Communication Site and using a Team Site? As an example, consider a COVID-19 research department where the team members have a Team Site that they use to collaborate on data and reports. During the preparation of these items, the team members have the option to work privately.

Another scenario would be an intranet where managers post news and other useful information for their employees. A Communication Site would be an ideal choice here, as the employees do not need to know how the published information is obtained; they just need to receive the information, provide feedback on it, and so forth.

For our site, let's choose a Communication Site, as shown in Figure 1-5.

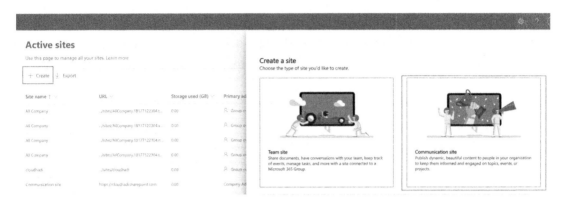

Figure 1-5. *Creating a site*

This will take you to a window where you can choose a design from the left-hand side of the screen; I chose Blank. If you were to select a Topic or Showcase, certain features would be added by default. This is a great option to use for getting started with a site, but for our site, let's use Blank.

As shown in Figure 1-6, you can enter the name, owner, and language for the site. In the Advanced Settings, there are additional options for you to choose from, including time zone and description. The availability of the site name will be checked immediately upon entering it.

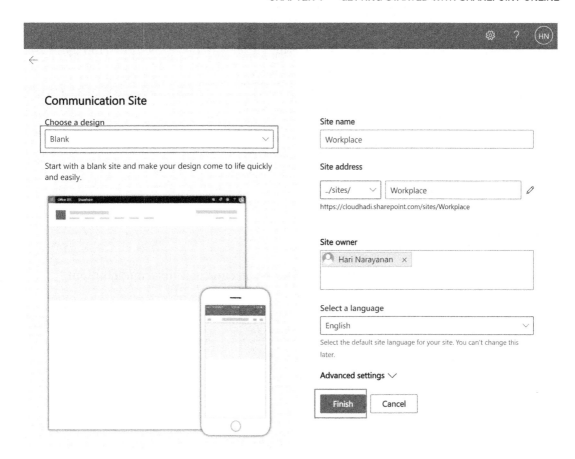

Figure 1-6. *Creating a Communication Site*

By clicking Finish, the site will be created in less than a minute. It will also be listed on the Active Sites screen, where you can navigate to the site by clicking the relevant URL, as show in Figure 1-7.

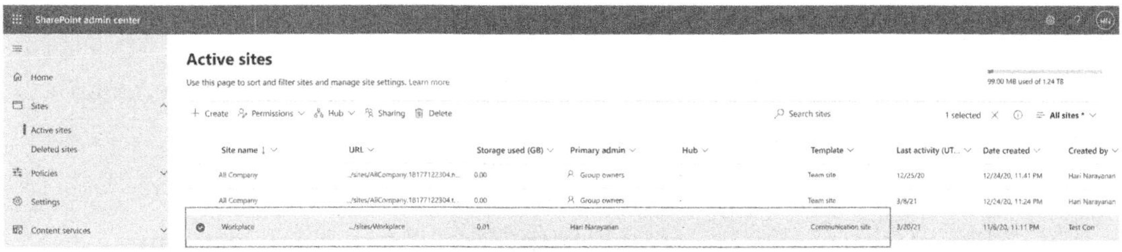

Figure 1-7. *Site is created and displayed in Active Sites*

Now you have created a Communication Site. By choosing the Blank template, the home page got created with only the headers and footers in place, as shown in Figure 1-8.

Figure 1-8. *Home page of a Blank site*

Configure and Customize

At the site level, what follows are the areas where you can customize and configure SharePoint based on the user's needs:

- Lists

- Libraries

- Pages

- Forms

- Search

- Web parts

- Workflows

- Security

Development Tools and Frameworks

We can customize SharePoint sites in different ways. Following are the modern and recommended tools for customizing sites with the platform:

- *JSON formatting*: Using JSON formatting, you can customize a list/ library form or view to a greater extent. We will go to this in detail in Chapter 3.

- *Power Apps*: Power Apps is a suite of apps, services, and connectors that helps you to quickly build custom apps or forms for SharePoint sites. Apps built using Power Apps have a responsive design and will run seamlessly in your browser or mobile device.

- *SharePoint Framework (SPFx)*: SPFx is a page and web part model that helps you develop client-side web parts and extensions for SharePoint. You can make use of Patterns and Practices client-side libraries (PnPjs) and Microsoft Graph to communicate with SharePoint inside an SPFx web part. The developer tool chain is based on open-source client development tools such as Node Package Manager (NPM), TypeScript, Yeoman, webpack, and Gulp. You can use any JavaScript framework for development, such as React, Angular, Knockout etc.

- *Power Automate*: Power Automate is a service that helps you create automated workflows. You can connect to SharePoint Online and communicate with many other programs using the service. In a nutshell, Power Automate helps you simplify business processes and manage them more effectively.

- *SharePoint REST service*: The Representational State Transfer (REST) service was created by SharePoint to help you interact remotely with SharePoint data by using any technology that supports REST web requests. PnPjs and Microsoft Graph are built using this.

- *PnPjs*: Patterns and Practices client-side libraries is a collection of fluent libraries for consuming SharePoint, Graph, and Office 365 REST APIs in a type-safe way. You can use it within SPFx, Node.js, or any JavaScript project. This open-source initiative complements existing Software Development Kits (SDKs) provided by Microsoft, offering you another way to consume information from SharePoint and Office 365.

- *Microsoft Graph*: Microsoft Graph (`https://graph.microsoft.com`) provides a unified programmability model that can be used to access data in Microsoft 365. Graph API offers a single end point that provides access to data in Microsoft cloud.

- *PowerShell*: PowerShell is a task automation and configuration management framework. You can make use of PowerShell to automate a huge number of things in SharePoint. It can interact with SharePoint using PnP modules, the REST API, and Microsoft Graph.

We will review all these tools in detail in the following chapters. In addition to the features just mentioned, we can make use of Azure services, such as Logic Apps and Functions, to customize SharePoint, although they are beyond the scope of this book. In the past, developers used the client-side object model, SharePoint designer, JavaScript Injection, Add-Ins, C#, .NET MVC, and other tools to customize SharePoint Online. Nowadays, these are no longer recommended unless there are no other options. They are also not covered in this book.

SharePoint Lists

A SharePoint list is a place where you can store and manage a collection of data. A list contains rows and columns, similar to an Excel table. The Calendar and Tasks are examples of Out Of the Box (OOB) lists offered in SharePoint. You can create a list with a variety of columns, including Text, Number, Date, and Time. Following are some of the types of lists available in SharePoint Online.

- *Announcements*: Announcements allows you to share news and status updates and to provide reminders. Announcements support enhanced formatting with images, hyperlinks, and formatted text.

- *Contacts*: Contacts allows you to store information about people or groups who you work with.

- *Discussion boards*: These boards provide a central place in which to record and store team discussions. The format is like that of newsgroups.

- *Links*: This list offers a central location for links to the Internet, your company's intranet, and other resources. For example, you might create a list of links to your customers' websites.

- *Calendar*: Here you can store all of your team's events or set a reminder of specific occasions, such as company holidays. A calendar provides visual views of your team's events in the form of features like a desk or wall calendar. You might record meetings, social events, or all-day events.

- *Tasks*: Tasks allows you to track information about projects and other to-do events for your group. You can assign tasks to people as well as track the status and percentage of a task completed.

- *Document Library*: A SharePoint library is a special type of list, the purpose of which is to create and store documents. Document Library, Site Assets, and others are OOB libraries in SharePoint.

In the site you created, if you go to the Settings column on the right side of the screen and navigate to Site contents row, you can see all the OOB lists and libraries offered (Figure 1-9). The Documents, Style Library, and other libraries are created by default, and once you set up your site, the Events list is created.

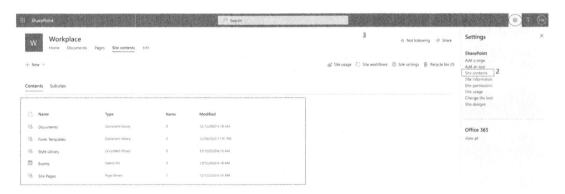

Figure 1-9. *Contents of your site*

Adding a Custom List

A Custom List is a SharePoint app in which you can store and manage content. It is like an Excel spreadsheet or a structured query language (SQL) table but with different capabilities. We can create any number of Custom Lists in a SharePoint site.

I will now take you through list creation and data entry in detail. If you're using SharePoint for first time, this can serve a strong basis to understand content management concepts in SharePoint.

For example, if you wanted to store your office's branch addresses, you could make a list called "Branch Information" with two columns, "Name" and "Address," and then enter information into the list. If you wanted to record the information for 15 branches, you would have 15 rows of information. Each row is called a list item, so you would have 15 list items.

Let's create a list from the site we set up earlier. To start, click the Settings button on the top right of the screen and then click Add an App, as shown in Figure 1-10.

Figure 1-10. *Adding an app in Settings*

Next, select Custom List from the set of available apps, give it a name, and then click Create, as shown in Figure 1-11.

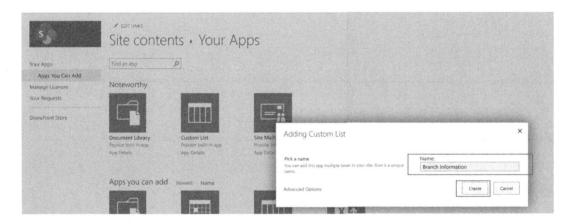

Figure 1-11. *Adding a Custom List*

The list will now be created, and displayed in the Site Contents section along with other items we created while making the site (Figure 1-12).

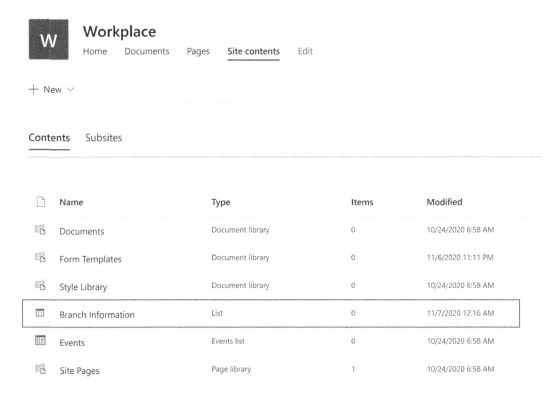

Figure 1-12. *New list added to the Site Contents interface*

Clicking Branch Information will take you to the list view, as shown in Figure 1-13. Here you can add a new list item, edit a list item, edit the list items together in grid view, export to Excel, and more.

As you can see in Figure 1-13, We only have the Title column available in the list. If we wanted to add more columns, such as "Name" and "Address," how would we create them? The best thing to do would be to create them at the site level so that the columns could be reused by other lists or libraries.

Figure 1-13. *Custom List interface*

Adding and Managing Site Columns

You can add a Site column to multiple lists. This type of column is reusable and ensures consistency of the metadata across sites and lists.

You can create Site columns using PnP PowerShell, which I will explain in upcoming chapters. For now, to understand how we can create and use a Site column, let's create one from a SharePoint interface.

To add a Site column, go to Site Settings from Site Contents interface, as highlighted in Figure 1-14.

Figure 1-14. *Navigating to Site Settings from Site Contents*

In the Site Settings interface, click the Site columns, as shown in Figure 1-15, to get to that interface.

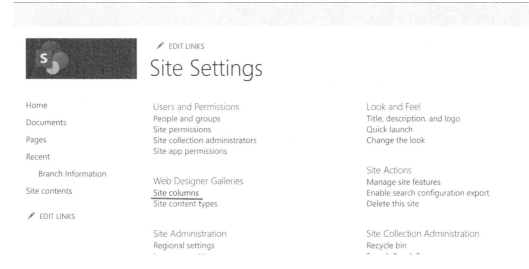

Figure 1-15. *Site Settings interface*

At the top of the Site Columns interface, click Create, as shown in Figure 1-16.

Figure 1-16. *Site Columns interface*

In this example, we need to create a column called "Branch Name" where we will enter the names of each branch.

As shown in Figure 1-17, add "Branch name" for the name of the branch and then type "Single line of text." For the Group, enter a new group name: "Workplace Columns."

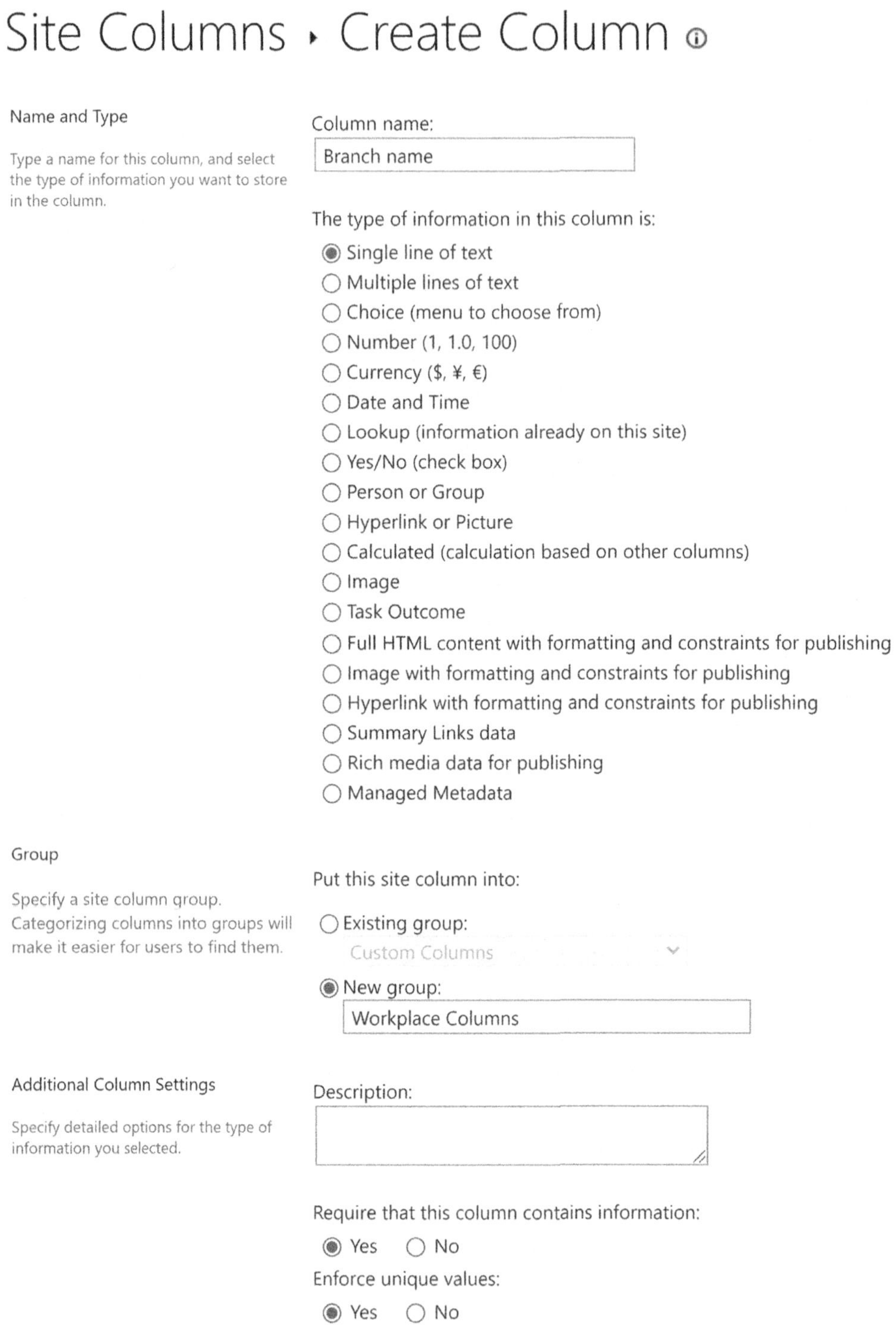

Site Columns › Create Column ⓘ

Name and Type

Type a name for this column, and select the type of information you want to store in the column.

Column name:

Branch name

The type of information in this column is:

- ⦿ Single line of text
- ◯ Multiple lines of text
- ◯ Choice (menu to choose from)
- ◯ Number (1, 1.0, 100)
- ◯ Currency ($, ¥, €)
- ◯ Date and Time
- ◯ Lookup (information already on this site)
- ◯ Yes/No (check box)
- ◯ Person or Group
- ◯ Hyperlink or Picture
- ◯ Calculated (calculation based on other columns)
- ◯ Image
- ◯ Task Outcome
- ◯ Full HTML content with formatting and constraints for publishing
- ◯ Image with formatting and constraints for publishing
- ◯ Hyperlink with formatting and constraints for publishing
- ◯ Summary Links data
- ◯ Rich media data for publishing
- ◯ Managed Metadata

Group

Specify a site column group. Categorizing columns into groups will make it easier for users to find them.

Put this site column into:

- ◯ Existing group:
  Custom Columns ⌄
- ⦿ New group:
  Workplace Columns

Additional Column Settings

Specify detailed options for the type of information you selected.

Description:

Require that this column contains information:

⦿ Yes ◯ No

Enforce unique values:

⦿ Yes ◯ No

Figure 1-17. *Creating a site column*

As shown in Figure 1-17, there are a number of different types of columns available in SharePoint, most of which are self-explanatory. The Group section allows you to add together a set of Site columns. Let's put all of our custom Site columns into a "Workplace Columns" group.

Figure 1-17 shows us that there are number of other properties we can assign, as well. The Require That This Column Contains Information option allows us to choose whether a column is mandatory or not. Let's make the branch name mandatory here. If you select Enforce Unique Values, the name of the branch will be unique and you won't be able to name two different branches the same thing. Let's select Yes here. Column formatting helps you to have a custom look for the column. I will explain formatting and column validation in detail in Chapter 3.

Click OK once you have filled in all the details. Since we chose to enforce unique values, you will get a warning. Click OK and the Site column will be created. You will be redirected back to the Site Columns page, shown in Figure 1-18. Here, you can filter Site columns based on the group and see the new column that we created.

Figure 1-18. *Site Columns filtered by group*

Let's next create another column called "Branch Address," as shown in Figure 1-19, by following the steps previously outlined. Select Multiple Lines of Text as the type of information since we will need to add multiple lines for the address. Choose No when asked whether it should be required that a column contains information and not required to allow unlimited length in document libraries as well. Select Workplace Columns in the Existing Group drop-down. Change the type of text to Plain Text. Leave the other properties as is.

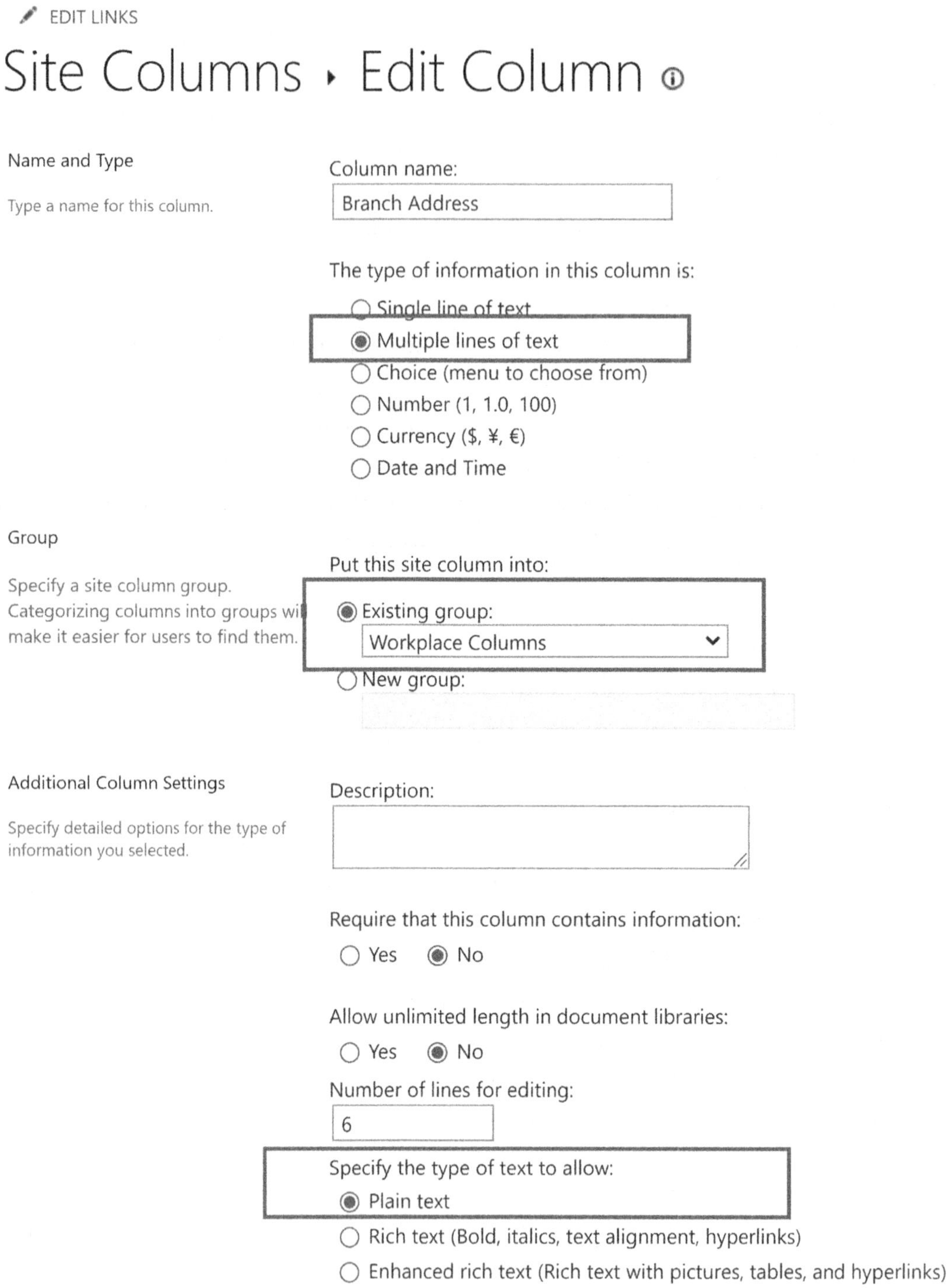

✎ EDIT LINKS

Site Columns ▸ Edit Column ⓘ

Name and Type

Type a name for this column.

Column name:

Branch Address

The type of information in this column is:

○ Single line of text

◉ Multiple lines of text

○ Choice (menu to choose from)

○ Number (1, 1.0, 100)

○ Currency ($, ¥, €)

○ Date and Time

Group

Specify a site column group.
Categorizing columns into groups will
make it easier for users to find them.

Put this site column into:

◉ Existing group:

Workplace Columns ⌄

○ New group:

Additional Column Settings

Specify detailed options for the type of
information you selected.

Description:

Require that this column contains information:

○ Yes   ◉ No

Allow unlimited length in document libraries:

○ Yes   ◉ No

Number of lines for editing:

6

Specify the type of text to allow:

◉ Plain text

○ Rich text (Bold, italics, text alignment, hyperlinks)

○ Enhanced rich text (Rich text with pictures, tables, and hyperlinks)

Figure 1-19. *Editing a column*

Once you've finished creating the second column, we'll add the two columns to the Branch Information list so that they will be available in the list for entering data. Go back to Site Contents by using the left navigation bar or the top right Settings button, as shown in Figure 1-20.

Figure 1-20. *Navigating to Site Contents from Site Columns*

From Site Contents, navigate to the Branch Information list as you did earlier (see Figures 1-12 and 1-13). From the list interface, select List settings as in Figure 1-21.

Figure 1-21. *Navigating to List Settings*

On the Settings page, select Add from existing site columns, as shown in Figure 1-22.

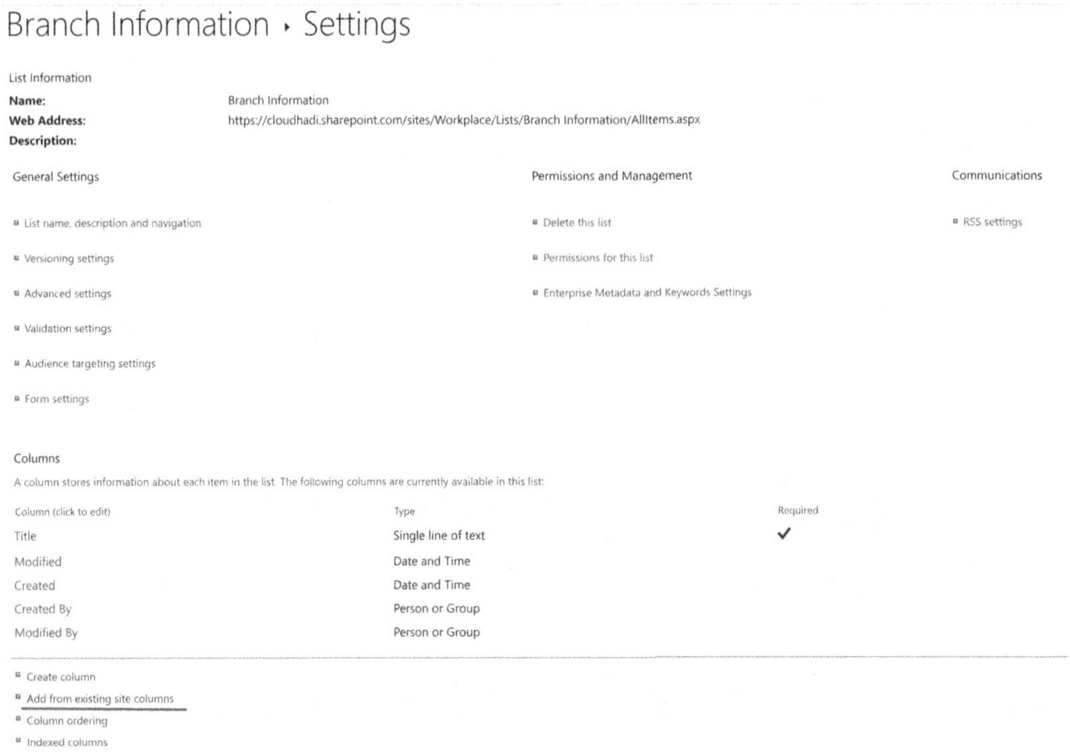

Branch Information ‣ Settings

List Information

Name:	Branch Information
Web Address:	https://cloudhadi.sharepoint.com/sites/Workplace/Lists/Branch Information/AllItems.aspx
Description:	

General Settings	Permissions and Management	Communications
▫ List name, description and navigation	▫ Delete this list	▫ RSS settings
▫ Versioning settings	▫ Permissions for this list	
▫ Advanced settings	▫ Enterprise Metadata and Keywords Settings	
▫ Validation settings		
▫ Audience targeting settings		
▫ Form settings		

Columns

A column stores information about each item in the list. The following columns are currently available in this list:

Column (click to edit)	Type	Required
Title	Single line of text	✓
Modified	Date and Time	
Created	Date and Time	
Created By	Person or Group	
Modified By	Person or Group	

▫ Create column
▫ Add from existing site columns
▫ Column ordering
▫ Indexed columns

Figure 1-22. *List settings*

As shown in Figure 1-23, select the group and then both Site columns. Click Add. Leave the Add to Default View box checked. Click OK.

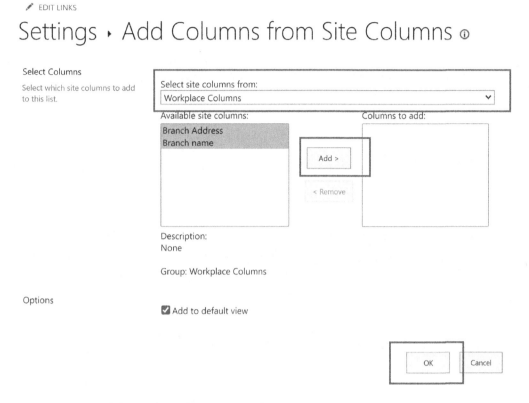

Figure 1-23. *Adding site columns to a list*

You will now be able to see both columns in List settings page (Refer Figure 1-22 above) under Columns.

Looking back at Figure 1-22, there is a Title column you can see on the first row of the section Columns, which is marked as required by default. Let's instead make it non-mandatory, as we do not need that column for this list. We can do that by clicking Title, changing Require This Column Contains Information to No, and clicking OK.

Scroll down and click All Items under Views section from the List settings page. List settings is page is shown in Figure 1-22, but you need to scroll down to see the section Views. A view is a way to show list or library data where you can define which columns to view and in which order. You can also define the filtering, grouping, and more. Clicking All Items will take you to the Edit View page, as shown in Figure 1-24. Uncheck Title and then click OK. The reason we're doing this is to remove the unnecessary Title column from view, so that you can get a basic idea of what a view is.

Figure 1-24. *Editing a view*

Clicking OK takes you to the list interface where you can see the two new columns in the view.

If you go to list settings, you can always add a column directly without having to add a site column. But in most of the cases, this is not recommended. The following table differentiates when you should use a site column and when you should use a list column.

Table 1-1. *Choosing Between Site and List Columns*

Scenario	Column	Reason
Column only needs to be used in a single list or library	List column	The list column is quick and easy to use here, as it will only be used only once.
Column needs to be reused across different lists and libraries	Site column	The site column can be reused across list and library boundaries.
Search	Site column	Creating a site column is easier for search functions, as doing so will create a managed property automatically.

In addition to the reasons for using site columns mentioned in the table, better maintenance is possible when using them.

Also, instead of adding Site columns directly to the list, you can add them to a Site Content type and later add the Content type to the list. A Content type is a reusable collection of metadata (columns)for a category of items or documents in a SharePoint list or Document Library. For example, you can create a Content type called "Product" and add multiple columns to it. From the list, you can add the Content type "product." All the columns in the Content type will be added to the list. Content types enable you to manage the settings for a category of information in a centralized, reusable way.

If you go to Site Settings ➤ Site Content Types, you can create a Content type. Once you create the Content type, you can add columns to it using the Create link. To add a Content type to a List or Library, you need to enable the management of Content types by clicking Advanced Settings from the List or Library settings. After that, you can add the Content type to the list. We will see this process in action in upcoming chapters.

Now, let's see how we can add a new item to a Custom List.

Data Operations in a Custom List

In this section, we will learn how to add and manage data in a Custom List. Let's start by clicking the New button from the List interface, as shown in Figure 1-25. A sliding window will then open on the right of the screen. You want to remove the Title column in the form and put the Branch Name on top of the Address. You can do this by clicking the pencil icon on the top right and click on Edit Columns. from the dropdown.

Figure 1-25. *New item form of a Custom List in SharePoint With the latest changes from Microsoft on OOB forms, you will see only a pencil icon in place of the 'Edit form' in Figure 1-25. Clicking on the icon will take you to Edit columns as in Figure 1-26)*

Clicking Edit Columns in the Form will give you the option to uncheck the Title box. (See the areas outlined in red in Figure 1-26 to follow along with the instructions here.) To move the Branch Name to the top, hover over Branch Name, click the three dots, and then select Move Up. Alternatively, you can just select Branch Name and drag it over Branch Address. Click Save to save your changes.

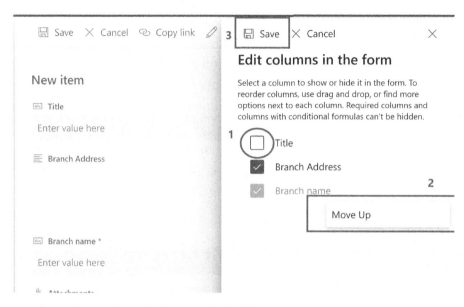

Figure 1-26.   Editing the columns in the list form

The Edit Columns in the Form window will now be closed and you can enter data in the New Item form. Save your changes using the top or bottom Save button. See Figure 1-27.

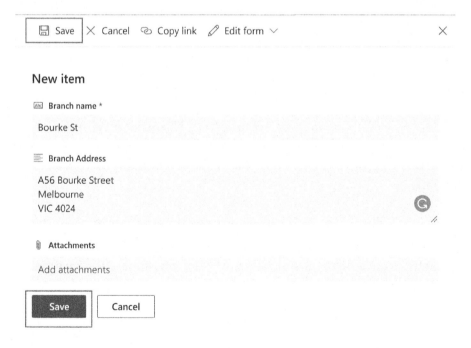

Figure 1-27.   Entering data in the New Item form

You have now created a new item, which will be displayed in the list view, as shown in Figure 1-28. You can select the item to edit or delete it.

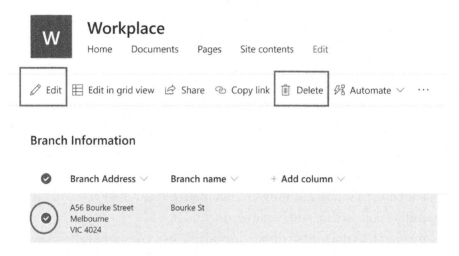

Figure 1-28. *List of items*

You also have the option to create and edit items in grid view (see Figure 1-29). Once you have created and/or edited an item, click Exit Grid View to save your changes.

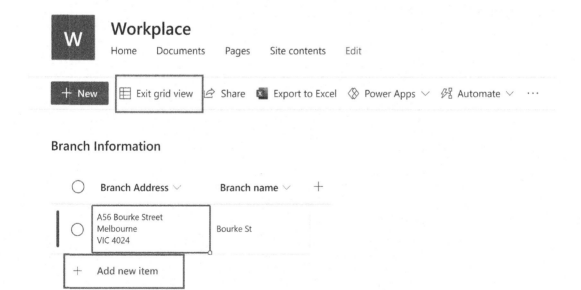

Figure 1-29. *Grid view*

You can add multiple items to this list either by using grid view, using New button or using the Add new item.

That should give you an overall idea of how to work with Custom Lists and site columns in SharePoint. You can explore more and play around with all the available options if you'd like to get more familiar with the features.

Document Library

Document Library is another SharePoint OOB app. In Document Library, you can store and manage documents, and add metadata to them. In a list, you can attach documents to a list item. However, list attachments cannot be searched as documents. Version control of a document is possible only in Document Library, which is what you should use if you want to collaborate and organize documents.

There are few OOB document libraries available in a communication site by default. Let's create a new one. We'll start by Clicking Add an App on the top right Settings button from anywhere on the site. Select Document Library from the Your Apps page, as shown in Figure 1-30.

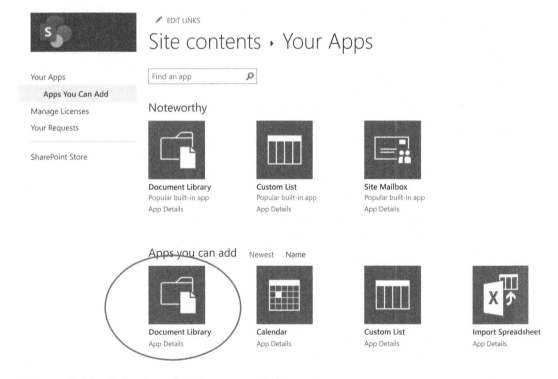

Figure 1-30. *Selecting the Document Library app*

A popup will appear where you can enter the library name. Enter "Policy" as the Document Library name and click Create. This is like adding a Custom List (see Figure 1-11); the only difference is that we're choosing a different app here. You'll be redirected to the Site Contents interface, where you can see that the Policy library has been created. Clicking this library takes you to the library interface.

Let's add the two site columns that we created earlier to this library. You can add more site columns if you'd like to. Go to the library settings and repeat the steps we took for the Branch Information list exactly (see Figures 1-21, 1-22, and 1-23). You do not have to update the Title field, as it is not a mandatory field by default here. After adding the site columns, the library interface will look like Figure 1-31.

Figure 1-31. *Site columns added to the library*

You can create a new document or upload the document from the library interface. To upload, you can use the Upload button or drag and drop. Once you upload a document, you can select the document and edit the Properties in the left-hand drop-down to fill in the metadata, as shown in Figure 1-32. Alternatively, you can use Edit in Grid View option like we did for the list.

Figure 1-32. *Editing document properties*

When the Properties window opens, click Edit All and fill in the metadata. Enter the data like you did for the Custom List in the "Data Operations in a Custom List" section (see Figure 1-27). You can fillin the properties as you filled it for the custom list item in Figure 1-27 Also, if you'd like to arrange the columns or want to remove any of the columns from the form, use Edit Form, as explained in the "Data Operations in a Custom List" section (see Figures 1-25 and 1-26). I advise keeping the Branch Name in the form, as it is a mandatory field.

Clicking the document will open it in Word. You can edit the content in a browser or desktop application. Save the changes once you're done and it will be updated in SharePoint.

This way, you can have multiple documents uploaded to a document library. What we just did is author the content. You uploaded the documents and set its metadata. But how will you ensure that it is visible to end users? How will you ensure that the documents are read-only for some users? How will you set up an approval before it is available to end users? How will you make sure that someone else from your organization/team can coauthor the content? We will get answers to all these questions. But before we do, let's have a quick look at the permissions in SharePoint.

Permissions in SharePoint

Permissions control access to the content in SharePoint. You can define who can read specific information and who can update that information. You can enable permission to access the entire site, a specific list or library, or even just a specific list item or document.

Let's take a look at the various permission levels and various security groups.

Permission Levels

What follows are the default permission levels for a site:

- *Full Control*: User has full control.

- *Design*: User can view, add, update, delete, approve, and customize.

- *Edit*: User can add, edit, and delete lists; and view, add, update, and delete list items and documents.

- *Contribute*: User can view, add, update, and delete list items and documents.

- *Read*: User can view pages and list items and download documents.

- *View*: User can view pages, list items, and documents, but not download.

Security Groups

On a site level, users can be added to security groups. Each group has an assigned SharePoint permission level. Permission levels tell the group what users can and cannot do. We can classify the user roles into the following three security groups:

- *Visitors*: Visitors can only read and download content from a site. The permission level assigned to them is Read.

- *Members*: In addition to reading and downloading, Members can add, share, edit, or delete content. Edit is their assigned permission level.

- *Owners*: Owners have a Full Control permission level assigned to them. They can do everything that Visitors and Members can do. In addition, they can manage settings, security, navigation, and other features. They can add users or remove users from the site.

To set site permission levels, go to the Site Contents interface (see Figure 1-12) and then Site Settings, where you will see a Site Permissions link (see Figure 1-15). Clicking that link will take you to the Permissions page, where the security groups and assigned permissions are selected. See Figure 1-33.

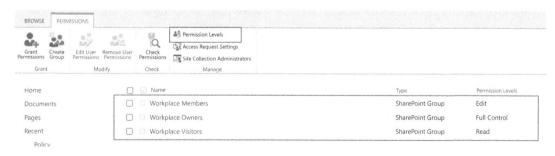

Figure 1-33. *Site permissions*

In addition to the groups just mentioned, you can create your own groups and assign custom-level permissions to them. But it is recommended that you avoid customizing these features unless required.

If you click Permission Levels on the Permissions page, (Figure 1-33), you will be taken to the Permission Levels page. Here, you can see the default permission levels and a list of additional permissions you can choose from (Figure 1-34).

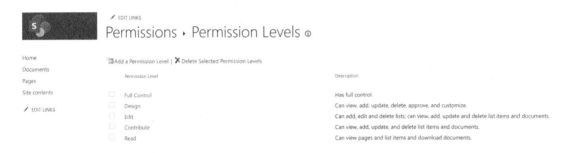

Figure 1-34. *Permission levels*

Permissions Inheritance

By default, Subsites, Libraries, and Lists inherit permissions from the site on which they were created (the parent site). If you break the permissions inheritance, the List, Document Library, or a document will be able to form its own unique permissions.

If you go to a list or library settings, you will be given the option to define permissions at the list or library level. Clicking Permission for this list will take you to the list permissions page. If you click Stop Inheriting Permissions, you will be able to stop the inheritance. You can then remove or add groups or users to the list. If you want to start inheriting permissions again, click Delete unique permissions. This will revert the permissions to being inherited from the site. We will look further at this action in upcoming chapters.

The best practice is to, as much as possible, have your lists and libraries inherit most of their permissions from the site. This enables easier management of permissions.

Now, let's go back to the Document Library and look further at the questions we had.

Version Control

Version control helps you easily track and manage data. For example, if more than one person wanted to update the content in a document called Bourke Branch Data.docx, version control could help you set that up. To get versioning set up, go to the library settings and click Versioning Settings, as shown in Figure 1-35.

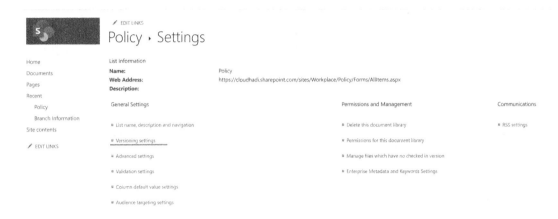

Figure 1-35. *Navigating to Versioning Settings*

In Versioning Settings, set Require Content Approval and Require Documents to Be Checked Out to "Yes." Leave the other settings as is. Then, click OK. See Figure 1-36.

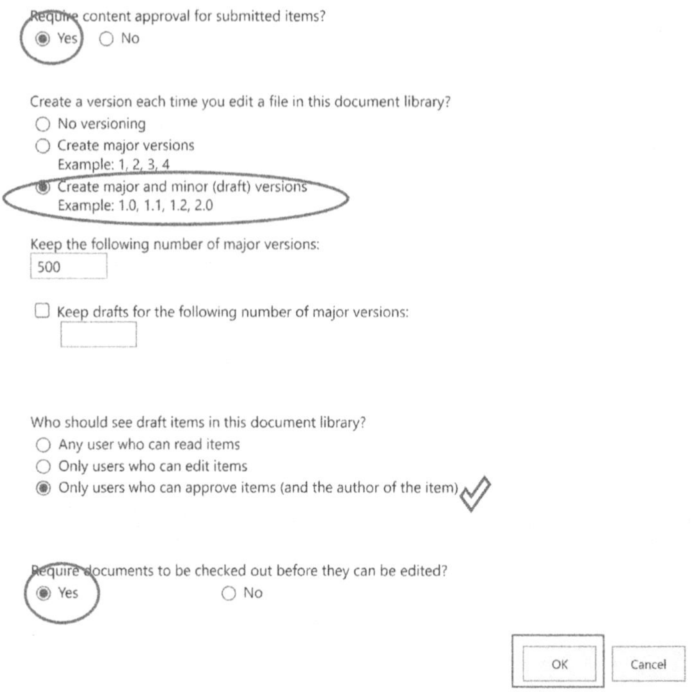

Require content approval for submitted items?
(● Yes)   ○ No

Create a version each time you edit a file in this document library?
○ No versioning
○ Create major versions
   Example: 1, 2, 3, 4
● Create major and minor (draft) versions
   Example: 1.0, 1.1, 1.2, 2.0

Keep the following number of major versions:
500

☐ Keep drafts for the following number of major versions:

Who should see draft items in this document library?
○ Any user who can read items
○ Only users who can edit items
● Only users who can approve items (and the author of the item)

Require documents to be checked out before they can be edited?
(● Yes)   ○ No

OK   Cancel

Figure 1-36. *Versioning Settings page*

Since we've enabled checkouts, documents will be checked out to users while they are editing a document. When they're finished making their changes, they can check the document back in. This guarantees that no two users can edit a document at the same time. As we enabled content approval and set Draft Item visibility for only certain set of users, users with only the Read permission won't be able to see a document unless they get approval. Let me explain this with an example.

If you upload a document to the Document Library, the document will be checked out to you by default. You can hover over the document and click the three dots to the right of it to navigate to the Version History, as shown in Figure 1-37.

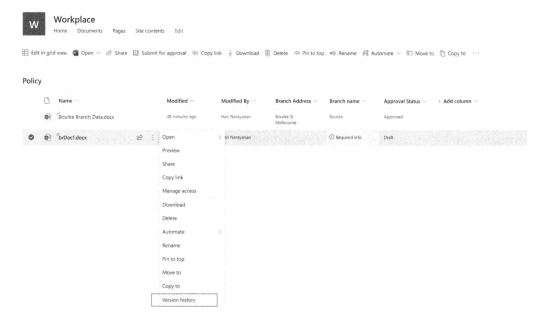

Figure 1-37. *Navigating to Version History*

When the Version History pop-up opens, you can see that the version is 0.1 and approval status is Draft. Close the pop-up and fill in the metadata as you did earlier by going to the context menu ➤ Properties ➤ Edit All. Until now, no other user could see the document, as it was not checked in yet. You can select the document and check it in using the context menu, as shown in Figure 1-38.

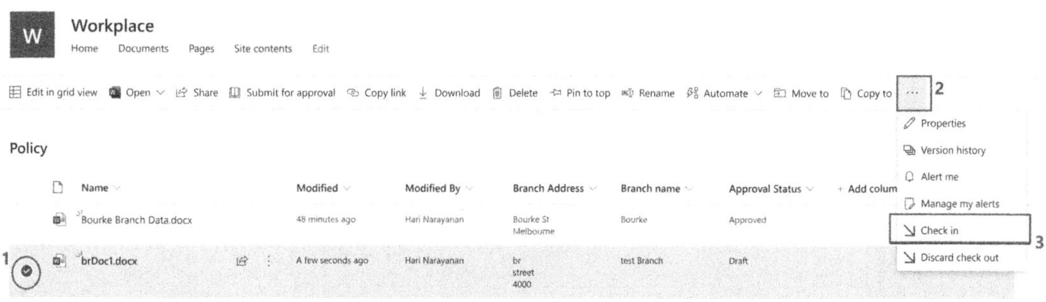

Figure 1-38. *Checking in a document*

A pop-up then opens. Select the major version and you provide comments if you choose, then click Check In. After the document is checked in, the document will be visible to all users with Approve permission. (See Figure 1-36, where we set the Draft visibility only to approvers).

In this site, all users added to the Workplace Owners group have Full Control permission. A Full Control level of permission is assigned when you have Approve permission and therefore users will be able to view, edit, or approve the document. Note that users with an Edit or Contribute permission will not even be able to view the document unless it is approved.

Select the document and click Approve/Reject on the context menu, as shown in Figure 1-39.

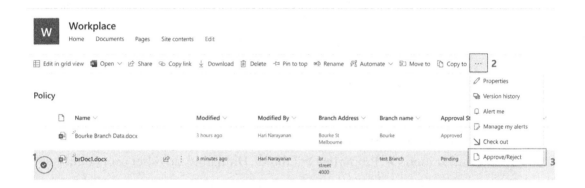

Figure 1-39. *Using the context menu to approve or reject a document*

The Approve/Reject window then pops up, giving you three options and explaining each option. Let's select Approved and then OK, as shown in Figure 1-40.

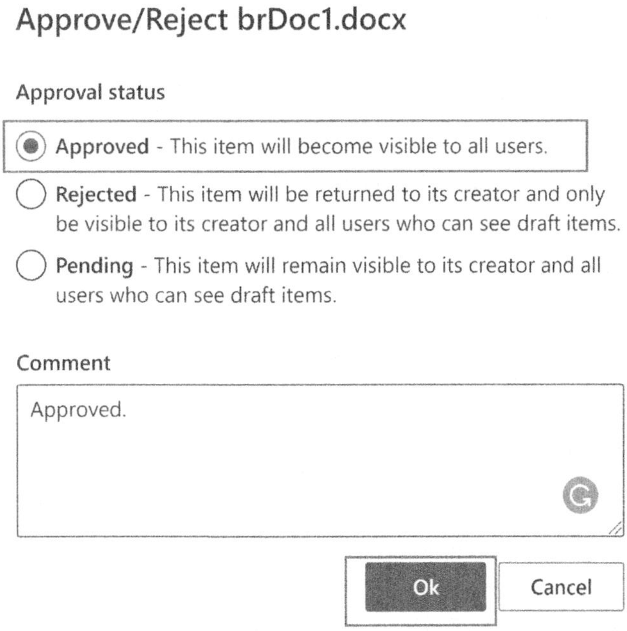

Approve/Reject brDoc1.docx

Approval status

(●) **Approved** - This item will become visible to all users.

( ) **Rejected** - This item will be returned to its creator and only be visible to its creator and all users who can see draft items.

( ) **Pending** - This item will remain visible to its creator and all users who can see draft items.

Comment

> Approved.
>
> ⟳

[**Ok**] [Cancel]

Figure 1-40. *Setting a document to Approved, Rejected, or Pending*

Since we set the draft visibility only to approvers, only users with Full Control can view a document unless it is approved. Since the document is now approved, all users with Read permission can view or download the document. Users with Edit or Contribute permission can edit the document content or metadata.

If you recheck the Version History (see Figure 1-37), you can see the current version as the published major version, 1.0, and the Approval Status as Approved.

Now that we've learned the basics of document management, you can go back to the questions at the end of the section "Document Library" and try to answer them yourself. I'm sure that you'll be able to. You've also learned about coauthoring, approval, and publishing, as well as how SharePoint maintains versions of a document and how you can define versioning settings. If you'd like, you can play around more with the Document Library, possibly enabling different users to edit one document, establishing different version settings, and anything else you'd like to try.

Pages and Web Parts

Pages in SharePoint are used to display content and web parts. A web part is something you use to store content and information. It is the building block of a page. Lists, libraries, and other features can be added to a page as web parts. The home page for our site is basically a page that got created as a blank page when we chose the Blank template. Let's now create a page and add some web parts to it to get a better idea of pages and web parts.

From anywhere on the site, click New ➤ Page from the context menu on the left side of the screen, as shown in Figure 1-41.

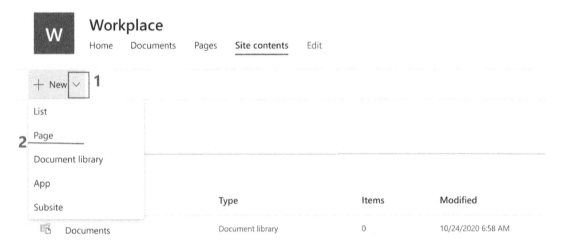

Figure 1-41. *Adding a new page*

A new page will be created, and you can provide a name for it. I named mine "Policy." If you click the Edit icon on the top toolbar, you can change the layout, alignment, and other features in the Title Area, as shown in Figure 1-42. Your changes will be autosaved upon closing. If you hover over your name below the Text, you can remove it using the Cross icon if you want to.

Figure 1-42. *Configuring the Title Area*

Clicking the + icon on left-hand side of the middle of the page brings up a Section Layout window, which allows you to add a section to the page and has different layout options. See Figure 1-43.

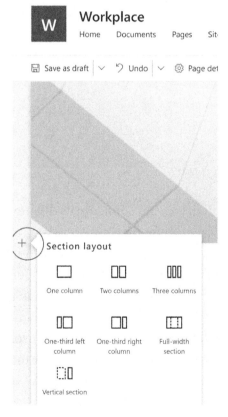

Figure 1-43. *Adding a section layout*

If we select two columns, a section with two columns will be created. Clicking the + icon in the first column will open different web parts that we can add. Selecting Highlighted Content, as shown in Figure 1-44, will display the most recent documents from the site.

Figure 1-44. *Adding a web part*

Once the web part is added, you can configure its different properties by using the Edit icon, in the same way as we did for the Title Area. You can try adding another web part of your choice to column 2. You can add multiple sections and web parts to the page. Have a look at different web parts available. The Properties pane will help you to configure the web part you choose. We will see how can add a web part in Chapter 6.

Once you finish adding the web parts, click Publish on the top right side of the screen. The page will then be published and visible to all users. If you want to make further changes, click Edit on the top right-hand corner of the screen (see Figure 1-45).

Figure 1-45. *Editing the page*

Now you can make changes and republish, as shown in Figure 1-46.

Figure 1-46. *Republishing the page*

You can customize the home page in the same way as you've done here.

Overview of Customization Needs

Let's take a look at what our custom requirements might be and how they will be addressed by various development tools.

When you approve a document or publish a page, it gets published. But what if you want to include few approvers and other conditions before publishing the page? We will need to bring in customized workflows to do that. Workflows are preprogrammed applications that allow you to automate the business process. We can use Power Automate or a third-party solution like Nintex workflow to create customized workflows. We will be covering Power Automate in detail in Chapter 5.

And what if you want to customize the list or library forms? We have option of using OOB JSON formatting to change the look and feel of the fields in the form to some extent. If you want to add complex validation and other such features, we can use Power Apps and SPFx forms. SPFx will give us more flexibility and performance.

If you want to create your own web parts and add them to a page, you can make use of SPFx web parts. In addition to this, you can use SPFx extensions to customize context menus, field behaviors, headers, footers, and more.

In SharePoint Online, we also have integration options with Teams, Power BI, and other options from the Microsoft 365 suite of products.

Summary

This chapter was mostly about getting you started. I gave you a quick overview of SharePoint Online and what is offered out of the box. You became familiarized with the Admin Center. You learned about site templates and different types of lists in SharePoint. We reviewed the different development tools and frameworks. You learned how columns, list items, documents, and web parts and pages are managed in SharePoint. We also went over how to manage security in SharePoint. In the upcoming chapters, I will take you through different customization options in detail and offer an application case study.

CHAPTER 2

Case Study

In the first chapter, we reviewed the basics of SharePoint Online. SharePoint Online can be integrated with many applications in and out of the Microsoft 365 suite. There are endless possibilities for designing an enterprise application using the platform. Let's look at an application case study and solve our business needs with the best available modern technology solutions.

From here on in, we will be doing a project together. At the end of the project, having finished converting some of the requirements into the final solution, you will have learned most of the modern customization scenarios and integration scenarios of SharePoint Online. This includes SharePoint out- of-the-box (OOB) capabilities; SharePoint Framework(SPFx) web parts; SPFx Extensions; the Patterns and Practices (PnP) provisioning framework; Search; Power Apps; Power Automate; Teams; and Power Virtual Agents (PVAs).

In case you do not understand the high-level solution mentioned for each use case, don't worry; I will be explaining each use case solution in detail in the following chapters. I provide the use cases mainly to give you an overview of the requirements before we design the solution.

By the end of this chapter, you will be familiar with how to design a solution in SharePoint Online. In addition, you will have learned about SharePoint site provisioning using PnP. This chapter will serve as a foundation for the upcoming chapters, as we will learn about requirements, design, and site preparation. Each upcoming chapter will concentrate on an area of technology while fulfilling the case study application requirements.

Business Use Cases

Let's say that an organization called Cloudhadi manufactures various types of products, including food, electronics, and furniture. Cloudhadi wants to build a portal where the employees can collaborate on documents and store and display product information.

© Harinarayanan V P 2021
Harinarayanan V P, *Building the Modern Workplace with SharePoint Online*,
https://doi.org/10.1007/978-1-4842-6945-9_2

The portal should serve as a central source where all of the information and its presentations are stored. The organization is the stakeholder for our project.

The stakeholder also wants to have a service desk option in the same portal. They want the home page to highlight the organization's products, achievements, news, and more.

Let's go through some of the use cases and see how SharePoint Online can be used to address them. Some of applications we will use are available OOB. Some will need customization and require that we use the best option available.

First, we will list out all of the use cases and mention the approach which can be used to solve each of the use case (high-level apprach). After that, we will organize the requirement and bring it into a design. In the following use cases, the use cases are denoted as "UC-" followed by respective category and number. The "Solution" that follows denotes the high-level approach of converting the use case into a business product.

Document Use Cases

There are many documents needs to be stored and published in relation to manufacturing each type of product: food, electronics, and furniture. The following use cases relate to managing the documents that accompany these products.

- *UC-D1*: "As a product executive, I need a place where I can create and upload product-related documents."

  - *Solution*: Create a Document Library called `Product Data`.

- *UC-D2*: "As a product executive, I want to create, upload, and read documents that are related to my product area."

  - *Solution*: Create a Document set for each product and set up permissions for the different groups of users.

- *UC-D3*: "As a product executive, I want to read and download documents related to other products."

  - *Solution*: Set Read permissions for other product Document sets.

- *UC-D4*: "As a product lead, I want to restore a previous version of my document in case of any wrong changes get made in the current version."

  - *Solution*: Enable versioning.

- *UC-D5*: "As a product lead, I want to see the history of changes made in the product document."

  - *Solution*: Use the version history feature.

- *UC-D6*: "As a product executive, I want my documents to be approved by the product lead before they are visible to end users."

  - *Solution*: Enable content approval and give the Approval permission to the appropriate product lead at the document set level.

- *UC-D7*: "As a product executive, I want the option to submit a product document for approval."

  - *Solution*: Create a field and use JSON formatting to provide a button so that it can call a Power Automate flow to submit for approval.

- *UC-D8*: "As a product executive, I want the option to choose a product lead from a set of product leads from different product areas."

  - *Solution*: Create SharePoint groups for each of the product leads in the different product areas and create a Person field to choose from the different groups.

- *UC-D9*: "As a product lead, I want to be notified if any user submits a document for approval."

  - *Solution*: Use Power Automate flow approvals.

- *UC-D10*: "As a product executive, I want to have the option to choose an inspection lead from out of the product leads in case a document needs their approval."

  - *Solution*: Create a Person field like we did in UC-D8 and use a Power Automate flow.

- *UC-D11*: "As an inspection lead, I want to be notified if any user submits a document for approval."

  - *Solution*: Use Power Automate flow approvals.

- *UC-D12*: "As a product lead, I want to enter metadata about my product and validate on a custom welcome page."

  - *Solution*: Use OOB forms with JSON formatting to create a custom welcome page for the Document set.

- *UC-D13*: "As a product executive, I want to enter information about a document I'm uploading and do basic validations for the metadata."

  - *Solution*: Use SharePoint OOB form.

- *UC-D14*: "As a product executive, I want to have a quick update option for the command set for documents where I can update only the document target date."

  - *Solution*: Create a custom list view command set extension using SPFx. The use case requirement cannot be achieved via OOB, as we need to introduce a custom button in the context menu.

Product List Use Cases

Let's say a stakeholder wants to maintain a list for storing product-related information. This list should contain all the products that are already manufactured, those where the manufacturing is in progress, and those that are in the pipeline.

- *UC-PL1*: "As a product lead, I want to enter project-related information into a product list and be able to update the status as needed. I want to have custom validations in the form such as autopopulating a field based on another field."

  - *Solution*: Use a Power Apps form. We won't be able to add the mentioned custom validation using OOB or JSON formatting. We won't require an SPFx web part for this task. Power Apps would be an ideal solution.

Page Use Cases

In this case, a stakeholder wants to set up a few webpages for an organization he is involved with, including a home page, an about us page, and other pages.

- *UC-P1*: "As a business user, I want to view recent company updates on the home page in a visually appealing way."

  - *Solution*: Use the Hero web part which is available OOB.

- *UC-P2*: "As a business user, I want to view the most recently manufactured products and details on the company's home page."

  - *Solution*: Use the OOB Highlighted content web part with product information.

- *UC-P3*: "As a business user, I want to be able to see the recent news and events on the home page."

  - *Solution*: Use OOB news and event web parts.

- *UC-P4*: "As a site administrator, I want to configure news and recent company updates on the home page."

  - *Solution*: Create a SharePoint group with Full Control permission to configure the information.

- *UC-P5*: "As a site administrator, I want to configure about us and employee offers pages on the site."

  - *Solution*: Create pages and provide a SharePoint group with Full Control permissions to configure the information.

Service Portal Use Cases

This scenario involves a stakeholder who would like to a set up a service portal on her company's site where employees can put in a request for services, like getting machinery and licenses, and the service desk team can respond to the request.

- *UC-SD1*: "As a business user, I want an interface where I can submit a request and view the status of existing requests."

  - *Solution*: Create SPFx web part and add it to a modern page, and also create a SharePoint list at the back end to store the requests. OOB JSON-formatted forms will not be suitable for this purpose, as we need to create a document with multiple forms that can handle different validations. You could, of course, do this using Power Apps forms, but we will opt for an SPFx for better performance in creating and retrieving service requests. Another scenario where you should choose SPFx is when you have more than 12 lookup columns in a list. Lookup columns include lookup, metadata, and person columns. Note that Power Apps forms cannot handle data if there are more than 12 lookup columns.

- *UC-SD2*: "As a business user, I want to have a live chat option where I can ask common questions and check the status of my request through Teams."

  - *Solution*: Create a chat bot using PVAs and deploy it to Teams.

- *UC-SD3*: "As a business user, I want to be notified via email when I put in a request and my request is responses to."

  - *Solution*: Create a Power Automate flow to get Outlook notifications.

- *UC-SD4*: "As a service desk executive, I want to be notified via both Outlook and Teams when a request is in my queue."

  - *Solution*: Create a Teams channel for service desk and set up a Power Automate flow for both notifications.

Navigation Use Cases

Navigation is an important part of a site. Users should be able to navigate to their desired location, where their access should be restricted according to their role.

- *UC-N1*: "As a business user, I want to have a link to view all products and a link to a service portal."

  - *Solution*: Make use of top navigation available OOB.

- *UC-N2*: "As a product executive, I should be able to navigate to product documents library where I can upload documents related to my product area."

  - *Solution*: Create SPFx Application Customizer to create a navigation link based on the current user. Because we need to add a link to the navigation and customize it based on the logged-in user, we should have an SPFx extension here.

- *UC-N3*: "As a site administrator, I want to configure a footer to provide a link to an about us page and other information about the company."

  - *Solution*: Use OOB footer settings.

- *UC-N4*: "As a business user, I want to be able to navigate to about us and employee offers pages."

  - *Solution*: Use OOB footer.

- *UC-N5*: "As a business user, I should be able to notify the Service Executives team immediately from the home page if an urgent issue arises, before raising a service request."

  - *Solution*: Use SPFx Application Customizer to create a link in the footer that posts an urgent issue message to the teams channel for service executives. As we need to communicate to Teams for this, we can make use of an SPFx extension to do the work.

Search Use Cases

Search is an important part of the requirements. Users should be able to search for documents or products and also refine their searches.

- *UC-S1*: "As a business user, I want to be able to search for all the documents related to all the products from the company's home page."

  - *Solution*: Use a SharePoint online OOB search box and search results page.

- *UC-S2*: "As a product executive, I want to be able to search for documents related to my product only."

  - *Solution*: Build a custom search page with a custom result source configured to filter for each product.

- *UC-S3*: "As a product executive, I want to be able to see specific metadata related to my product documents while searching for it."

  - *Solution*: Use a PnP modern search solution and update the display templates to reflect the required metadata.

- *UC-S4*: "As a product executive, I want to be able to filter documents based on metadata."

  - *Solution*: Use PnP modern search filters.

High-Level Design

Now we have identified the use cases and high-level approach for building a modern workplace for our theoretical company, Cloudhadi. In the following sections, let's analyze the above identified requirements and put them into a high-level design.

Identifying the Roles

If you were to go through all use cases, you could identify few roles, each of which needs to have its own access levels. Let's take a look at what the roles are.

- *Product executives*: Product executives are all the employees working to make a certain product, including the product lead. Product executives need to have access to view all the information on the site. In addition, they need to have access to creating and uploading documents for their respective products.

- *Product leads*: Product leads are responsible for approving the documents. Each product lead needs to have access to view all information on the site. In addition, they need to have Approval permission for their product document set. You might have come across an inspection lead in use cases. This is part of the same role.

- *Service executives*: This role needs to have access to viewing all information on the site. In addition, they need to have Edit access to the service portal list.

- *Site administrators*: This group needs to have Full Control access to the site.

- *Business users*: This category of users includes all the previous four sets of users, plus all the employees of the stakeholder. These users should be able to view all the information on the site. In addition, they should have access to add an item to the service portal list so that they can raise service requests. These users should not have access to editing the service requests, however.

One of the important things that we have identified is that business users require the most basic level of access for the site. For all the other roles, we need to set up permissions on top of the business users' permissions.

Designing the Security Level

Let's now decide on the SharePoint groups and permission levels. The following steps should satisfy the security requirements. These permission settings follow the principle of minimum privilege. The steps outline how we're planning to design the security for the site.

1. Let's start by creating a SharePoint group called `Cloudhadi Users` with Read permission for the site, and then add "Everyone except external users" to the group, thereby adding all business users. Once the service portal list is created, let's set unique permissions for the list and provide Add Item access for `Cloudhadi Users`.

2. Next, let's create three groups called `Food Executives`, `Electronics Executives`, and `Furniture Executives`, all with Read permission for the site. Once the library product data is created, set up unique permissions for each document set. For example, give Edit access to the `Food Executives` for the Food Product document set.

3. Now, we will create three groups called `Food Leads`, `Electronics Leads`, and `Furniture Leads`, each with Read permission to the site. Once the library product data is created, set unique permissions for each document set. For example, give Approve access to the `Food leads` for the Food Product document set.

4. Let's go on to create a group called `Service Executives` with Read permission for the site. Once the service portal list is created, set unique permission to the service portal list and give Edit access to the `Service Executives`.

5. Finally, we should create a group called `Site Administrators` with Full Control permissions for the site.

We now have a total of nine groups. Except for the `Site Administrators` group, all the other groups will only have Read permission at the site level. This is our base design for the security level. If required, we can make any adjustments during our project development and update the design accordingly.

Identifying and Designing Items

At this stage, we need to identify all the items that we will create.

We'll be creating all the items using Patterns and Practices (PnP) Schema and then deploy them to the SharePoint site using PnP PowerShell.

Site Columns and Content Types

Let's start with the Site columns. Table 2-1 shows all the Site columns that we need to create for the portal. Of course, we may need to alter or add some columns during development, and we can update the design accordingly. For now, let's start with the information we already have to design the solution.

In Table 2-1, the first column shows the site column title; the second column shows the type of column; the third column shows any special requirements for the column; and the last column displays the content types to which the site column belongs.

A Content type is a reusable collection of Site columns. A list or library can inherit Content types. In this case, we will need to create four Content types: `Cloudhadi Product` for the Product List; `Cloudhadi Document` for documents in the Product Data document library; `Cloudhadi Service` for the service portal; and `Cloudhadi Document Set` for Document sets. The latter will inherit from the existing OOB Document Set Content type in SharePoint.

Note   If you're new to SharePoint and find the terms here confusing, don't worry. They will be clarified in the upcoming chapters. And you can always refer back to the design if you need to later on.

Table 2-1. *Site Columns and Content Types*

Site Column Title	Type	Special conditions	Content Type
Product Name	Single line of text	Mandatory	Cloudhadi Product, Cloudhadi Document
Product Type	Choice	MandatoryPossible values: food, electronics, furniture no default value	Cloudhadi Product, Cloudhadi Document, Cloudhadi Service, Cloudhadi Document Set
Product Lead	Person or group	Single person, restrict to product lead group, mandatory	Cloudhadi Document, Cloudhadi Product
Materials Used	Multiple lines of text		Cloudhadi Product
DateInspection Completed	Date	Mandatory	Cloudhadi Product
Date ofManufacture	Date	Mandatory	Cloudhadi Product
Expiration Date	Date		Cloudhadi Product
Product Features	Multiple lines of text		Cloudhadi Product
Product Status	Choice	Mandatory, possible values: new, in production, completed Default is new	Cloudhadi Product
Review Date	Date	Mandatory	Cloudhadi Document
Required to Do Inspection?	Boolean	Yes or No toggle	Cloudhadi Document
Inspection Lead	Person or group	Single person, restrict to product lead group	Cloudhadi Document
Document Type	Choice	Mandatory, possible values: product information, product inspection details, product tooling data, product materials information, other	Cloudhadi Document

(*continued*)

Table 2-1. (*continued*)

Site Column Title	Type	Special conditions	Content Type
Date of Activity	Single line of text	Mandatory	Cloudhadi Document Set
Date Started On	Date	Mandatory	Cloudhadi Document Set
Capacity	Number	Mandatory	Cloudhadi Document Set
License Valid Until	Date	Mandatory	Cloudhadi Document Set
Goal	Single line of text	Mandatory	Cloudhadi Document Set
Quality Rating	Number	Mandatory	Cloudhadi Document Set
Request Title	Single line of text	Mandatory	Cloudhadi Service
Request Description	Multi line of text	Mandatory	Cloudhadi Service
Related To	Choice	Possible values: Access, Materials, Equipment, General	Cloudhadi Service
Request Status	Choice	Mandatory Possible values: New, In Progress, Resolved, Completed, Rejected, Reopened, Default Is New.	Cloudhadi Service
Request Assigned To	Person or group	Person only, restricted to service executive groups	Cloudhadi Service

Lists and Libraries

Table 2-2 shows the possible lists and libraries for the solution.

Table 2-2. *Lists and Libraries*

List/Library name	Content type	Purpose
Products	Cloudhadi Product	List to capture the product information
Product Data	Cloudhadi Document Set, Cloudhadi Document	Document Library for document upload, approval, and publishing
Service Portal	Cloudhadi Service	List to capture service request information

Site Pages

Table 2-3 shows the possible pages we can create for the solutions.

Table 2-3. *Site Pages*

Page title	Web parts	Purpose
Home	Hero, news, events, Highlighted content, SPFx custom Application Customizer	Home page of the site
About Us	Text	About us page
Employee Offer	Text	Employee offers page
Service Portal	SPFx custom web part	To display the service requests by pulling data from the service list
Search Product	PnP modern search box, search filter and search results web parts	Custom search page for products

Custom Web Parts and Extensions (SPFx)

There are few custom web parts and extensions we need to create according to the use cases. Table 2-4 identifies and lists them.

Table 2-4. *SPFx Components*

Web part/ extension	Purpose	Use case
Welcome Set	A custom form for entering metadata for each product area. It will be added to the welcome page of the document set.	UC-D12
Quick Updater	An extension for quickly updating the metadata of documents from the library interface.	UC-D14
Navigator	Application Customizer extension for creating navigation links based on the current user.	UC-N2
Notify App Customizer	Application Customizer extension for notifying service executive team of urgent issues	UC-N5
Service	SPFx web part for service portal page to display the service request.	UC-SD1

Custom Form (Power Apps Form)

Table 2-5 identifies some of the list/library form/forms that can be developed using Power Apps.

Table 2-5. *Power Apps Forms*

Form	Purpose	Use case
Product List form	For product list form and validations	UC-PL1

Workflows (Power Automate)

Table 2-6 shows the scenarios where we need to create a workflow in Power Automate.

Table 2-6. *Power Automate Workflows*

Workflow	Purpose	Trigger
Product Document Publishing	For the document approval process, which includes inspection and product leads approval and notifications	On custom button
Product Document Reset	To reset the document status when editing the document	On file modified
Service Request	To notify the service desk via teams and email on raising a service request	On item created in service portal
Service Action	To notify a requester once a service request has been activated	On item modified in service portal

Integration Scenarios for Teams and PVAs

Related to the service chat bots, we have some requirements to have Teams and PVAs integrated. See Table 2-7.

Table 2-7. *Integration Scenarios*

Action	Purpose
Teams channel creation	To create a channel for service executives to receive request notifications
Chat bot	To create a chat bot using PVAs and deploying to Teams
Integration	To integrate the Teams channel and bot to the service portal in SharePoint

A Quick Recap

To summarize what we have done so far, we planned how to build the solution, and we decided on the security, creation of items, customization scenarios, and more. During development, we can make minor changes to this design if required.

The purpose of this requirement gathering and design is to familiarize you with how to design a solution in SharePoint. Also, in this requirement I included all the technical areas I'm going to cover in this book. In the upcoming chapters, we will work on each of the technical areas and learn the technical solution and its real implementation. We will implement at least one of the use cases for each of the technical areas, such as Power Apps, SPFx web parts, extension, and Teams.

Creation of Items

In the first chapter, we went over how to create site columns, lists, and other tools from a SharePoint interface. In a real project, we would have three or four environments. There are multiple approaches to creating and deploying the items.

We could create all the items from SharePoint interface in a development site, then run a PowerShell command to take them all out in an Extensible Markup Language (XML) format. This is called the Get Provisioning Template command. We would then run another PowerShell command to deploy all the items to test and prod environments. The Apply Provisioning Template command is used here. In this approach of getting the template and then applying it to a site in another environment, there will be lot of unnecessary items and properties in the XML. So, we always need to do a cleanup before applying to another site.

Another approach is to create all the items in an XML format by referring to the PnP provisioning schema. Then use the Apply Provisioning Template command to deploy it to dev, test, and prod environments. Here, we're not taking any manual action from the SharePoint interface. The disadvantage of this approach is that you initially need more time to analyze and create the schema and may not be a practical solution for larger projects. Also, you need to acquire some knowledge of the schema. The advantage is that you will become aware of the schema and have much cleaner code. We will use this approach for creating items for our workplace project.

Whenever you want to make any updates to the schema, even if they are minor modifications, you can edit the schema and then deploy it using PowerShell without touching the SharePoint interface. This keeps the site protected from any manual changes.

PnP XML Provisioning Schema

We will use the PnP Provisioning Schema to prepare the items. The XML PnP Provisioning Schema is an open-source solution. The SharePoint PnP community is an open-source initiative coordinated by SharePoint engineering. The PnP Provisioning Schema is available in the GitHub community source code location: `https://github.com/pnp/PnP-Provisioning-Schema`.

At the time of writing, the latest schema available is the February 2020 version, which you can find here: `https://github.com/pnp/PnP-Provisioning-Schema/blob/master/ProvisioningSchema-2020-02.md`.

Before start creating this schema, let's have quick look at what development tools are needed for writing this schema.

Development Tools
Visual Studio Code

We will use an awesome code editor to create our XML schema. You can download and install it from the Visual Studio Code site: `https://code.visualstudio.com/`.

Once the code is installed, you can get an extension called Guid that allows you to generate GUID by pressing Ctrl+Shift+[. As shown in Figure 2-1, select the extension icon from VS code (selected in red), search for "guid," and click Install.

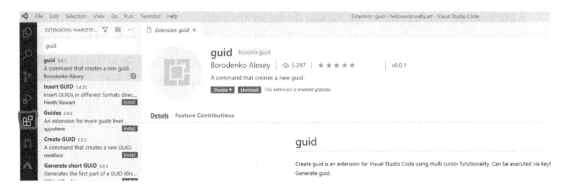

Figure 2-1. *Installing the Guid extension*

In a similar way, you can search for and install any XML formatter extension of your choice. I personally use an extension called XML for XML formatting.

SharePoint Online Management Shell

SharePoint Online Management Shell is a Windows PowerShell module that helps you to connect to SharePoint and deploy SharePoint items. You can download and install it here: `https://www.microsoft.com/en-au/download/details.aspx?id=35588`.

You also have the option of using Windows PowerShell Integrated Scripting Environment (ISE), which will make the PowerShell scripting easier.

Creating the Provisioning Schema

Let's create a new XML file and name it "ProvisioningWorkplace.xml" and open it in Visual Studio Code. Then, let's add the schema section by section and then put all of the sections into the parent schema. This "bottom-to-top" approach should help you to learn easier.

Security Groups

We can start creating the XML provisioning schema by setting up security groups and assigning them the permissions required at the site level. The design is based on the analysis we did earlier. If you want to refer back to it, go to the "Designing the Security Level" section.

Similar to HTML, a PnP element will have an opening and closing tag. Every PnP element will have properties in property name = property value format. Each property is a separated by a space.

Following is an example of a site group element that is called `pnp:SiteGroup`. Since we have a total of nine groups, there will be nine site groups and role assignment tags to add.

```
<pnp:SiteGroup Title="Cloudhadi Users" Description="Group for all business
users" Owner="i:0#.f|membership|CHWorkplaceAdmin@cloudhadi.onmicrosoft.com"
AllowMembersEditMembership="false" AllowRequestToJoinLeave="false"
AutoAcceptRequestToJoinLeave="false" OnlyAllowMembersViewMembership="true" />
```

Each site group will have the following properties: title, description, and owner. You can add a specific user account as the owner for all groups. The user should have Full Control permissions for the site. You will need to have at least one user with a Full Control permission, as an owner needs to be specified while creating the site. The other properties are explained as follows:

- AllowMembersEditMemberShip set to false implies a member can't add or remove another member.

- AllowRequestsToJoinLeave set to true means users can request to join or leave the group to a specified email ID. We're setting it to false.

- AutoAcceptRequestToJoinLeave set to true means users can request to join or leave the group and it will be autoaccepted. We are also setting this to false.

- OnlyAllowMembersViewMembership set to true means only members can view the list of group members.

All the `pnp:sitegroup` elements are be wrapped under the parent element `pnp:SiteGroups`.

Here is an example of a role assignment for the previous site group:

```
<pnp:RoleAssignment Principal="Cloudhadi Users"
RoleDefinition="{roledefinition:Reader}" />
```

Role Assignment has a role definition for each site group, which is the element Principal. In our requirement, only `Site Administrators` have the Administrator role definition, and all others have the Reader definition.

As you can see from the code, all the pnp:RoleAssignment elements are wrapped under the parent element pnp:RoleAssignments, which is in turn is a child element of pnp:Permissions.

It is important to follow this structure while designing the schema.

The final schema for all the site groups and its role assignments is given in the following code section. We will not add any users to any of the groups for now.

Note The source code for this book is available on GitHub via the book's product page: https://github.com/Apress/building-modern-workplace-sharepoint-online. You can use it for reference any time during our review. The files are organized chapter wise.

```
<pnp:Security>
<pnp:SiteGroups>
 <pnp:SiteGroup Title="Cloudhadi Users" Description="Group for all business
 users" Owner="i:0#.f|membership|CHWorkplaceAdmin@cloudhadi.onmicrosoft.com"
 AllowMembersEditMembership="false" AllowRequestToJoinLeave="false"
 AutoAcceptRequestToJoinLeave="false" OnlyAllowMembersViewMembership="true" />
 <pnp:SiteGroup Title="Food Executives" Description="Group for product
 executives for Food" Owner="i:0#.f|membership|CHWorkplaceAdmin@cloudhadi.
 onmicrosoft.com" AllowMembersEditMembership="false" AllowRequestToJoinLeave=
 "false" AutoAcceptRequestToJoinLeave="false" OnlyAllowMembersViewMembership=
 "true" />
   <pnp:SiteGroup Title="Electronics Executives" Description="Group for
   product executives for Electronics" Owner="i:0#.f|membership|
   CHWorkplaceAdmin@cloudhadi.onmicrosoft.com" AllowMembersEditMembership=
   "false" AllowRequestToJoinLeave="false" AutoAcceptRequestToJoinLeave=
   "false" OnlyAllowMembersViewMembership="true" />
   <pnp:SiteGroup Title="Furniture Executives" Description="Group for
   product executives for Furniture" Owner="i:0#.f|membership|
   CHWorkplaceAdmin@cloudhadi.onmicrosoft.com" AllowMembersEditMembership=
   "false" AllowRequestToJoinLeave="false" AutoAcceptRequestToJoinLeave=
   "false" OnlyAllowMembersViewMembership="true" />
```

```
  <pnp:SiteGroup Title="Food Leads" Description="Group for product leads
  for Food" Owner="i:0#.f|membership|CHWorkplaceAdmin@cloudhadi.onmicrosoft.
  com" AllowMembersEditMembership="false" AllowRequestToJoinLeave="false"
  AutoAcceptRequestToJoinLeave="false" OnlyAllowMembersViewMembership="true" />
  <pnp:SiteGroup Title="Electronics Leads" Description="Group for product
  leads for Electronics" Owner="i:0#.f|membership|CHWorkplaceAdmin@
  cloudhadi.onmicrosoft.com" AllowMembersEditMembership="false"
  AllowRequestToJoinLeave="false" AutoAcceptRequestToJoinLeave="false"
  OnlyAllowMembersViewMembership="true" />
  <pnp:SiteGroup Title="Furniture Leads" Description="Group for product
  leads for Furniture" Owner="i:0#.f|membership|CHWorkplaceAdmin@
  cloudhadi.onmicrosoft.com" AllowMembersEditMembership="false"
  AllowRequestToJoinLeave="false" AutoAcceptRequestToJoinLeave="false"
  OnlyAllowMembersViewMembership="true" />
  <pnp:SiteGroup Title="Service Executives" Description="Group for
  service desk executives" Owner="i:0#.f|membership|CHWorkplaceAdmin@
  cloudhadi.onmicrosoft.com" AllowMembersEditMembership="false"
  AllowRequestToJoinLeave="false" AutoAcceptRequestToJoinLeave="false"
  OnlyAllowMembersViewMembership="true" />
  <pnp:SiteGroup Title="Site Administrators" Description="Group for
  site administrators" Owner="i:0#.f|membership|CHWorkplaceAdmin@
  cloudhadi.onmicrosoft.com" AllowMembersEditMembership="false"
  AllowRequestToJoinLeave="false" AutoAcceptRequestToJoinLeave="false"
  OnlyAllowMembersViewMembership="true" />
</pnp:SiteGroups>
<pnp:Permissions>
  <pnp:RoleAssignments>
    <pnp:RoleAssignment Principal="Cloudhadi Users" RoleDefinition="{rolede
    finition:Reader}" />
    <pnp:RoleAssignment Principal="Food Executives" RoleDefinition="{rolede
    finition:Reader}" />
    <pnp:RoleAssignment Principal="Electronics Executives" RoleDefinition="
    {roledefinition:Reader}" />
```

```
    <pnp:RoleAssignment Principal="Furniture Executives" RoleDefinition=
    "{roledefinition:Reader}" />
    <pnp:RoleAssignment Principal="Food Leads" RoleDefinition=
    "{roledefinition:Reader}" />
    <pnp:RoleAssignment Principal="Electronics Leads" RoleDefinition=
    "{roledefinition:Reader}" />
    <pnp:RoleAssignment Principal="Furniture Leads" RoleDefinition=
    "{roledefinition:Reader}" />
    <pnp:RoleAssignment Principal="Service Executives" RoleDefinition=
    "{roledefinition:Reader}" />
    <pnp:RoleAssignment Principal="Site Administrators" RoleDefinition=
    "{roledefinition:Administrator}" />
  </pnp:RoleAssignments>
</pnp:Permissions>
</pnp:Security>
```

Note   In the previous schema, make sure you replace the user
CHWorkplaceAdmin@cloudhadi.onmicrosoft.com with a user from your
site. To create a user, go to the Users section in the M365 Admin Center. See
Chapter 1 Users section for details.

We now have security schema ready that we can add to our provisioning schema file,
ProvisioningWorkplace.xml.

Site Fields

We can start creating the provisioning schema XML by defining our site fields.

To create a field, we can use <Field> element. For example, let's create XML for the
site field Product Name. The field will look like this:

```
<Field ID=" B9114FE0-6AB0-4AC8-986F-6E8EF9515B56" DisplayName="Product
Name" Name="ProductName" Type="Text" Group="Cloudhadi Columns" />
```

The field ID can be generated by pressing Ctrl+Shift+[in Visual Studio Code. The
GUID should be unique across all fields. DisplayName is the name that should be
displayed in forms. Name denotes the internal name of the column that we'll use in the

SPFx components, Representational State Transfer (REST) application programming interface (API) calls, and more. The type is set to Text, as the column is a single line of text. The Group property helps us to group site columns, which can all be grouped into Cloudhadi Columns.

Similarly, we can create the field XML for all the site columns that are listed in Table 2-1. Press Shift+Alt+Down to easily copy and paste the field XML below one line and then modify according to the field type and other properties. Once all fields are added, we need to wrap all the pnp:SiteField elements with its parent element, pnp:SiteFields.

Use the following code for the final XML for the site fields. See the site columns in Table 2-1 for the design.

```
<pnp:SiteFields>
    <Field ID="B9114FE0-6AB0-4AC8-986F-6E8EF9515B56" DisplayName="Product
    Name" Name="ProductName" Type="Text" Group="Cloudhadi Columns" />
    <Field ID="4298CA83-4D90-4826-903C-755649CFB45C" DisplayName="Product
    Type" Name="ProductType" Type="Choice" Group="Cloudhadi Columns">
        <CHOICES>
            <CHOICE>Food</CHOICE>
            <CHOICE>Electronics</CHOICE>
            <CHOICE>Furniture</CHOICE>
        </CHOICES>
        <Default>Draft</Default>
    </Field>
    <Field ID="746D7D9C-7A08-4E7D-9480-804601EF2111" DisplayName="Product
    Lead" Name="ProductLead" Type="User" UserSelectionMode="PeopleOnly"
    Group="Cloudhadi Columns" />
    <Field ID="28FF0BE4-2408-46F2-AA7E-A3B7EA1A93F8" DisplayName="Materials
    Used" Name="MaterialsUsed" Type="Note" Group="Cloudhadi Columns" />
    <Field ID="C88176A1-20F0-451D-AB09-C72EE53944CF"
    DisplayName="Inspection Completed Date" Name="InspectionCompletedDate"
    Type="DateTime" Format="DateOnly" Group="Cloudhadi Columns" />
    <Field ID="DF798B76-8622-439D-BF85-E47202A8B72C"
    DisplayName="Manufactured Date" Name="ManufacturedDate" Type="DateTime"
    Format="DateOnly" Group="Cloudhadi Columns" />
```

```
<Field ID="728C8D74-8364-4531-9396-8D74267C069B" DisplayName="Expiry
Date" Name="ExpiryDate" Type="DateTime" Format="DateOnly"
Group="Cloudhadi Columns" />
<Field ID="B6555F8B-946A-4EF3-8C19-5344D52F6A2F" DisplayName="Product
Features" Name="ProductFeatures" Type="Note" Group="Cloudhadi Columns" />
<Field ID="4C2DA4DD-3AF6-4775-8967-8C45411518CB" DisplayName="Product
Status" Name="ProductStatus" Type="Choice" Group="Cloudhadi Columns">
    <CHOICES>
        <CHOICE>New</CHOICE>
        <CHOICE>In production</CHOICE>
        <CHOICE>Completed</CHOICE>
    </CHOICES>
    <Default>New</Default>
</Field>
<Field ID="B1970C42-76FB-4FE4-AF12-65A3AE8A4E49" DisplayName="Review
Date" Name="ReviewDate" Type="DateTime" Format="DateOnly"
Group="Cloudhadi Columns" />
<Field ID="6757A127-3692-4548-878A-6596F4DED93B" DisplayName="Do
inspection required" Name="InspectionRequired" Type="Boolean"
Group="Cloudhadi Columns" />
<Field ID="555653F3-12BC-4487-8ED9-C1F87D73DC91"
DisplayName="Inspection Lead" Name="InspectionLead" Type="User"
UserSelectionMode="PeopleOnly" Group="Cloudhadi Columns" />
<Field ID="8D6E884A-C16B-430D-8410-415E1F4E3981" DisplayName="Document
Type" Name="DocumentType" Type="Choice" Group="Cloudhadi Columns">
    <CHOICES>
        <CHOICE>Product Information</CHOICE>
        <CHOICE>Product Inspection details</CHOICE>
        <CHOICE>Product Tooling Data</CHOICE>
        <CHOICE>Product Materials Information</CHOICE>
        <CHOICE>Other</CHOICE>
    </CHOICES>
    <Default>New</Default>
</Field>
```

```
<Field ID="F65BB8F3-D1E0-4FDF-B783-45940F23638E" DisplayName="Activity"
Name="Activity" Type="Text" Group="Cloudhadi Columns" />
<Field ID="73610C4A-C4E8-4C90-AE1D-A9955D6E2FBC" DisplayName="Started
on" Name="Startedon" Type="DateTime" Format="DateOnly" Group="Cloudhadi
Columns" />
<Field ID="5BDDD9A5-DDEA-4976-B5C2-BE2247C1CB4E" DisplayName="Capacity"
Name="Capacity" Type="Number" Group="Cloudhadi Columns" />
<Field ID="F7AD6719-9669-4D32-AFE8-2BC8FA7E8DB7" DisplayName="Licence
valid till" Name="Licencevalidtill" Type="DateTime" Format="DateOnly"
Group="Cloudhadi Columns" />
<Field ID="F3512954-565F-4AEB-AD29-A080FFE34D88" DisplayName="Goal"
Name="Goal" Type="Text" Group="Cloudhadi Columns" />
<Field ID="11D219F2-E845-47F2-B9E4-75F904659783" DisplayName="Quality
Rating" Name="QualityRating" Type="Number" Group="Cloudhadi Columns" />
<Field ID="05D34EF6-9F98-42D5-99D4-63EC96086302" DisplayName="Request
Title" Name="RequestTitle" Type="Text" Group="Cloudhadi Columns" />
<Field ID="0B501881-098F-45F9-89BD-77A0C4443C9C" DisplayName="Request
Description" Name="RequestDescription" Type="Note" Group="Cloudhadi
Columns" />
<Field ID="94FA1F37-2171-4E46-A20E-2B8ED283A92F" DisplayName="Related
to" Name="Related to" Type="Choice" Group="Cloudhadi Columns">
    <CHOICES>
        <CHOICE>Access</CHOICE>
        <CHOICE>Materials</CHOICE>
        <CHOICE>Equipments</CHOICE>
        <CHOICE>General</CHOICE>
    </CHOICES>
    <Default>New</Default>
</Field>
<Field ID="F4F0127E-E953-4D86-92D0-EDCAC10BC05A" DisplayName="Request
Status" Name="RequestStatus" Type="Choice" Group="Cloudhadi Columns">
    <CHOICES>
        <CHOICE>New</CHOICE>
        <CHOICE>In progress</CHOICE>
        <CHOICE>Resolved</CHOICE>
```

```
            <CHOICE>Completed</CHOICE>
            <CHOICE>Rejected</CHOICE>
            <CHOICE>Reopened</CHOICE>
        </CHOICES>
        <Default>New</Default>
    </Field>
    <Field ID="079FF054-1F50-4BD5-932F-9F651A1958AF" DisplayName="Request
    Assigned To" Name="RequestAssignedTo" Type="User" UserSelectionMode=
    "PeopleOnly" Group="Cloudhadi Columns" />
</pnp:SiteFields>
```

For choice columns, possible values can be added using the CHOICE element, and the default choice value using Default. For the Person field, the Type of which is of User, we need to specify UserSelectionMode as PeopleOnly to restrict it to only selected people and not groups.

Content Types

Now we can create XML for content types on the site and then put it in the same XML file. To create an ID for content types, we need to generate GUID and append it to its parent Content type. For example, the Cloudhadi Document Content type inherits from the Document Content type. So, while adding the content type ID, we should generate GUID like we did for site fields and then append it to 0x0101, which is the ID for the Document Content type. While appending the generated GUID, remove the dash characters from it and append the two zeros.

Table 2-8 shows the ID of parent content types for each of the Content types.

Table 2-8. *Content Type ID*

Content type	Parent content type	ID of parent content type
Document	Document	0x0101
Cloudhadi Product	Item	0x01
Cloudhadi Service	Item	0x01
Cloudhadi Document Set	Document set	0x0120D520

So, a GUID for the Document content type looks like this: **0x0101**00C1B123C08DD74EB7B8ABE22C7D89C293. The parent ID is highlighted in bold, the two zeros are appended, and then there is the generated ID without the dashes.

Let's create a schema for the Cloudhadi Document Content type. Part of the XML will be similar to the following:

```
<pnp:ContentType ID="0x010100C1B123C08DD74EB7B8ABE22C7D89C293"
Name="Cloudhadi Document" Description="For product documents."
Group="Cloudhadi Content Types">
    <pnp:FieldRefs>
            <pnp:FieldRef ID="B9114FE06AB04AC8986F6E8EF9515B56"
            Name="ProductName" Required="true" UpdateChildren="true" />
    </pnp:FieldRefs>
<pnp:ContentType>
```

The Content type has a child property, pnp:FieldRefs, which can include all the Site columns. Each of the Site columns needs to be referred to using the pnp:FieldRef element. With respect to the properties, the ID refers to the ID of the column, which we specified while creating the XML for site fields, and Name refers to the Name property of site field. As the product name is a required field for the Document Content type, we need to set Required to true. Setting UpdateChildren to true ensures that if any changes are made to the Content type or Site column, those changes will be propagated to all the lists and libraries that inherit the Content type. Similarly, we can add all the Site columns that are specified for documents to the Content type using pnp:FieldRef.

Likewise, we can create templates for the remaining Content types and add Site columns. Once XML is prepared for all Content types, wrap it inside the pnp:ContentTypes element.

The final XML for Content types follows, which is per Table 2-1. Check the Content Type column in the table against the Site Column Title column.

```
<pnp:ContentTypes>
  <pnp:ContentType ID="0x010100C1B123C08DD74EB7B8ABE22C7D89C293"
  Name="Cloudhadi Document" Description="For product documents"
  Group="Cloudhadi Content Types">
    <pnp:FieldRefs>
      <pnp:FieldRef ID="B9114FE0-6AB0-4AC8-986F-6E8EF9515B56"
      Name="ProductName" Required="true" UpdateChildren="true" />
```

```
      <pnp:FieldRef ID="4298CA83-4D90-4826-903C-755649CFB45C"
      Name="ProductType" Required="true" UpdateChildren="true" />
      <pnp:FieldRef ID="746D7D9C-7A08-4E7D-9480-804601EF2111"
      Name="ProductLead" Required="true" UpdateChildren="true" />
      <pnp:FieldRef ID="B1970C42-76FB-4FE4-AF12-65A3AE8A4E49"
      Name="ReviewDate" Required="true" UpdateChildren="true" />
<pnp:FieldRef ID="6757A127-3692-4548-878A-6596F4DED93B"
Name="InspectionRequired" Required="false" UpdateChildren="true" />
      <pnp:FieldRef ID="555653F3-12BC-4487-8ED9-C1F87D73DC91"
      Name="InspectionLead" Required="true" UpdateChildren="true" />
      <pnp:FieldRef ID="8D6E884A-C16B-430D-8410-415E1F4E3981"
      Name="DocumentType" Required="true" UpdateChildren="true" />
    </pnp:FieldRefs>
  </pnp:ContentType>
  <pnp:ContentType ID="0x0120D52000A0759C7CB1BD41F3A46AC682755F0FA1"
  Name="Cloudhadi Document Set" Description="For product document set"
  Group="Cloudhadi Content Types">
    <pnp:FieldRefs>
      <pnp:FieldRef ID="4298CA83-4D90-4826-903C-755649CFB45C"
      Name="ProductType" Required="true" UpdateChildren="true" />
      <pnp:FieldRef ID="F65BB8F3-D1E0-4FDF-B783-45940F23638E"
      Name="Activity" Required="true" UpdateChildren="true" />
      <pnp:FieldRef ID="73610C4A-C4E8-4C90-AE1D-A9955D6E2FBC"
      Name="Startedon" Required="true" UpdateChildren="true" />
      <pnp:FieldRef ID="5BDDD9A5-DDEA-4976-B5C2-BE2247C1CB4E"
      Name="Capacity" Required="true" UpdateChildren="true" />
      <pnp:FieldRef ID="F7AD6719-9669-4D32-AFE8-2BC8FA7E8DB7"
      Name="Licencevalidtill" Required="true" UpdateChildren="true" />
      <pnp:FieldRef ID="F3512954-565F-4AEB-AD29-A080FFE34D88" Name="Goal"
      Required="true" UpdateChildren="true" />
      <pnp:FieldRef ID="11D219F2-E845-47F2-B9E4-75F904659783"
      Name="QualityRating" Required="true" UpdateChildren="true" />
    </pnp:FieldRefs>
  </pnp:ContentType>
```

```
<pnp:ContentType ID="0x010067B88C4E585D4F2BA6496757590983F2"
Name="Cloudhadi Product" Description="For products" Group="Cloudhadi
Content Types">
  <pnp:FieldRefs>
    <pnp:FieldRef ID="B9114FE0-6AB0-4AC8-986F-6E8EF9515B56"
    Name="ProductName" Required="true" UpdateChildren="true" />
    <pnp:FieldRef ID="4298CA83-4D90-4826-903C-755649CFB45C"
    Name="ProductType" Required="true" UpdateChildren="true" />
    <pnp:FieldRef ID="28FF0BE4-2408-46F2-AA7E-A3B7EA1A93F8"
    Name="MaterialsUsed" Required="false" UpdateChildren="true" />
    <pnp:FieldRef ID="C88176A1-20F0-451D-AB09-C72EE53944CF"
    Name="InspectionCompletedDate" Required="true" UpdateChildren="true" />
    <pnp:FieldRef ID="DF798B76-8622-439D-BF85-E47202A8B72C"
    Name="ManufacturedDate" Required="true" UpdateChildren="true" />
    <pnp:FieldRef ID="728C8D74-8364-4531-9396-8D74267C069B"
    Name="ExpiryDate" Required="true" UpdateChildren="true" />
    <pnp:FieldRef ID="B6555F8B-946A-4EF3-8C19-5344D52F6A2F"
    Name="ProductFeatures" Required="true" UpdateChildren="true" />
    <pnp:FieldRef ID="4C2DA4DD-3AF6-4775-8967-8C45411518CB"
    Name="ProductStatus" Required="true" UpdateChildren="true" />
  </pnp:FieldRefs>
</pnp:ContentType>
<pnp:ContentType ID="0x0100C0C6636718D340F1B92019A3D33D5DE8"
Name="Cloudhadi Service" Description="For service requests"
Group="Cloudhadi Content Types">
  <pnp:FieldRefs>
    <pnp:FieldRef ID="05D34EF6-9F98-42D5-99D4-63EC96086302"
    Name="RequestTitle" Required="true" UpdateChildren="true" />
    <pnp:FieldRef ID="0B501881-098F-45F9-89BD-77A0C4443C9C"
    Name="RequestDescription" Required="true" UpdateChildren="true" />
    <pnp:FieldRef ID="94FA1F37-2171-4E46-A20E-2B8ED283A92F" Name="Related
    to" Required="false" UpdateChildren="true" />
    <pnp:FieldRef ID="F4F0127E-E953-4D86-92D0-EDCAC10BC05A"
    Name="RequestStatus" Required="true" UpdateChildren="true" />
```

```
        <pnp:FieldRef ID="079FF054-1F50-4BD5-932F-9F651A1958AF"
        Name="RequestAssignedTo" Required="true" UpdateChildren="true" />
      </pnp:FieldRefs>
    </pnp:ContentType>
  </pnp:ContentTypes>
```

We have four Content types and the respective columns are added inside using pnp:FieldRef elements. You can see that some of the columns, like Product Type, are reused across multiple Content types. We now have the schema for both site fields and Content types in the ProvisioningWorkplace.xml file along with the Security schema.

Lists and Libraries

Let's create a list schema and add those Content types to it. By default, all Site columns will be added to the list while we add the Content types. The schema for the Product Data Document Library will be as follows:

```
<pnp:ListInstance Title="Product Data" Description="Product Data
library" TemplateType="101" Url="ProductData" EnableModeration="true"
ContentTypesEnabled="true" EnableVersioning="true" MinorVersionLimit="0"
MaxVersionLimit="500" DraftVersionVisibility="2">
 <pnp:ContentTypeBindings>
  <pnp:ContentTypeBinding ContentTypeID="0x010100C1B123C08DD74EB7B8ABE22C7D
  89C293" Default="true" />
  <pnp:ContentTypeBinding ContentTypeID="0x0120D52000A0759C7CB1BD41F3A46AC6
  82755F0FA1" />
  <pnp:ContentTypeBinding ContentTypeID="0x0101" Remove="true"/>
 </pnp:ContentTypeBindings>
</pnp:ListInstance >
```

As you can make out from this schema, pnp:ListInstance is the root element for creating a list or library. TemplateType denotes the type of list. 101 stands for "library," whereas 100 for "list." Content approval will be enabled if EnableModeration is set to true. You need to set ContentTypesEnabled to true to use the content types. DraftVersionVisibility determines who can see the draft items in the library. In this case, it is set to Only Users with Edit Permissions. Basically, all the versioning properties in this instance of the list point to the versioning settings of the library.

pnp:ContentTypeBinding adds a content type to the library. In our case, Cloudhadi Document and Cloudhadi Document Set are added, and Cloudhadi Document being the default. There will be a Content type called Document that gets added by default; we can remove it as it is not needed. Add it as another binding with its ID and Remove equals true in properties. Once all Content type bindings are added, wrap it inside the parent element pnp:ContentTypeBindings.

Lastly, we need to place all the list instances under the parent element pnp:Lists. The final schema for lists follows. See Table 2-2 for a design reference.

```
<pnp:Lists>
  <pnp:ListInstance Title="Product Data" Description="Product Data
library" TemplateType="101" Url="ProductData" EnableModeration="true"
ContentTypesEnabled="true" EnableVersioning="true" MinorVersionLimit="0"
MaxVersionLimit="500" DraftVersionVisibility="2">
    <pnp:ContentTypeBindings>
      <pnp:ContentTypeBinding ContentTypeID="0x010100C1B123C08DD74EB7B8ABE2
      2C7D89C293" Default="true" />
      <pnp:ContentTypeBinding ContentTypeID="0x0120D52000A0759C7CB1BD41F3A4
      6AC682755F0FA1" />
      <pnp:ContentTypeBinding ContentTypeID="0x0101" Remove="true"/>
    </pnp:ContentTypeBindings>
  </pnp:ListInstance >
  <pnp:ListInstance Title="Products" Description="Products list"
TemplateType="100" Url="Products" ContentTypesEnabled="true">
    <pnp:ContentTypeBindings>
      <pnp:ContentTypeBinding ContentTypeID="0x010067B88C4E585D4F2BA6496757
      590983F2" Default="true" />
      <pnp:ContentTypeBinding ContentTypeID="0x01" Remove="true"/>
    </pnp:ContentTypeBindings>
  </pnp:ListInstance>
  <pnp:ListInstance Title="Service Portal" Description="Service portal
list" TemplateType="100" Url="ServicePortal" ContentTypesEnabled="true">
    <pnp:ContentTypeBindings>
      <pnp:ContentTypeBinding ContentTypeID="0x0100C0C6636718D340F1B92019A3
      D33D5DE8" Default="true" />
      <pnp:ContentTypeBinding ContentTypeID="0x01" Remove="true"/>
```

```
        </pnp:ContentTypeBindings>
    </pnp:ListInstance>
</pnp:Lists>
```

We have the schema ready for the Product Data library and the lists, Products, and Service Portal. The lists inherit their respective Content types: Product and Service Portal. For lists, the default Content type which is set to be removed is the Item Content type. As you can see, we're not required to add the versioning for the lists per the requirements.

Next, append the pnp:Lists schema to the ProvisioningWorkplace.xml. Now the site security, site fields, content types, and lists are ready in the base template.

Final Base Template

To deploy the ProvisioningWorkplace.xml template, we need to wrap all the prepared schema into parent elements. See the below parent element section.

```
<pnp:Provisioning xmlns:pnp="http://schemas.dev.office.com/PnP/2020/02/
ProvisioningSchema">
    <pnp:Templates ID="CONTAINER-TEMPLATE-57A385BB2A25469BB111BF5A8
    4D34815">
        <pnp:ProvisioningTemplate ID="TEMPLATE-57A385BB2A25469BB111BF5
        A84D34815" Version="1" BaseSiteTemplate="SITEPAGEPUBLISHING#0"
        Scope="RootSite">
            <! - - Add all schema code here -->
        </pnp:ProvisioningTemplate>
    </pnp:Templates>
</pnp:Provisioning>
```

Now add the schema for site security, site fields, content types, and lists inside the element pnp:ProvisioningTemplate. See the comment Add all schema code here in the previous code. We need to provide ID, Version, BaseTemplate and Scope properties to the pnp:ProvisioningTemplate element, as in the code. You can generate the ID by pressing Ctrl+Shift+[as mentioned earlier and append to the respective text as in the previous code.

`pnp:Templates` acts as a parent element to `pnp:ProvisioningTemplate`. `pnp:Provisioning` is the topmost element of the schema. Always follow this structure while building a provisioning schema. Also note that the property `xmlns:pnp` of the `pnp:Provisioning` element is pointing to the latest schema available. In future, you can update this URL when a new schema is published. All updates will be available in the PnP GitHub repository: `https://github.com/pnp/PnP-Provisioning-Schema`.

Note   The ProvisioningWorkplace.xml template is available in the Chapter 2 folder in the GitHub repository. Other individual schema files and the PowerShell scripts in the section Preparing the Site, are also available there. You can refer to it via book's product page, `https://github.com/Apress/building-modern-workplace-sharepoint-online`. You can also use the upgraded version of PnP PowerShell (Install-Module -Name PnP.PowerShell) instead of the version used in the below section - Preparing the Site (Install-Module SharePointPnPPowerShellOnline). With the latest module, You use 'Get-PnPSiteTemplate' command in place of 'Get-PnpProvisioningTemplate' and 'Invoke-PnPTenantTemplate' in place of 'Apply-PnPProvisioningTemplate'. New commands also available in the same Chapter 2 folder location.

Preparing the Site

Let's deploy this base template to our workplace site and get started. Once the template is deployed, all items will be provisioned and we can start with form development in the next chapter. Search for command prompt, right-click, and run as administrator. Enter the following commands in the order they appear here.

1. `Install-Module SharePointPnPPowerShellOnline`: This command installs all the required PnP modules. You are only required to enter it the first time.

2. `Connect-PnPOnline -Url [SiteURL] -UseWebLogin`: This command connects you to the SharePoint site. Provide a site URL in place of "[*SiteURL*]." I'm using `https://cloudhadi.sharepoint.com/sites/Workplace`. `UseWebLogin` will help you supply your credentials to connect from the browser.

3. `Enable-PnPFeature -Identity 3bae86a2-776d-499d-9db8-fa4cdc7884f8 -Scope Site -ErrorAction Stop`: This command will enable the document set feature, which is a requirement for our site.

4. `Apply-PnPProvisioningTemplate -Path .\Provisioning Workplace.xml`: This command will create all the schema in the site. Make sure ProvisioningWorkplace.xml is placed in your directory or provide the exact path to the XML file location.

In a few minutes, the site will be provisioned with all the items. You can see the progress in the Management Shell. Once the provisioning is completed, browse to the site and you will see that all the groups, fields, content types, lists are there now without even having touched the site manually until this point. Go through the site and have a look at all those items.

If you go to Site Settings ➤ Site Columns, you can see all the site columns that have been created, as in Figure 2-2.

Figure 2-2. *Site columns that have been created*

Similarly, you can go to Site Settings ➤ Site Content Types to view the content types that have been created. To view site groups, you can go to [*SiteURL*]/_layouts/15/ `groups.aspx` and view the groups, settings, and permission levels.

Figure 2-3 is a screenshot of the Site Contents page that shows the lists.

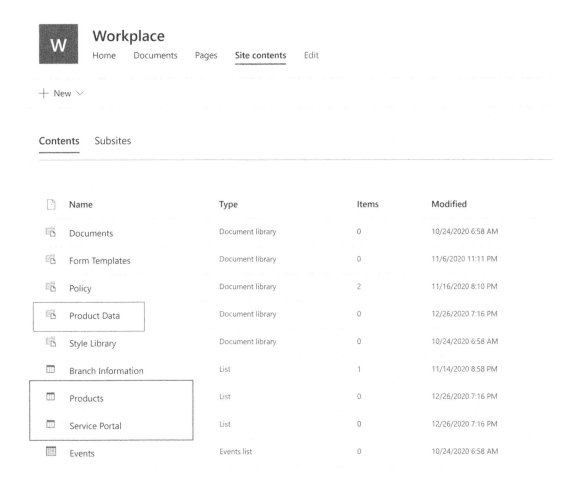

Figure 2-3. *Site Contents page*

You can click each list to go to its interface, and click ... on the right of the list or library to go to settings and verify the respective list or library settings.

Note   If you followed along with Chapter 1 using the same site, the Policy and Branch Information lists you previously created may now be shown on the site. Feel free to delete them.

Summary

In this chapter, we went through the requirements of a project, planned a design, and identified the components that need to be developed. Now you have an idea of the project and its design.

In addition to that, we created the base provisioning schema for the site items, which are site security, site fields, content types, lists, and libraries. The provisioning template ProvisioningWorkplace.xml will serve as a base template. We can also add other components such as pages, web parts, and navigation to the same template once we have completed their development.

We also deployed the base template and prepared the site to get started with the development. The site is now provisioned with all the required items and we are ready to kick of the OOB forms development. That will be the focus of the next chapter.

CHAPTER 3

Forms and Formatting

In the last chapter, we went over planning and designing a SharePoint Online solution based on a case study. You learned about provisioning and provisioned the site with basic items. The next step in building our solution is to provide the users with an option to enter data into SharePoint in a user-friendly manner.

SharePoint serves as both a front end and back end of your application. Lists and libraries store various information. Forms serve as the front end where you can enter data, validate data, and so forth. There are many ways to customize forms in the platform. Within the scope of this book, we will be focusing only on the most modern and recommended ways to customize forms.

SharePoint Online out-of-the-box (OOB) forms offer quite a number of functionalities with a stylish look and feel. However, they do have lot of limitations when it comes to customizing. There are number of modern options to customize forms such as Power Apps, SharePoint Framework (SPFx) web parts, and Nintex forms. You will learn about SharePoint OOB forms in this chapter and how to implement them in a workplace site. I will cover Power Apps and SPFx forms in the upcoming chapters.

We will touch upon the views and how to set up a default view quickly from the modern interface. In addition to the forms and views, one of the other things this chapter will focus on will be formatting columns and views in a list and library. We will go through some examples of how to format columns and views in the Product Data library and Products list.

At the end of this chapter, you will learn about OOB forms and views. You'll become familiar with setting up a SharePoint form, validations, views, formatting, and other features. You'll be able to customize the columns and views using OOB design and JSON formatting.

© Harinarayanan V P 2021
Harinarayanan V P, *Building the Modern Workplace with SharePoint Online*,
https://doi.org/10.1007/978-1-4842-6945-9_3

Form Requirements

Our requirements for Cloudhadi mainly consist of four forms: the Product Data document set form, the Product Data document properties form, the Products List list properties form, and the Service Portal list form. Let's develop the Product Data document form using SharePoint OOB. For other forms, we'll be using custom solutions, as mentioned in the use cases. Let's get started.

Document Properties Form

The Product Data library is where the user uploads documents, which will go into three document sets. We'll be creating document sets in a later section. We'll start by uploading a document to the library and then we'll organize the Document Properties form according to our requirements. In the process, you will learn about using SharePoint OOB forms.

In the first chapter, we looked at about the basics of a Document Library and how you can edit and save properties of a document. Let's now get into a little more detail and see how we can set up a good-looking form for the properties of a Product Data document and provide some validations. We'll start by going to the Product Data library from the Site Contents interface and uploading a document. As shown in Figure 3-1, select the document and go to the top context menu and click the ... icon in the right-hand corner, then click Properties.

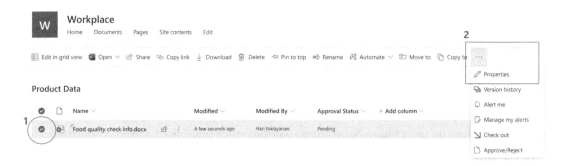

Figure 3-1. *Selecting document properties*

The properties window will then open, as shown in Figure 3-2. You can see that the mandatory fields will be marked per the Content type properties.

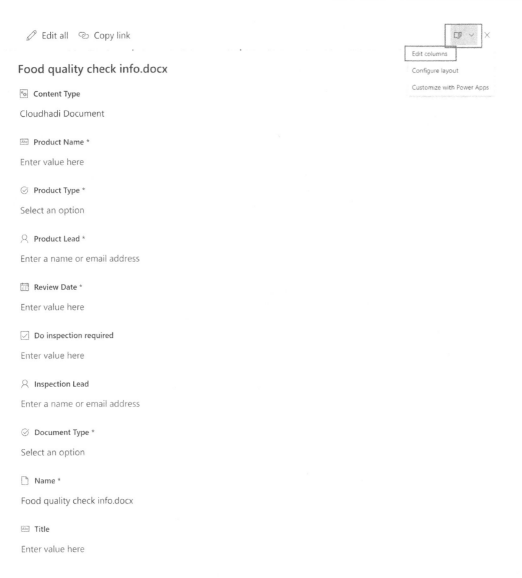

Figure 3-2. *Document Properties form*

Note   In some cases, the UpdateChildren property of Patterns and Practices (PnP) schema may not work as expected. This is a known bug. If this happens, the mandatory fields will not get reflected at the library level. To fix this, go to Site Contents ➤ Content Types ➤ Cloudhadi Document. Click each required column inside the content type and then click OK at the bottom of the screen. This will ensure that the library fields reflect the required property. The same applies to other content types as well.

Let's arrange the fields using the options selected on the right-hand side of the form, as shown in Figure 3-2. To do so, click the selected icon in the right-hand corner, choose Edit Columns, and then drag the fields to the required position. Alternatively, you can use the Move Up and Move Down options, as selected in Figure 3-3. Once you're done, save your work.

If you want to hide a column, uncheck the checkbox on the left side of its name. You only want to show the Inspection Lead column when the Do Inspection Required is selected. You can use Edit Conditional Formula to do that. These options are shown in Figure 3-3 along with the move options.

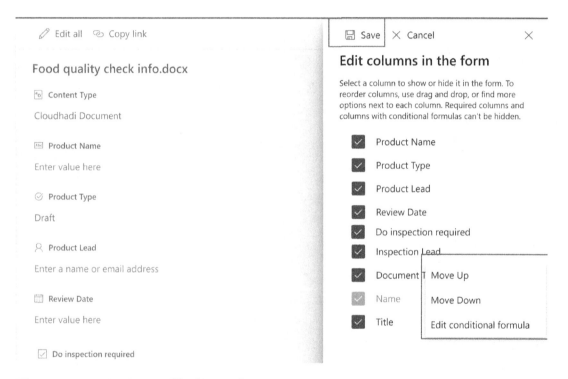

Figure 3-3. *Moving and hiding columns*

Let's now see how we can use conditional formula to show or hide a column. Click the ... icon next to the Inspection Lead column and select Edit Conditional Formula. In the pop-up window, enter the condition. See Figure 3-4.

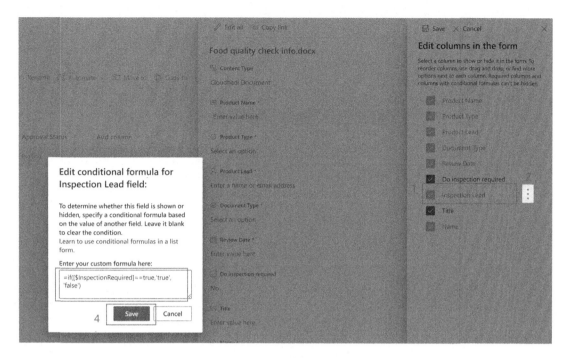

Figure 3-4. *Conditional formula for columns*

The condition =if([$InspectionRequired]==true,'true', 'false') means the Inspection Lead column will be visible only if Do Inspection Required is selected as Yes. Note that we use the internal name of the column here. Save the pop-up as well as the form once the formula is entered.

Note   Be aware that we will not be able to hide the Content Type column from the form with SharePoint OOB. The only way to hide the Content Type column is to disallow the management of content types, but we don't want to do this here, as we need to use the content types.

Now you can enter the properties for the document and save. To do so, select document and properties like we did before, type in the values, and it will be saved when you enter it. See Figure 3-5.

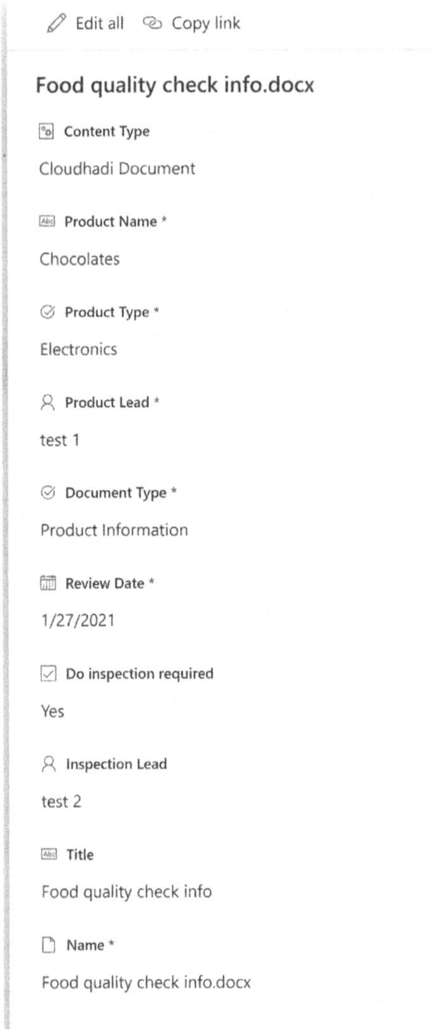

Figure 3-5. *Doing a quick edit of Document properties*

You can see that the Inspection Lead column is hidden, but as soon as you select Yes for Do Inspection Required, the Inspection Lead column will appear again. For the Product Lead and Inspection Lead columns, you can enter any person for now. Each field data will be saved when you enter data into it. This is called the quick edit option.

Alternatively, you can click Edit All and put in the properties, as shown in Figure 3-6. In this case, you will need to click Save at the top or bottom of the screen once you enter the data.

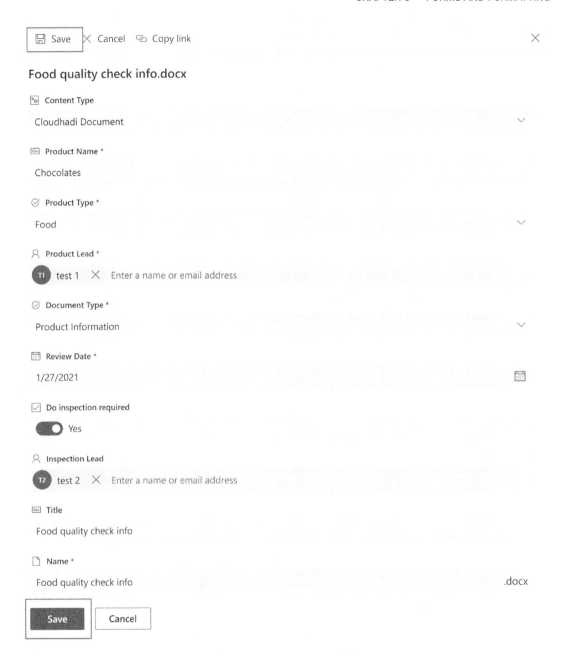

Figure 3-6. *Editing the document properties using Edit All*

We have now set up the OOB list form now with the field arrangements, validations, and visibility settings. You learned how to organize fields, how validation works, how to conditionally show and hide columns, and different ways to edit the properties of a document.

Pros and Cons of OOB Forms

SharePoint OOB forms are quite powerful, but they do have some limitations. The following pros and cons of the OOB forms will help you to choose whether they are the right choice for your needs:

Pros:

- *Look and feel*: OOB forms have the modern look and feel that align well with that of the rest of the SharePoint site. If you were to choose Power Apps, SPFx, or Nintex forms, you'd have to explicitly match their style with the site theme.

- *Built-in validation*: Because they have built-in validation, OOB forms allow you to validate mandatory columns, show or hide a column based on another, calculate a column value from another, and more without having to do any custom coding.

- *Organizing fields*: These forms offer the option to move fields and show or hide the columns using the Edit Form option, which comes in very handy.

Cons:

- *Headers*: You cannot add a custom header to a form with OOB forms. For example, if you wanted to add "Enter your Product Data properties here" to the top of the Properties form, it wouldn't be possible. You would have to choose a different type of form to do that.

- *Visibility of Content Type*: You don't have the option to hide content types other than disallowing their management when using these forms. This can be a deal breaker when deciding on which form to choose.

- *Editing form security*: The Edit Form option to arrange or hide the fields can sometimes be a problem when using OOB forms. This option is available to all users who have Edit permission in the library. Therefore, if any of the users updates the column arrangements, all users will be affected. Ideally, site administrators should have the option to hide this option from other users.

- *Custom watermarks*: The watermarks of the columns can't be changed. For example, if the watermark in the Product Name field says, "Enter value here" and you want to change it to "Enter product name here," this wouldn't possible with OOB forms.

Restricting the Selection of People

As of now, you can select any user from the site as the product or inspection lead. With an OOB form, we can restrict the Lead field to only one SharePoint group. So, if you wanted to restrict it to Food Leads, Electronics Leads, and Furniture Leads, three groups, it would not be possible to achieve using this form.

The only way we could achieve this with an OOB form is to create a common SharePoint group, say "Product Leads," where all the leads from the three groups could be added, and then restrict the Person field to the Product Leads group.

Note   To avoid the extra work of having to add the same user to both groups, we can automate this process by using a Power Automate flow to add a user to the Product Leads group when a user is added to any of the three lead groups.

Let's see how we can make this change using PnP. To do so, we'll create a new provisioning template called ProvisioningWorkplace_CH03.xml, and at the end of this chapter, we'll integrate it into our main template, ProvisioningWorkplace.xml.

1. Let's start by creating a new XML file called ProvisioningWorkplace_CH03.xml and adding the parent elements to it like we did in Chapter 2 Final Base Template section (see Step 2 for an example). The only difference is that in this case, we going to use a unique GUID for `pnp:Templates` and `pnp:ProvisioningTemplate`.

2. Now, let's add a Site Security section to the XML with a new site group within the site groups tag. We don't need role assignments here as the individual product lead groups already have the permissions assigned. The template will look the following now:

```
<pnp:Provisioning xmlns:pnp="http://schemas.dev.office.com/PnP/2020/02/
ProvisioningSchema">
    <pnp:Templates ID="CONTAINER-TEMPLATE-AAE59FE314734AFAA5C86866441D8A98">
        <pnp:ProvisioningTemplate ID="TEMPLATE-67AB254EB99240DFA53F78C
        C753AE8D7" Version="1" BaseSiteTemplate="SITEPAGEPUBLISHING#0"
        Scope="RootSite">
            <pnp:Security>
                <pnp:SiteGroups>
                    <pnp:SiteGroup Title="Product Leads"
                    Description="Group for all product leads"
                    Owner="i:0#.f|membership|CHWorkplaceAdmin@cloudhadi.
                    onmicrosoft.com" AllowMembersEditMembership="false"
                    AllowRequestToJoinLeave="false" AutoAcceptRequestToJoin
                    Leave="false" OnlyAllowMembersViewMembership="true" />
                </pnp:SiteGroups>
            </pnp:Security>
        </pnp:ProvisioningTemplate>
    </pnp:Templates>
</pnp:Provisioning>
```

3. Next, we'll connect to the site using the `Connect-PnPOnline`
    `-Url [SiteURL] -UseWebLogin` command. Replace the site
    URL with your site URL. Apply the provisioning template using the
    command `Apply-PnPProvisioningTemplate -Path`
    `.\ProvisioningWorkplace_CH03.xml`. Provide the full path to the
    provisioning template

4. Once Step 3 is completed, execute the command
    `Get-PnPGroup -Identity 'Product Leads'`. This will give
    you the ID of the group.

5. Now go to the main template ProvisioningWorkplace.xml
    and copy the `Product Lead` and `Inspection Lead` columns
    to ProvisioningWorkplaceCH03.xml. Add a new property
    UserSelectionScope to both columns and set it to the ID from
    Step 4.

The final template will now look like the following:

```
<pnp:Provisioning xmlns:pnp="http://schemas.dev.office.com/PnP/2020/02/
ProvisioningSchema">
    <pnp:Templates ID="CONTAINER-TEMPLATE-AAE59FE314734AFAA5C86866441D8A98">
        <pnp:ProvisioningTemplate ID="TEMPLATE-67AB254EB99240DFA53F78C
        C753AE8D7" Version="1" BaseSiteTemplate="SITEPAGEPUBLISHING#0"
        Scope="RootSite">
            <pnp:Security>
                <pnp:SiteGroups>
                    <pnp:SiteGroup Title="Product Leads" Description=
                    "Group for all product leads" Owner="i:0#.f|membership|
                    CHWorkplaceAdmin@cloudhadi.onmicrosoft.com" AllowMembers
                    EditMembership="false" AllowRequestToJoinLeave="false"
                    AutoAcceptRequestToJoinLeave="false" OnlyAllowMembers
                    ViewMembership="true" />
                </pnp:SiteGroups>
            </pnp:Security>
            <pnp:SiteFields>
                <Field ID="746D7D9C-7A08-4E7D-9480-804601EF2111"
                DisplayName="Product Lead" Name="ProductLead" Type="User"
                UserSelectionMode="PeopleOnly" UserSelectionScope="24"
                Group="Cloudhadi Columns" />
                <Field ID="555653F3-12BC-4487-8ED9-C1F87D73DC91"
                DisplayName="Inspection Lead" Name="InspectionLead"
                Type="User" UserSelectionMode="PeopleOnly"
                UserSelectionScope="24" Group="Cloudhadi Columns" />
            </pnp:SiteFields>
        </pnp:ProvisioningTemplate>
    </pnp:Templates>
</pnp:Provisioning>
```

6. Connect to the site and apply the provisioning template like we did in Step 3.

In the previous steps, you created a site group and restricted the selection of people for that group in the Product Lead and Inspection Lead columns.

If you go to the library settings and click Product Lead in the Columns section, you can see that the column is now limited to the group Product Leads (see Figure 3-7). The same applies to the Inspection Lead.

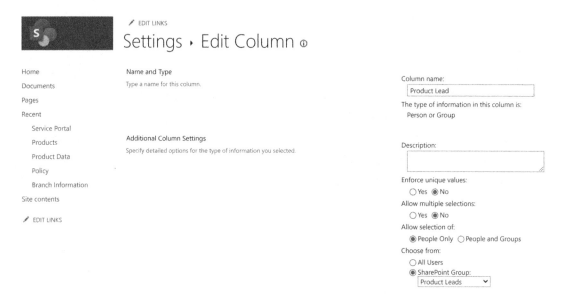

Figure 3-7. *Person field column settings*

Note   Every time you deploy PnP site fields for the Inspection Lead column, you need to manually re-add the condition allowing the column's visibility, or it will be lost. As the conditional formula for columns is a recent feature introduced by Microsoft, this is still not incorporated into PnP and the manually added conditional formula gets lost on PnP deployments.

Let's add some users to the Product Lead group now.

Go to Site Settings ➤ Peoples and Group. Click More... from the left navigation bar, and you will be redirected to the Groups page. There, you can click the Product Lead group. Alternatively, you can access the group directly using [`SiteURL`]`/_layouts/15/ people.aspx?MembershipGroupId={Id}`.

For example, I use `https://cloudhadi.sharepoint.com/sites/Workplace/_ layouts/15/people.aspx?MembershipGroupId=24` to access the group in my site.

Now if you go back to the document we edited before and try to enter product lead or inspection lead, you will only be able to select the members of product leads.

Note   If you don't have enough test users, go to the Microsoft 365 Admin Center and add few users. See Chapter 1. When assigning the licenses, choose the Microsoft 365 and Power Automate free licenses. Both will be available with a developer trial E3 or E5 account. Newly added users may take few hours to appear in the SharePoint site.

Views

Views are virtual representations of content in a list or library. Different views may show different columns and have different sorting, filtering, grouping, and styles. We touched on views in Chapter 1. Here, I want to take you through how we can edit the columns of a view quickly from the modern interface without having to go to the list or library settings.

Go to the Product Data library, upload a few documents, and update the properties for each document. To view the properties of an individual document, you need to select and click the properties.

To view the properties of multiple documents from the library interface, we depend on the view. By default, the library is in the All Items view, as shown in Figure 3-8.

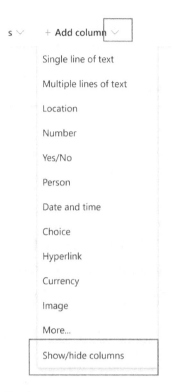

Figure 3-8. *Library default view*

If we want to view the product details such as Product Name and Product Type, as well as set an order for how they appear in the view, we can take the following steps.

Start by clicking Add Column in the library interface and then clicking Show/hide Column, as selected in Figure 3-8.

From the sliding panel, you can select and deselect the columns, and order them using drag and drop or the up and down arrows. Click Apply to save the view. See Figure 3-9.

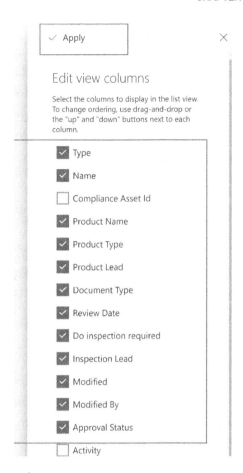

Figure 3-9. *Customizing the view*

By clicking Apply, the library view will be updated with the changes you made and all the columns in the view will be in the order you chose. Now let's add a button to the view that we can use later to initiate a Power Automate flow for approval. We'll create the button using JSON formatting.

Column Formatting with JSON

Column formatting and view formatting allow you to make front-end changes to a list or library view. These kinds of customizations won't make any changes to the underlying data; they are only intended for customizing the presentation of the data for the user.

If you want to add a custom button to a library view, you can do it without having an SPFx extension. Column formatting with JSON can help you with that. JSON data is written as name-value pairs. Let's learn about it by implementing a custom button for the initiation of document approval.

Initially we need to create a text column, which we didn't do during our initial PnP deployment. Let's add this column to the ProvisioningWorkplaceCH03.xml and execute. Update the site fields element and add a Content types element to include the new field Cloudhadi Document. Remember to comment out the Inspection Lead field to avoid having to add the conditional formula again. Just put your cursor in front of the Inspection Lead <Field> line and press Ctrl+/. If you'd like to, you can comment out the SiteGroups element as well. The template ProvisioningWorkplaceCH03.xml will now look like the following:

```
<pnp:Provisioning xmlns:pnp="http://schemas.dev.office.com/PnP/2020/02/
ProvisioningSchema">
    <pnp:Templates ID="CONTAINER-TEMPLATE-AAE59FE314734AFAA5C86866441D8A98">
        <pnp:ProvisioningTemplate ID="TEMPLATE-67AB254EB99240DFA53F78C
        C753AE8D7" Version="1" BaseSiteTemplate="SITEPAGEPUBLISHING#0"
        Scope="RootSite">
            <pnp:Security>
                <pnp:SiteGroups>
                    <pnp:SiteGroup Title="Product Leads"
                    Description="Group for all product leads"
                    Owner="i:0#.f|membership|CHWorkplaceAdmin@cloudhadi.
                    onmicrosoft.com" AllowMembersEditMembership="false"
                    AllowRequestToJoinLeave="false" AutoAcceptRequestToJoin
                    Leave="false" OnlyAllowMembersViewMembership="true" />
                </pnp:SiteGroups>
            </pnp:Security>
            <pnp:SiteFields>
                <Field ID="746D7D9C-7A08-4E7D-9480-804601EF2111"
                DisplayName="Product Lead" Name="ProductLead" Type="User"
                UserSelectionMode="PeopleOnly" UserSelectionScope="24"
                Group="Cloudhadi Columns" />
                <!-- <Field ID="555653F3-12BC-4487-8ED9-C1F87D73DC91"
                DisplayName="Inspection Lead" Name="InspectionLead"
                Type="User" UserSelectionMode="PeopleOnly"
                UserSelectionScope="24" Group="Cloudhadi Columns" /> -->
```

```
        <Field ID="F7EE4F85-3496-4CB6-B8AE-310644769F45"
        DisplayName="Initiate Approval" Name="InitiateApproval"
        Type="Text" Group="Cloudhadi Columns" />
    </pnp:SiteFields>
    <pnp:ContentTypes>
        <pnp:ContentType ID="0x010100C1B123C08DD74EB7B8ABE22C7D8
        9C293" Name="Cloudhadi Document" Description="For product
        documents" Group="Cloudhadi Content Types">
            <pnp:FieldRefs>
                <pnp:FieldRef ID="F7EE4F85-3496-4CB6-B8AE-
                310644769F45" Name="InitiateApproval"
                Required="false" UpdateChildren="true" />
            </pnp:FieldRefs>
        </pnp:ContentType>
    </pnp:ContentTypes>
  </pnp:ProvisioningTemplate>
 </pnp:Templates>
</pnp:Provisioning>
```

Run the apply provisioning template command using `Apply-PnPProvisioningTemplate -Path .\ProvisioningWorkplace_CH03.xml`. The field `Initiate Approval` will be created and added to the Content type. It will now be available in the Product Data library.

Note   You may find it a bit tedious to do each small step using PnP templates. Let's stick to it, though, and by the end of development we'll have a final provisioning script with minimum number of templates. Moving the code to another environment will be fully automated and much easier with this approach.

Let's go back to the Product Data library and add the column Initiate Approval to the view we made earlier (see Figures 3-8 and 3-9 for the existing view). While adding the column, we can move it up. Let's put it below to the Product Name column. Once the column is added to the view, click the downward-facing arrow next to the column, go to Column Settings, and then click Format This Column, as shown in Figure 3-10.

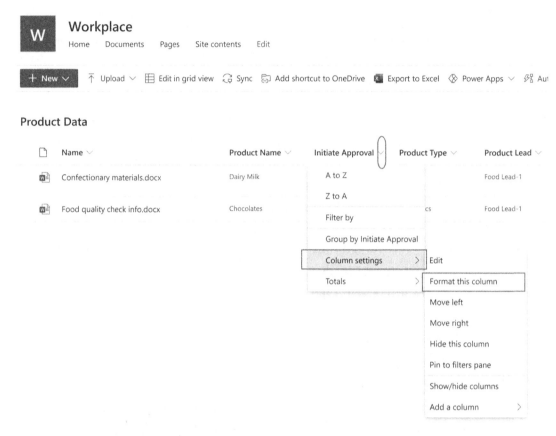

Figure 3-10. *Formatting a column*

In the window that opens, click Advanced mode on the bottom and a JSON editor will become available. While in advanced mode, you can Switch to design mode using the same button. Drag it to the left to give yourself more space to enter the JSON code. Leave Intake Approval as the choice for Apply Formatting To. See Figure 3-11.

Figure 3-11. *Advanced mode for JSON formatting*

We will keep the formatting simple for now. The button text will be `Initiate Approval` and it will have a `flow` icon to its left. We will add some basic styling and placeholders for custom actions.

Following is the JSON code, after which I'll explain each property.

```
{
  "elmType": "span",
  "style": {
    "color": "white",
    "background-color": "#3d7b80",
    "border": "1px solid",
    "border-radius": "8px",
    "padding-left": "8px",
    "visibility": true
  },
```

```
"children": [
  {
    "elmType": "span",
    "attributes": {
      "iconName": "flow"
    }
  },
  {
    "elmType": "button",
    "style": {
      "background-color": "inherit",
      "border": "none",
      "color": "white",
      "cursor": "pointer"
    },
    "txtContent": "Initiate Approval",
    "customRowAction": {
      "action": "",
      "actionParams": ""
    }
  }
]
}
```

In the code, we are placing the value of the Initiate Approval field into a span element. It is set to a style where we choose the span text color, background color, and so forth.

The span has two child elements, a span and a button. The child span element is set to the flow icon. The button element is also set to have some styles. The text content of the button is set using the txtContent property. There is also a customRowAction property, which sets an action on the button click. For now, we will leave the action and actionParams blank.

In upcoming chapters, we will modify this same formatting to invoke a flow, to set the visibility based on Content type, to set conditions for disabling the button and for text change of the button based on approval status, and so forth.

As shown in Figure 3-12, by clicking Preview, you can see that the field is now changed to a button.

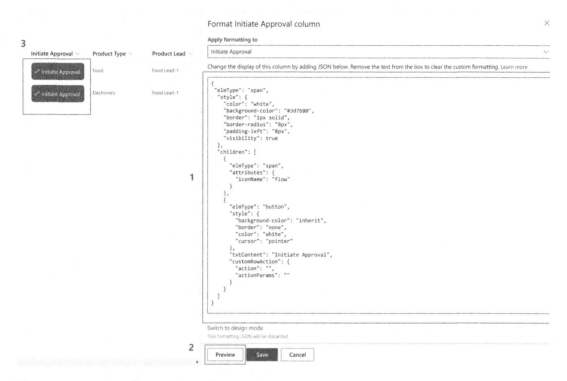

Figure 3-12. *Applying JSON formatting*

Click Save to save the changes.

You can use Visual Studio Code to create the JSON and then copy and paste it here to have a better editing experience.

You can update the field Initiate Approval in ProvisioningWorkplaceCH03.xml to include the JSON using CustomFormatter property, but you need to formatting of the JSON content. I updated this in the template. Refer to Chapter 3 folder of the GitHub repository.

There are a lot of options available for formatting columns. You can create various rules and apply different styles. Figure 3-13 shows how we can add colors to choices in the Document Type column.

Figure 3-13. *Using Choice Pills*

As seen in Figure 3-10, if you click Format This Column under Document Type, you will be given an option called Choice Pills. From here, click Edit Styles to choose your desired color. Let's keep the preselected colors for our example. If you click Advanced mode on the bottom of the screen, you can see the JSON code that was created.

In the same way, you can add different conditional styling using the built-in column formatting. If you want to add a people icon to the Product Lead column, you can do that using the default formatting options. I recommend spending some time playing around with different options the formatting provides. We will have a look at conditional formatting in the next section, which is also similar in the case of columns.

Conditional View Formatting

In the previous section, we went over formatting individual columns using JSON code as well as using the design options available. Now let's see how we can format the entire item view.

Let's say we're required to highlight an item if the review date has already passed. We can make this happen by viewing the formatting.

To view the formatting, click All Documents in the drop-down list on the right side of the screen, then click Format Current View, as selected in Figure 3-14.

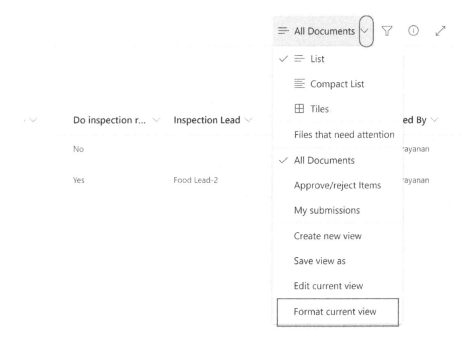

Figure 3-14. *Selecting the format view*

Now the Format View window will open as shown Figure 3-15. Choose Conditional Formatting, then click on Manage Rules.

Figure 3-15. *Conditional formatting*

In the window that opens, click Add Rule, as shown in Figure 3-16.

Figure 3-16. *Adding a rule*

Now create a rule, as shown in Figure 3-17. The rule sets the color of the item row to light yellow if the review date is before the current date.

Figure 3-17. *Creating and saving a rule*

After selecting an option in Show List Item As, click More Styles from the pop-up, which will give you different options, such as standard colors, fonts, and borders. When you add a rule, the library view will reflect that. I updated the review date to the previous day before formatting the view. You'll be able to add multiple rules like this. Save and close once you're done. You can edit or delete the created rules using the same settings.

Custom Image Cards on Hover Event

Now that we've done some formatting for the library columns and view, let's head to the product list and do some work there in terms of displaying the data.

Go to Site Contents ➤ Products and click Show/Hide More Columns like we did for the library (look back at Figure 3-8). Then check off the columns as done in Figure 3-18, and click Apply.

Figure 3-18. *Product list columns*

Next, add few items to the product list using the New button. Make sure you have at least one product for each status. See Figure 3-19.

Products

	Title	Product Name	Product Type	Materials Used	Manufactured ...	Expiry Date	Product Features	Product Status	Inspection Com...
	Chocolates	Chocolate CH	Food	Sugar, Cocoa	12/23/2020	12/22/2022	Dark chocolate	In production	12/23/2020
	Breakfast products	WheetEat	Food	Wheat, Cashew, Almonds	12/15/2020	12/15/2022	Breakfast food	New	12/23/2020
	Breakfast products	BananaApple	Food	Banana, Apple, Cashew, Almonds	11/1/2020	12/15/2022	Breakfast food	Completed	12/9/2020

Figure 3-19. *Products added to the product list*

We want to add a hover to the Production Status column that displays three different images for three different status values. To do this, first navigate to Site Contents ➤ Documents Library and upload three images of your choice. Make sure the names of the files are "Completed.jpg," "InProduction.jpg," and "New.jpg," respectively. See Figure 3-20.

Note   You're free to use the same images I used here. Refer to the images folder from Chapter 3 section of the GitHub repository: `https://github.com/Apress/building-modern-workplace-sharepoint-online/tree/main/Chapter%203/Images/Documents%20Library`.

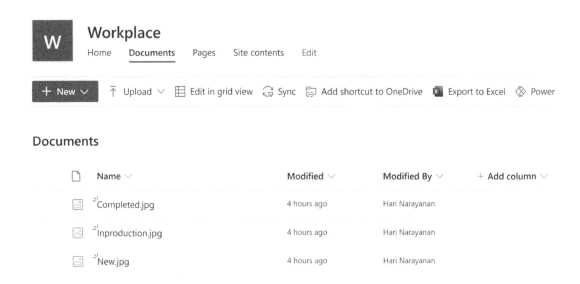

Figure 3-20. *Uploading images in the Documents library*

Now, go to the product list, click the Production Status column arrow, and choose format this column, as you did for the library, and paste the following code and save. I will explain the code in detail after it.

```
{
    "elmType":"div",
    "style":{
        "font-size":"12px"
    },
    "txtContent":"[$ProductStatus]",
    "customCardProps":{
        "formatter":{
            "elmType":"img",
            "style":{
                "width":"150px",
                "height":"100px",
                "border-radius":"8px",
                "border":"1px solid #ddd",
                "padding":"10px"
            },
            "attributes":{
                "src":"=if([$ProductStatus]=='Completed', '/sites/Workplace/
                Shared%20Documents/Completed.jpg', if([$ProductStatus] == 'In
                production','/sites/Workplace/Shared%20Documents/Inproduction.
                jpg', '/sites/Workplace/Shared%20Documents/New.jpg')",
                "title":"[$ProductStatus]"
            }
        },
        "openOnEvent":"hover",
        "directionalHint":"bottomCenter",
        "isBeakVisible":true,
        "beakStyle":{
            "backgroundColor":"blue"
        }
    }
}
```

By setting `elmType` as `div`, we're placing the `ProductStatus` field into a `div`. The content of the `div` is set to `ProductStatus`. After that, we're creating a custom card and setting its properties using `customCardProps`. We're putting an image element inside the card and setting its style and attributes. In the `attributes` section, we're adding a condition to check the `ProductStatus`. If the `ProductStatus` is `Completed`, the `src` is set to the relative path of `Completed.jpg`. The path to the Documents library is [*SiteURL*]/ `Shared Documents/`. In my case the complete path is `sites/Workplace/Shared%20 Documents/Completed.jpg`.

If the status is `In Production`, `src` should be set to the path `inproduction.jpg`. In all other cases, it will point to `New.jpg`.

In the next line, we will set the `openOnEvent` property, which means the custom card will open only on an event, the even being `hover` in this case. The `directionalHint` ensures that the card will appear on the bottom center when we hover over the `ProductStatus` column. The `isBeakVisible` and `beakStyle` properties are to make the arrow point to the card.

If you hover over the product status for each of the items and see how it appears. In Figure 3-21, you can see how it appears for an item where the product status is Completed.

Figure 3-21. *Column formatting image that appears upon hover event*

In the `Completed.jpg` image that appears upon hovering, note that the color of the top arrow is blue as we set it to be. The image style, direction, and other elements are all appearing as expected. If you hover over items with the New or In Production status, the image that appears will be different, as we have conditionally based images.

This is one of example where you can customize the front end of the list using column formatting. Using JSON formatting, you can make quite number of customizations, such as displaying a progress bar in columns, setting text as a hyperlink, and setting custom layouts for list or library items.

Integrating the PnP Schema Files

Now that we're approaching the end of the chapter, it's time to merge the ProvisioningWorkplace-CH3.xml file with our main template, ProvisioningWorkplace. xml. But before we do that, let's review the changes we made manually in this chapter.

We customized the `ProductStatus`, `InitiateApproval`, and `DocumentType` columns using JSON. We added the `CustomFormatter` property for those columns to the provisioning template files. The product data and product list views will also be added to both templates. Inside the `pnp:ListInstance`, you will be able to see `pnp:Views`. The All Items view is added inside that root element using the View element. Go to ProvisioningWorkplace-CH3.xml and have a detailed look at the changes we made in this chapter.

Note   If you would like to, feel free to skip the PnP integration sessions in each chapter. When doing deployment at the end of the development, you can go through the templates in detail and understand them better. As mentioned earlier, all code samples used in this book are available in the GitHub repository.

Now go to each section and copy each of the modified child elements from ProvisioningWorkplace-CH3.xml to ProvisioningWorkplace.xml For example, copy the `pnp:SiteGroup` element for `Product Leads` and paste it inside `pnp:SiteGroups`. Do the same with each of the site fields and content types. For any fields that are changed, replace the old `<Field>` line with the new one. `Product Lead` is an example, as we added the `UserSelectionScope` property to it. For content types, copy the new `FieldRef` into the `pnp:FieldRefs`. `InitiateApproval` is the new column that needs to be added to the content type. For list instances, replace the `pnp:ListInstance` for both `Products` and `Product Data` to include the views, or just copy the `pnp:Views` section.

Like the Inspection Lead column formatting, we are limited in adding the custom formatting of the view to the PnP. These are the two things we need to add manually after the PnP XML is deployed.

See the Chapter 3 folder of GitHub repository for the final ProvisioningWorkplace. xml at this stage.

Project Development Review

Let's do a quick review of where we're at in terms of developing a modern workplace for Cloudhadi. Each chapter is like a sprint for us where we develop a functionality along with the learning process.

We already provisioned the basic items in the last chapter. In this chapter, we developed the form for Product Data documents. Users can now upload documents to the Product Data library and set their properties. The mandatory column validation is in place now. The Inspection Lead column will not be shown if inspection isn't required. The Product Lead and Inspection Lead columns are now restricted to the Product Lead group. Product executives can't select a random person for approval.

The default view is also set up with the columns and desired order. The Initiate Approval button is now available and it can be modified later to invoke the approval flow. The documents that are past their due date will be highlighted in the view.

In the product list, we set up the view with a custom image card when you hover over the product status. We Will develop the product list form in the next chapter using Power Apps.

Summary

In this chapter, we started learning about SharePoint forms and views. You learned about how a default SharePoint form can be used for validating and saving data to a SharePoint library. You learned how to use a conditional formula to show and hide a column based on another. We had a look at the advantages and disadvantages of using an OOB form.

We also went over different options for customizing columns and views using JSON formatting without having to update the underlying data. You learned about conditional formatting, the creation of rules, and how to edit the formatting in advanced mode. We looked at how to set a hover event on a list column and display an image. In addition to what we have discussed so far, there are recent developments in the JSON formatting space. You can customize the list and library forms look and feel with the help of JSON formatting. This brings in a lot of flexibility while developing a list or library form. You might not need to use PowerApps for most of the scenarios. You can achieve most of the requirements using JSON configured OOB forms. I could not cover it in this chapter as the chapter was written well before this new capability got introduced. To learn more about configuring the form with JSON, refer to Microsoft documentation at `https://docs.microsoft.com/en-us/sharepoint/dev/declarative-customization/list-form-configuration`. Also, I added some of the JSON list form example samples in the Chapter 3 folder of the GitHub repository

In the next chapter, we'll begin our custom forms development. The chapter will be all about Power Apps form development. You'll learn about the Power Platform and how it can be integrated with SharePoint Online to achieve various business needs. In the process, we'll build a custom Power Apps form for the product list.

CHAPTER 4

Power Apps

In the last chapter, we reviewed SharePoint forms and how to validate and format columns. You learned a few custom solutions for using column formatting and viewed formatting with the help of JSON. In this chapter, we will look at one of the most modern solutions for customizing your list or library forms: Power Apps. You don't have to do any extensive coding when using this software.

Power Apps is a low-code app solution that can satisfy business requirements in a quick and efficient manner. You can connect to your business data using Power Apps. For our purposes, we'll be using SharePoint Online as the data source, but there are various other data sources that Power Apps can interact with as well.

We'll start learning about Power Apps by becoming familiar with the canvas- and model-driven apps. We'll then create a stand-alone canvas app for adding, editing, and deleting products from the Cloudhadi products list. You'll learn how to make the app responsive to creating forms that automatically adapt to any type of screen, such as that of a mobile device.

In addition to this, we'll customize the new and edited forms of our Products list for Cloudhadi. By the end of this chapter, you'll be familiar with creating a canvas app in Power Apps, configuring the user interface, and implementing the business logic. You'll learn about different components, properties, and integrations of Power App forms with SharePoint Online lists.

Canvas and Model-Driven Apps

Power Apps developers can build either canvas or model-driven applications. Canvas apps provide you with a blank canvas onto which you can drag and drop components to design a user interface, which you can apply formatting to complete. You can connect to a data source like SharePoint. After that, you can apply field and data logic, and preview and publish the app. Canvas apps can integrate with more than 200 data sources out of

© Harinarayanan V P 2021
Harinarayanan V P, *Building the Modern Workplace with SharePoint Online,*
https://doi.org/10.1007/978-1-4842-6945-9_4

the box (OOB). By design, canvas apps are not responsive. They come programmed with a portrait or landscape orientation. We can make these apps responsive by setting up some properties.

Model-driven apps are based on underlying data, specifically the data stored in Microsoft Dataverse. Dataverse is a cloud-based storage space. Model-driven apps follow a data-first approach, and much of the layout is determined for you and largely designated by the components you add. When developing canvas apps, on the other hand, you have complete control over the app layout.

Model-driven apps are usually used for platforms like Dynamics 365 to develop end-to-end business solutions by making use of Dataverse. For development in SharePoint, we use canvas apps and they are therefore the focus of this book.

Getting Started with Canvas Apps

Let's get familiar with the Power Apps Studio and start creating an app. First, go to `https://make.powerapps.com/` and follow the steps to sign up for Power Apps. Since you already got the Microsoft 365 developer trial license, you don't need to now acquire a separate license for Power Apps. Just follow the steps for signing up, and a window, like the one in Figure 4-1, will open.

Figure 4-1. *Power Apps designer*

Select SharePoint as your data source. As shown in Figure 4-2, you'll be taken to a page where you can enter the SharePoint site URL and select the connection, which will consist of your SharePoint credentials. In the next window, select Products and click Connect on the bottom of the screen.

Figure 4-2. *Connecting to the data source*

After clicking Connect, it will take few seconds to load the canvas. You can skip the dialog box that appears. Once the canvas loads, you will be able to see your product list items.

In the screenshot in Figure 4-3, you can see all the product items. Observe that there are three screens available in the tree view on the left-hand side. In BrowseScreen1, you'll see the list of products. In DetailScreen1, you'll see THE details of the selected products; if you use EditScreen1, you can see the same details but in Edit mode. Preview App is selected in in the top right-hand corner of the screen and IS also available by pressing F5 on your keyboard.

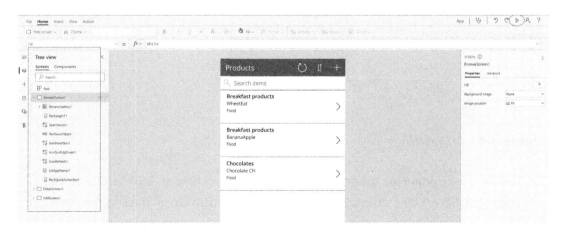

Figure 4-3. *Products home screen*

The app will load in preview form. You can conduct several operations here. Click each item to view its details. On the view page, there will be a pencil icon with which you can edit any of the field values. You'll also be given a delete icon to delete an item if required. Use the vertical scrollbar to view and edit more fields. Once you're finished editing, you can use the tick mark on the top to save your changes to SharePoint. If you go back to the home screen, you can use the + icon to add a new item, enter details, and save the changes like you did for the Edit Screen.

In addition to this, you can search, sort, and refresh items from the home screen. If you add more products using the app, you'll have more items to play around with.

Now let's go back to the designer, save the current app, and see how each functionality works. After that, we can add some more logic to the form. Note that, by designer I mean the canvas where you work with the controls.

Let's save the current form and then make changes to it. Click File, which is located on the top left side menu. The Settings page for the app will open. Provide a Name, Icon, Background Color, and Description for the app as highlighted in Figure 4-4.

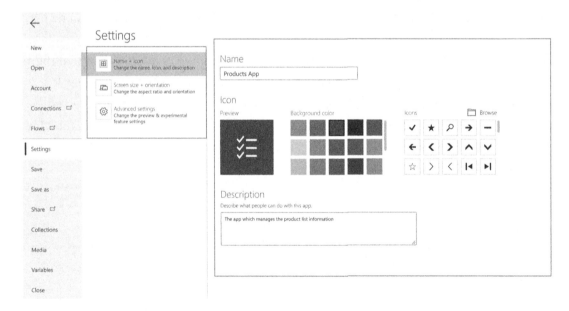

Figure 4-4. *App settings*

You can also update the other settings such as Screen Size and Advanced Settings and then click Save. Once saved, you can use the back arrow to go back to the designer. You can save your changes to the canvas at any time during development using the keyboard shortcuts Ctrl+S.

Understanding the Canvas Better

Let's take a deep look at the screens and their properties before implementing some business logic. As I mentioned earlier, we have three screens. The main one shows the list of products; the other two are for the display and editing of forms.

So, where does the data for this form come from? We connected to the product list while creating the app itself. You can see the Products data connection if you click the Data icon on the left side of the designer, as shown in Figure 4-5.

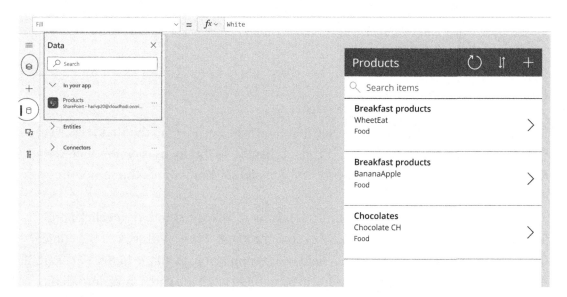

Figure 4-5. *Data source*

Go back to the tree view by clicking the Tree View icon on the top of the screen as shown in Figure 4-6.

Figure 4-6. *Properties and expressions*

From the tree view, click any of the Products; Breakfast Products, for example.

As shown in Figure 4-7, in the Text pane on the right-hand side of the screen, you can see a number of properties for the selected field, which you can configure according to your needs.

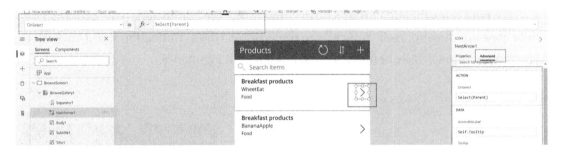

Figure 4-7. *Icon properties*

On the top of the pane, you can see that the Text value is set to the `ThisItem.Title` expression. Change it to `ThisItem.'Product Name'`, as our focus is on Product Name field. Similarly, if you open the drop-down, you can see number of other properties you can configure.

Each field value displayed on the screen is set to an expression. If you click Food, for example, you can see it is set to `ThisItem.'Product Type'.Value`, as it is a choice field. The properties you set for each field will be applicable to all the items. For example, if you set Red color font for the title, it will be applied to all the cards, meaning all the items. Each item is displayed as a card on the canvas.

If you click the > sign on the right side of any card, you can view an `OnSelect` property in the Advanced section of the Text pane, which is set to the expression `Select (Parent')`. This will help you redirect the item to specific item details screen. You can also set a different icon, tool tip, or any other properties. You can view or modify the properties in the drop-down at the top as well.

You can customize the other two screens and properties in a similar way. Click each screen to have a look at the properties and play around with them. In the Edit and Details Screens, the properties you configure for a field will be applicable only to that field. This is because these screens represent a single card, whereas the Browse Screen represents a bunch of cards.

If you notice, in between the Tree View and data icons, there is a + button. You can insert controls like Label, Button, and Date Picker using that screen. Below the Home menu at the top, there is a New Screen option, which you can use to create a new screen and add to the app. There are few other options, too, such as the Theme option, which you can use to set a different theme.

If you select BrowseGallery1, you can see and modify the properties of the gallery on the right, such as replacing the layout with a different one. See Figure 4-8.

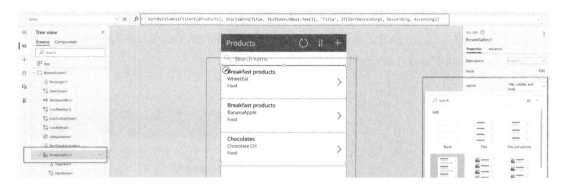

Figure 4-8. *Browsing, sorting, and filtering the gallery layout*

In Figure 4-8, you can also see how the sorting and filter expression is given on the top:

```
SortByColumns(Filter([@Products], StartsWith(Title, TextSearchBox1.Text)),
"Title", If(SortDescending1, Descending, Ascending))
```

This expression allows you to sort the products in ascending order based on the Title. The last two sections denote the sorting part in Field, Order. You can sort any other field in either ascending or descending order. I updated it to sort by the Product Name. To do that, I just replaced Title with Product Name. By default, the order is ascending; by clicking the Sort icon, the default order will be reversed to descending.

Filter denotes the search. Whenever you search for a keyword, the screen will display all the products cards with Title starts with the keyword. For example, if you search for "Break," the first two products will be displayed on the screen. If you replace StartsWith with EndsWith, the products whose Title ending with the keyword will be displayed.

This section has been focused on giving you an overall idea of screens, property configurations, and so on. Next, let's look at some customizations for the Edit and Details screens with respect to our Cloudhadi requirements.

Multiple Edit Screens

We created the app by connecting to the data source and all the fields got populated by default. If you go to the edit screen, you'll notice there is a vertical scrollbar. Let's create two different screens and split the columns into screens for a better user experience.

So, we have an edit screen and we need to create another one and link them together. To start, click the ... icon to the right of EditScreen1 and then Duplicate Screen to create a copy of the screen, as shown in Figure 4-9.

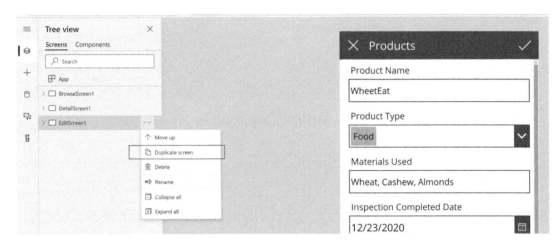

Figure 4-9. *Duplicating a screen*

A new EditScreen1_1 screen will now be created.

Under EditScreen1, expand EditForm1. Let's keep Product Name, Product Type, Materials Used, and Product Status on the screen by selecting all other data cards except these and clicking Delete. See Figure 4-10. To select multiple data cards, press Ctrl on your keyboard and click each card.

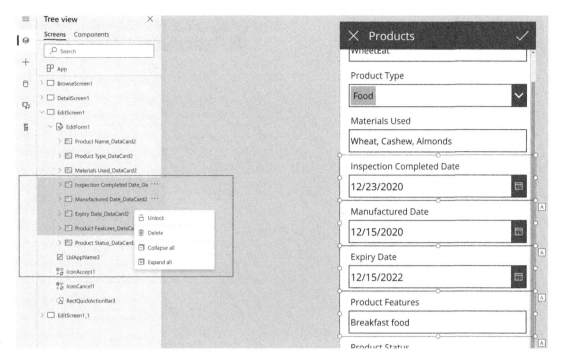

Figure 4-10. *Deleting data cards*

Now, again under EditForm1_1, repeat the same steps, but this time delete the Product Name, Product Type, Materials Used, and Product Status cards. Keep the others. We now have four fields in EditScreen1 and the remaining four in EditScreen1_1.

Let's give a heading to both forms. Select EditForm1 using the top circle on the line and drag it little below to give a space for a header text. See Figure 4-11.

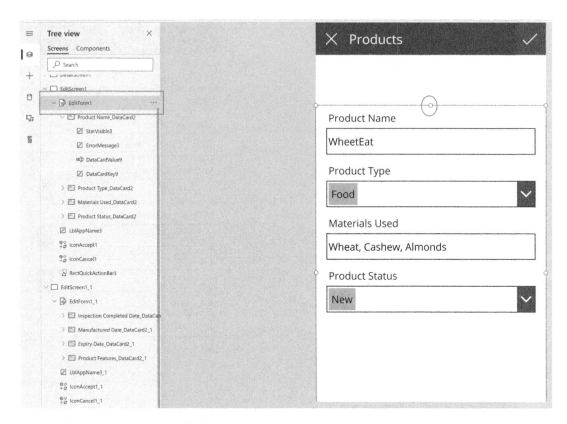

Figure 4-11. *Dragging EditForm1*

Click the + icon to insert a text label, as shown in Figure 4-12. A label that says Text will be created. Drag it to fit into the Edit Screen space. Type in "Product Info." You can configure the style using the right hand side properties window as you wish. The styling I applied is selected in the figure.

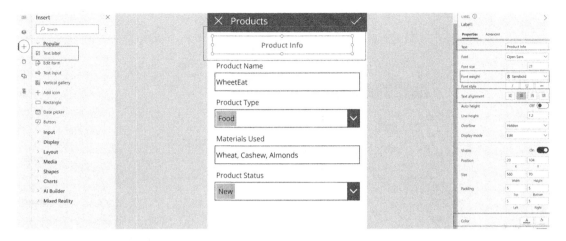

Figure 4-12. *Inserting and styling a header text*

Now go back to the tree view and repeat the same steps for EditScreen1_1. Name the heading "Quality Info," and then click File and save. Give some type of version note, such as "Multiple screens added." You don't have to publish now. If you click See All Versions, you can see all the versions and restore an older one if required.

Note   You can always save the changes by pressing the Ctrl+S shortcuts. This will create a new version. However, I recommend you save the major changes with a version note. This will help you to identify the right version in case you need to restore it.

Now we need to link both screens. Click the back arrow to return to the canvas. Let's add an arrow icon on EditScreen1 to navigate to EditScreen1_1. Go to EditScreen1, select EditForm1, and free up the extra space below Product Status using the drag feature. Use the + icon, scroll down and click to expand Shapes. Then select the Next arrow. The Next arrow component will be inserted in the screen. Drag it to the bottom of EditForm1. See Figure 4-13.

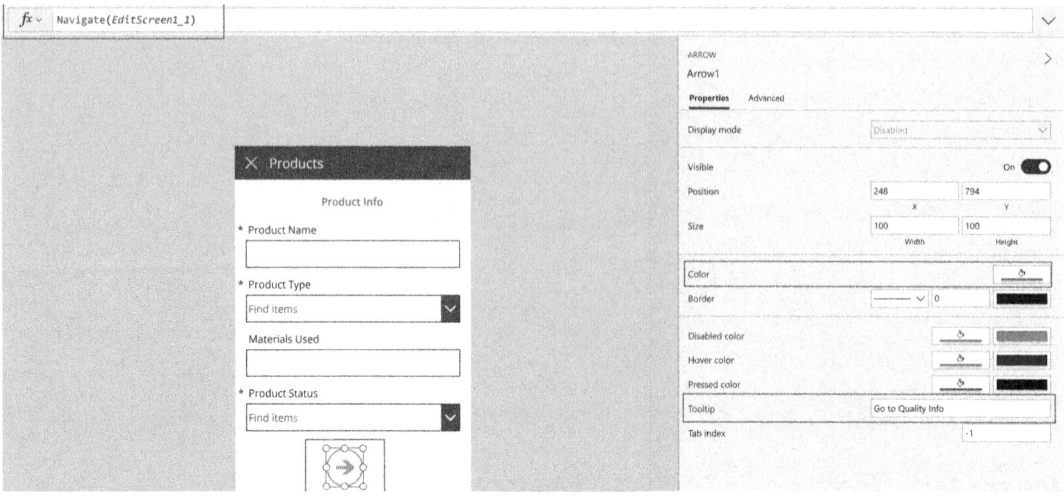

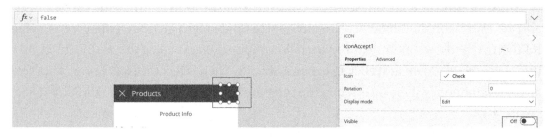

Figure 4-13. *Setting the navigation and style for the Next arrow*

As selected in Figure 4-13, you can set the `OnSelect` property of the arrow icon. Select the Next arrow, `OnSelect` property will be visible on top to edit. Set the value to `Navigate(EditScreen1_1)` This ensures that by clicking the icon, you will get to the next screen. Go to the properties window on the right and set the styles, as selected in Figure 4-13.

Let's hide the submit icon (tick) from the top, as we don't want to submit the form from the first Edit Screen. We should submit it from the Quality Info screen after filling in the details for both screens. Select the submit icon and then set the Visible toggle to off. See Figure 4-14.

Figure 4-14. *Hiding the tick icon from EditForm1*

We'll take similar steps for the Quality Info screen, which is EditForm1_1. Use the back arrow and set `OnSelect` to `Navigate(EditScreen1)`. Set similar styles for this screen.

Press F5 to preview the app. Try navigating between the screens to make sure everything is working as expected. Then, close the preview and save the changes with a version note. Let's have a look at validation next.

Validation

We now have two screens for the Edit Form of a product. Let's include some validations. On the Product Info screen, except Materials Used, the other three fields should be mandatory. Also, the validation should occur within Product Info screen when you click the Next arrow not on submit on the Quality Info screen.

As shown in Figure 4-15, select Product Name_DataCard2 and go to the Advanced tab. Click Unlock to Change Properties and set the Required property to True.

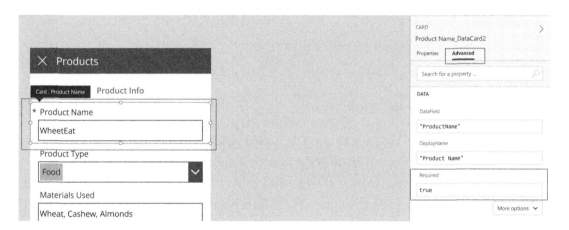

Figure 4-15. *Making a field mandatory*

The * icon will now be visible to the left of Product Name. Repeat the same steps for the Product Type and Product Status fields.

We can create a new product to test this. But before we do that, we need to ensure that users cannot go to the next screen unless all mandatory fields are filled in. Click the arrow and select `DisplayMode` property from the top and set it to `If(EditForm1.Valid, DisplayMode.Edit, Disabled)`. See Figure 4-16.

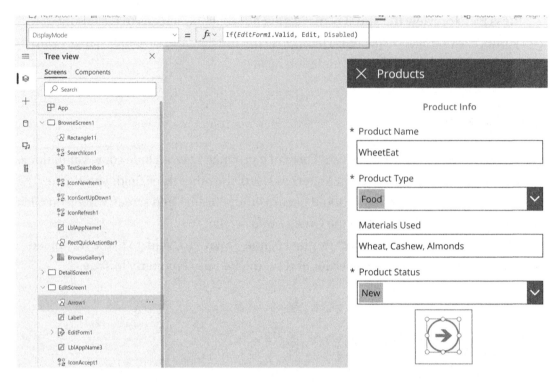

Figure 4-16. *Screen validation*

This expression If (EditForm1.Valid, DisplayMode.Edit, Disabled) checks if edit form is valid, enabling the arrow if if it is and disabling it if it isn't.

Click the Browse Screen from the Tree view, press F5, and try to create a new product using + button. Unless you enter values for Product Name, Product Type, and Product Status, the arrow will be disabled. See Figure 4-17.

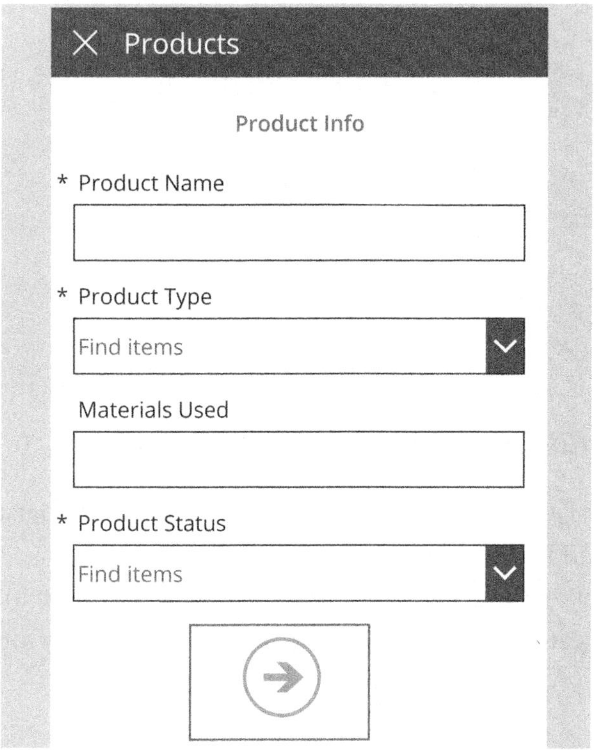

Figure 4-17. *Product Info preview for multiple screens*

Now go to EditScreen1_1 for Quality Info and make all three date fields mandatory like we did for Product Info.

We can configure the display mode property of the tick button (submit) in the same way we did for the arrow in the Product Info screen. But let's set the visibility here, as the tick button will not provide a good user experience with the disabled effect. Set the Visible property to If(EditForm1_1.Valid, true, false). This ensures that the submit option will be visible only if the form is valid. See Figure 4-18.

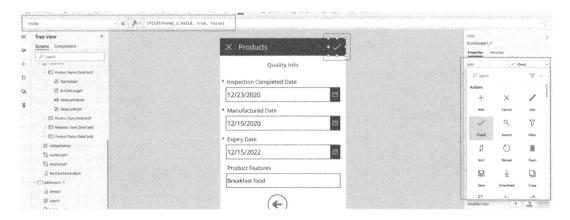

Figure 4-18. *Setting the visibility for submit*

If you'd like to set a different icon for submit, you can do so using the Properties pane, as selected in Figure 4-18.

We need to set up the home screen, navigation, and submit functions before we can use the form to create or edit data. We can also set up a display form.

Connecting the Screens

Go to BrowseScreen1 using the Tree view. For navigating between the screens, always use the Tree view. The Tree view is shown in Figure 4-8. There are three fields set for each data card. Update the properties for all three fields. Set the text property of the three fields to `This.'ProductName'.Value`, `This.'ProductStatus.Value`, and `This.'ProductType'.Value` respectively. This will highlight these values on the home screen for each product. Also drag the data card to reduce its size, keeping some space on the right side. Drag the view icon from right to left to get space for another icon. Then, go to DetailScreen1, select the pencil icon, and copy and paste it to the right side of the view icon in one of the items in BrowseScreen1. Select it and change the color to blue. It will appear for all datacards now. The form will look like Figure 4-19.

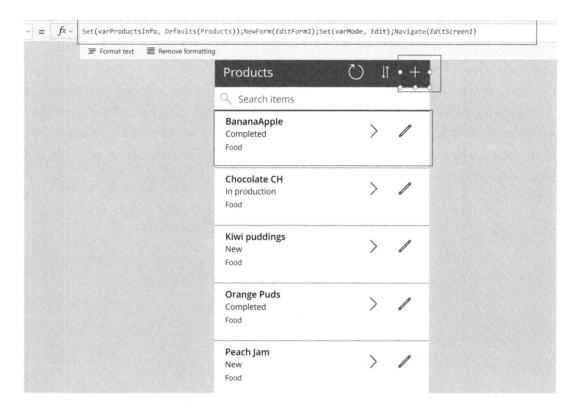

Figure 4-19. Browse Screen Edit icon and OnSelect for New icon

Select the + icon on the top right as highlighted in Figure 4-19. Put the expression Set(varProductsInfo, Defaults(Products));NewForm(EditForm1);Set(varMode, FormMode.Edit);Navigate(EditScreen1) into the OnSelect property. Set(varProductsInfo, Defaults(Products)) creates a variable and assigns the default data source value to it. NewForm(EditForm1) sets the EditForm in New Form mode. We're also setting the varMode variable to edit, which will be required at a later stage to differentiate with view mode. Finally, we're setting the navigation to the first Edit Screen, which is EditScreen1. Now when you click the icon, the app will open EditScreen1.

Repeat these steps for editing and viewing icons. For the edit icon, set varProductsInfo to ThisItem instead of to Defaults(Products). This ensures that the current item is passed to Edit Form. The final expression will be as follows:

```
Set(varProductsInfo, ThisItem);Set(varMode, FormMode.Edit);
Navigate(EditScreen1)
```

For the view icon, the only difference is the variable varMode should be set to
FormMode.View. The expression is Set(varProductsInfo, ThisItem);Set(varMode,
FormMode.View);Navigate(EditScreen1).

Now, we have all three icons set up to redirect to the right form in the right mode.
Now go to EditScreen1 ➤ EditForm1 and set DefaultMode to varMode and set Item value
to varProductsInfo. Setting the item property ensures that the form updates refer to the
same record. The mode helps to use the same form for the view data when view mode is
passed. See Figure 4-20.

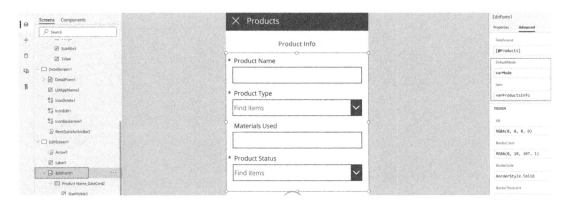

Figure 4-20. *Setting the Item property and mode*

Repeat the same steps for EditScreen1_1 ➤ EditForm1_1. In addition, select the
accept icon (tick mark) and set the OnSelect property as follows:

```
Patch(Products, varProductsInfo, EditForm1.Updates, EditForm1_1.Updates);
If(
    IsEmpty(Errors(Products)),    Notify("Products updated",
    NotificationType.Success); Navigate(BrowseScreen1),
    Notify(First(Errors(Products)).Message, NotificationType.Error)
)
```

The patch function will create or modify the product item for you. It accepts the data
source, Products, as a parameter. The second parameter is the varProductsInfo, which
references the items from each screen. In addition, the updates to both the forms are
passed as parameters. If the patch is successful, the app will send a success message, and
if it fails, it will send an error notification.

Also, update the visible property of the tick icon to If(EditForm1_1.Valid &&
varMode = FormMode.Edit, true, false). This ensures that the icon will not be visible
to view forms. Also, the quality info details (EditForm1_1) should be valid for the icon to
be displayed. We have already hidden the icon from EditForm1.

Figure 4-21 shows how to set OnSelect and visible properties to the tick icon.

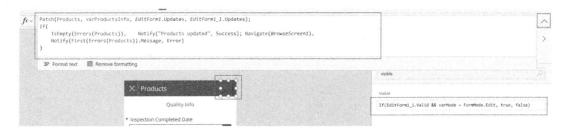

Figure 4-21. *Patch function*

Note   You can delete DetailScreen1 since we're not using it. Also, you can add a
delete function for BrowseScreen1. I'll leave it for you to explore.

Save the changes and try to create, edit, and validate the items using the app. But
before trying to create items, make sure that the Title column in the product list in
SharePoint is set to nonmandatory. Otherwise, you won't be able to create items, as we
don't have a title for our form. Once everything looks good, you can publish the form.
Click File, save the changes, and then click Publish and then Publish This Version on the
pop-up, as in Figure 4-22.

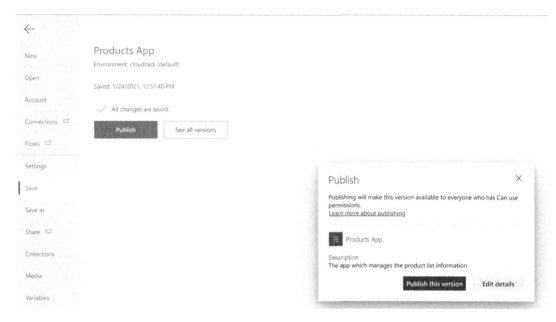

Figure 4-22. *Publishing the App*

Once the App is published, a Share Products App button will become available. Click it to share the App with the users you choose. Once you close the Share Products App window, you'll be able to see the App details. A web link will be available, which you can use to create or edit products to SharePoint List from Power Apps. See Figure 4-23.

Figure 4-23. *App details*

You might have noticed that the Products App is mobile friendly. But if you're looking at the App on a desktop browser, it will appear on the center of the page. The current user interface is suitable for a mobile device. We need to make the App suitable for desktop and tablet devices as well. We'll see how to do that in the next section.

You can always come back to the App screen by going to Apps on the `make.powerapps.com` page.

If you install Power Apps on your mobile or tablet and log in with your Microsoft 365 credentials, you can insert, edit, and delete data from the Products list on your device. But, as I mentioned earlier, the App will not be responsive by design. We'll take a look at how to make it responsive in the next section.

Making a Power App Responsive

Let's start by going to `make.powerapps.com` and clicking Apps. As shown in Figure 4-24, select Products App and click the Edit icon on the context menu or on the top toolbar. This will open the canvas for you.

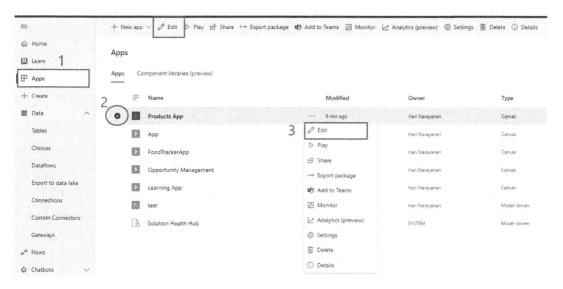

Figure 4-24. *Editing the published app*

Click File from the top left of the canvas and then click Settings in the left navigation bar, as shown in Figure 4-25. Select Screen Size + Orientation. Set the Orientation to Portrait mode, turn off Scale to Fit, and click Apply. This ensures that the app won't scale anymore but will instead fill the screen.

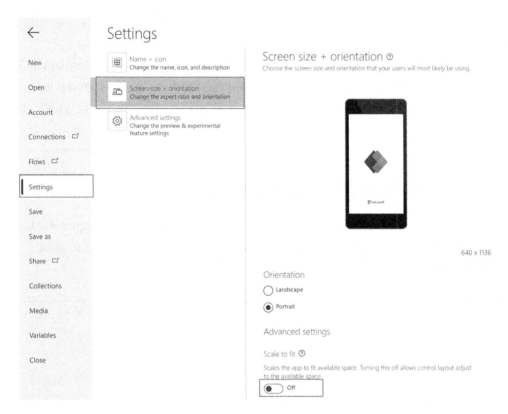

Figure 4-25. *Turning off Scale to Fit*

Now, click the back arrow to return to the canvas. To preview the screen, click the preview button or F5 from BrowseScreen1. You can see that the screen now fits the desktop view. Click any of the items using the right arrow. You will be redirected to the Details Screen. In the Details Screen, you can see that the form is floating on the left side of the screen and there's a lot of empty space on the right side. See Figure 4-26.

Products
Product Info
Product Name
BananaApple
Product Type
Food
Materials Used
Banana, Apple, Cashew, Almonds
Product Status
Completed

Figure 4-26. *View item desktop appearance*

Let's close the preview and go back to the canvas. Go to EditScreen1 ➤ EditForm1. Update the Columns to 4. This will set it up so that there are four columns in one row. See Figure 4-27.

Tree view
Products
Product Info
Prod...
Prod...
Mate...
Prod...
Banan
Food
Banan
Com...

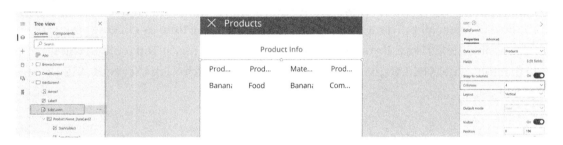

Figure 4-27. *Updating the number of columns in EditForm1*

If you're also viewing this on a mobile screen, you'll see four columns in one row, which will look weird. You can preview the app, minimize the browser, and try to simulate mobile and tablet views.

To overcome this, we need to make sure that four columns per row only appear in the desktop view and that there is only one column per row in the mobile view. Similarly, there should be only two columns per row in the vertical view on a tablet and three for the horizontal view. The screen size will be 1 for the mobile view; 4 for the desktop view; and 2 and 3, respectively, for the vertical and horizontal views on a tablet.

By default, the size break points for the width in the app are 1 (small), which ranges from 0 to 1200; 2 (medium), ranging from 1200 to 1800; and 3 (large), ranging from 1800 to 2400. 2400 and above is considered 4 (extra large). If you click App from Tree view, you can see the size break points defined in the properties window on the right. See Figure 4-28.

Figure 4-28. *Predefined size break points*

If we divide the screen width by size, it will be a perfect width for each data card column. The data cards will become responsive.

You can select all the data cards in the form at the same time by clicking your mouse and pressing the Ctrl key. If you select the Width property on the top toolbar, you'll see that the value is 640. Replace it with `EditScreen1.Width/ EditScreen1.Size`. See Figure 4-29.

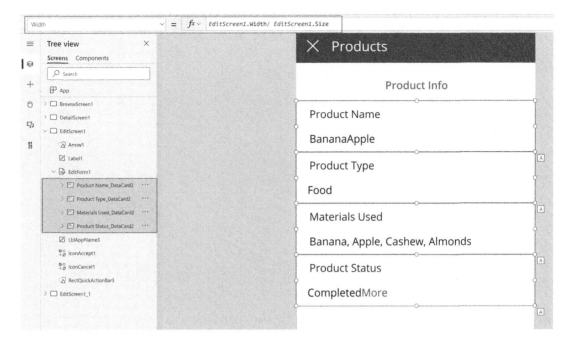

Figure 4-29. *Setting the width of the data cards in EditForm1*

Doing this will set the width of all columns based on screen size to simulate desktop, mobile, and tablet screens. The number of columns will also get adjusted based on the screen size. Repeat the same steps for setting width for EditForm1_1. Set `columns` to `4` and set the `width` to `EditScreen1_1.Width/ EditScreen1_1.Size`. Now both of the screens are responsive for Details Screen. As we use the same screens for Edit and New, Edit and New Screens are also responsive now.

For EditScreen1_1, for the icon submit tick, update property X to the screen width of 90. This will ensure the icon floats to the left. See Figure 4-30.

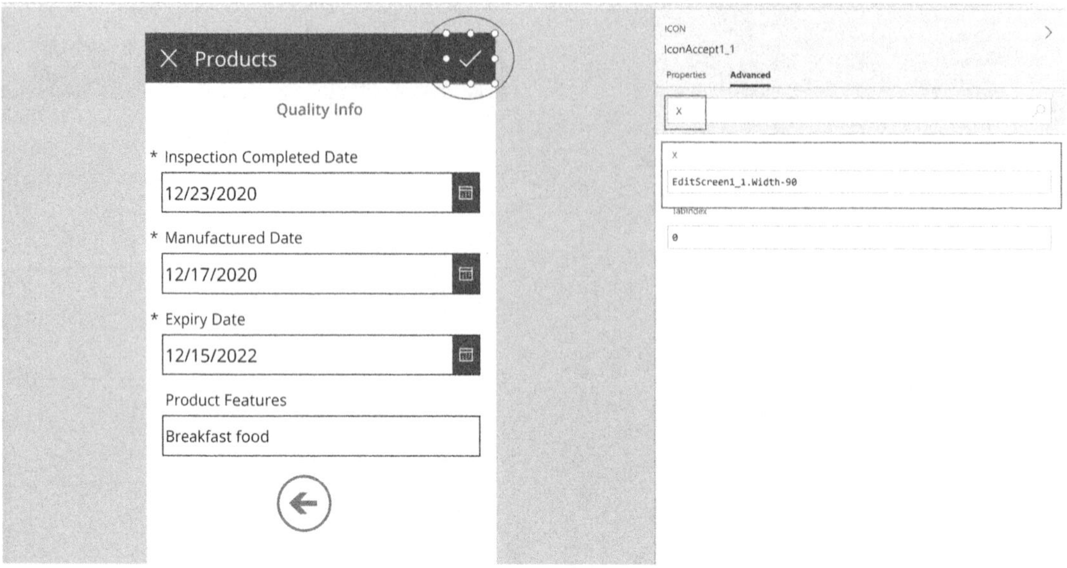

Figure 4-30. *Setting the responsiveness for the icon tick*

Go ahead and preview the App. The New Edit and Details forms are now responsive in both screens. Figure 4-31 shows the second Edit Screen in desktop view.

Figure 4-31. *Responsive forms*

Note   For reference, you can download the final app package from Chapter 4 folder of the GitHub repository at `https://github.com/Apress/building-modern-workplace-sharepoint-online/tree/13fe6c9973a5f3c1066f4 b16a53a67afd31a0e1f/Chapter%204`. You can import the package by going to `http://make.powerapps.com`, then Apps ➤ Import Canvas App.

Power Apps List Forms

We now have the Products App that works across all devices. Next, let's create a form that can be used within a SharePoint list as new and edit form. How can we achieve that?

If you go to the product list, you can see Power Apps option in the context menu. Click it and then Customize Forms, as shown in Figure 4-32.

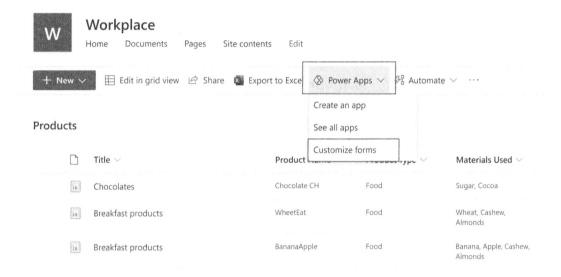

Figure 4-32. *Customizing list forms in Power Apps*

This will take you to Power Apps. Delete everything in the designer and start fresh. Click Choose the Fields … and add the fields to the form. Select all the fields that we previously used in the app. By clicking Add once, all the fields will be selected. See Figure 4-33.

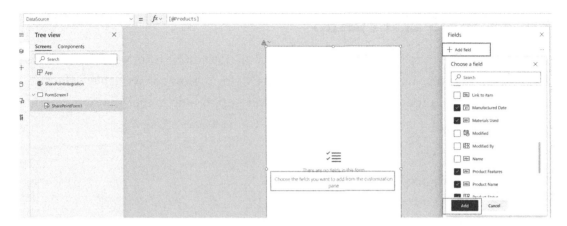

Figure 4-33. *Adding fields to the form*

The fields will be populated inside the form. Select each data card that needs to be mandatory and set Required to true. Figure 4-34 shows the Product Name data card as an example.

Figure 4-34. *Setting the properties of data cards*

Let's publish this form to SharePoint. Go to File and save the changes with a version note like you did for the app. You'll see a Publish to SharePoint button. Click it and a pop-up will open telling you that publishing the form will make it visible to everyone who uses the SharePoint list. Click Publish to SharePoint again and all of your changes will be published. Go back to the product list and refresh. Then go to New ➤ Item. The Power Apps form will open instead of the SharePoint OOB form. Select an item and click Edit to view the edited form in Power Apps. Basically, the SharePoint OOB form has been replaced with the Power Apps form. See Figure 4-35.

Figure 4-35. *SharePoint form using Power Apps*

You can validate and save the data using this form. We can customize the form with different logics and user interfaces in Power Apps and publish it to SharePoint. We can implement multiple screens, tabs, and so on. Let's split the columns into two sections like we did for the app, but instead of multiple screens, we'll use the tabbed form. Next, let's get familiar with creating these forms.

Note   If you'd prefer to remove the Power Apps form and revert the list forms to SharePoint, go to List Settings ➤ Form settings. Select Use the Default SharePoint Form.

Tabbed Forms

We're going to create two tabs: Product Info and Quality Info. While creating the multiple screen design for the App, we set up two screens and split the column so that it could be viewed in them. In the tabbed design, we'll use a single screen and set the visibility of columns based on tab.

To start, go to Tree View ➤ FormScreen1 ➤ SharePointForm1. Drag SharePointForm1 to the bottom of the screen and add two buttons to the top using the + icon. Name the buttons "Product Info" and "Quality Info" and drag the them so that they position properly at the top. Set the style for the Product Info button, as shown in Figures 4-36 and 4-37.

Figure 4-36. *Setting the text and width for the Product Info button*

Figure 4-37. *Setting the radius for the Product Info button*

Create the width for the Product Info button by setting the top-left and top-right radius to 15 to make it look like a tab. To create the radius, search for "radius" in the Advanced Properties section. Repeat the styling for the Quality Info button.

Now we need to show and hide the tabs based on the selection. To do this, you need to understand the concept of variables. Mainly, there are two ways to set the variables of a screen in Power Apps: by using Set() or by using UpdateContext({}). If you use Set, Power Apps will create a global variable that can be used across multiple screens. UpdateContext is used for local variables, and can't be used for global ones. In this scenario, we can make use of UpdateContext since we're using only one screen.

We'll have two Boolean variables, tab1 and tab2. By selecting the Product Info tab, we can set tab1=true and tab2=false. By selecting the Quality Info tab, we can do the reverse. Set the visibility of each field to tab1 or tab2 based on which tab the field needs to fit in. You don't need to create these variables explicitly; Power Apps will create them the first time you set the UpdateContext for the variables.

For clarity, take a look at Figure 4-38 and the explanation that follows.

Figure 4-38. *Setting* `OnSelect` *and* `Fill` *for the tab*

As shown in Figure 4-38, set the `OnSelect` property of the Product Info tab to `Upda teContext({tab1:true});UpdateContext({tab2:false});`. This will create two local Boolean variables `tab1` and `tab2` for the screen. By selecting the Product Info tab, the `tab1` variable will be set to true and the `tab2` variable will be set to false.

Next, configure the `Fill` property to differentiate the selected tab with a background color. I set it to `If(tab1, Blue, LightBlue)`, which means the Product Info tab will be a blue color when `tab1` is set to true. This happens when the tab is selected. So, if selected the tab will be blue, and if not selected it will be light blue.

Repeat these steps for the Qualify Info button by replacing `tab1` with `tab2` and vice versa. `OnSelect` should be `UpdateContext({tab1:true});UpdateContext({tab2:false});` and `Fill` should be `If(tab1, Blue, LightBlue)`.

Additionally, we need to have the Product Info button get selected by default while the form loads. To set this, select `FormScreen1` and set the `OnVisible` property to `Update Context({tab1:true});UpdateContext({tab2:false});`. See Figure 4-39.

Figure 4-39. *Setting the Product Info button to get selected by default on load*

The next step is to set the visibility for each field. Select each data card from the left and configure the property `visible` with respective tab variables. For Product Name, Product Type, Materials Used and Product Status, set it to `tab1` and for the remaining fields, set it to `tab2`. Figure 4-40 shows the `Product Name` field as an example.

Figure 4-40. *Setting the visibility for each field based on the tab*

Note   When you're setting the visibility, fields may disappear from the canvas. If you'd like to modify any field properties later on, you can always select the data card from the left side to do so.

Now you can publish the form to a SharePoint list. But before you do so, check the Variables section to see that the two variables are there, as shown in Figure 4-41.

Figure 4-41. *Variables in Power Apps*

Once the form is published to SharePoint, go to the product list and hit Refresh. Click New. The customized form will look like the one in Figure 4-42. You can click the tabs to verify the changes you made in both new and edit mode.

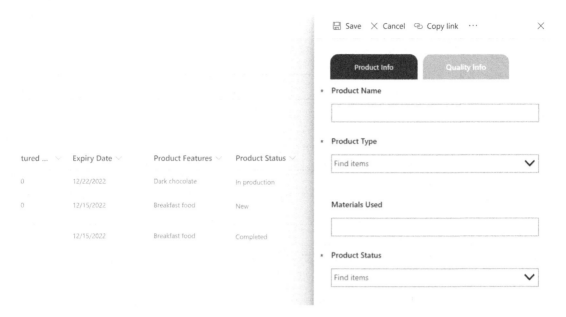

Figure 4-42. *SharePoint List: Customized Power Apps form*

Summary

In this chapter, we went over creating a stand-alone canvas app in Power Apps. You got familiar with the Power Apps designer and learned how to use various icons and components. You learned how to create multiple screens and link them together. We reviewed on-form validations and how to set different properties for different components. We looked at how to publish an app and use it with different devices.

In addition to this, we took a look at how to customize a list form within SharePoint. You learned about variables and different ways of setting them. You got familiar with how to create tabbed forms by making use of variables and properties. In the process, we also satisfied the requirement for the Cloudhadi project by developing a custom form and a stand-alone app for product data operations. Now, you have experience with creating and customizing user interface forms using Power Apps with SharePoint as a data source.

In this chapter, I focused on getting you aligned with Power Apps by stressing the basics. We took a learning-by-doing approach. I'd suggest you explore different ways of customizing the forms on your own, so that you can become an expert in Power Apps.

In the next chapter, we'll move on to Power Automate. I'll introduce you to SharePoint workflows and how Power Automate can bring modern automation capabilities.

CHAPTER 5

Power Automate

In the previous chapters, we looked at creating and customizing SharePoint Online forms. In this chapter, our focus will be on building business process automation using workflows. Forms allow users to enter and view data. Workflows are applications that contain a preprogrammed set of tasks. A simple example of a time when a workflow would be used with respect to our case study would be if you need to send an email when a new product is created in the Products list.

Power Automate is a service that allows you to create automated workflows. You can connect to hundreds of data sources with Power Automate or send automatic reminders based on a due date. Here, we use SharePoint Online as the primary data source for Power Automate. Power Automate is a widely used tool for the automation of business processes. The workflows that we create within Power Automate are called flows.

In this chapter, we'll focus on creating flows within Power Automate and communicating with SharePoint. You'll learn about different triggers and actions. We'll go over expressions, variable, and approvals and explore solutions, child flows, and how to connect different flows. We'll touch upon how to prepare flows to move from one environment to another. In the final section, we'll do a quick review of how Power Apps and Power Automate communicate with each other. By the end of this chapter, you'll be familiar with Power Automate and how to use it for various business requirements. Along with learning the process, we'll develop a few flows to bring some of the workplace site requirements into action.

Creating Your First Flow

Let's start by creating a flow for product document approval. If you recall the requirement in Chapter 2, when the product executive requests approval using the Initiate Approval button, the appropriate product lead should receive the request and activate it. Once the document is approved by the product lead, it will be published for end users.

© Harinarayanan V P 2021
Harinarayanan V P, *Building the Modern Workplace with SharePoint Online*,
https://doi.org/10.1007/978-1-4842-6945-9_5

Type `flow.microsoft.com` in your browser and follow the steps that come up. The license you already have for Microsoft 365 will be adequate for this purpose. There are premium connectors, some of which we'll use in this chapter. You can make use of the trail license for those.

Once the home page is loaded, click Create, then select Instant Cloud Flow, as shown in Figure 5-1.

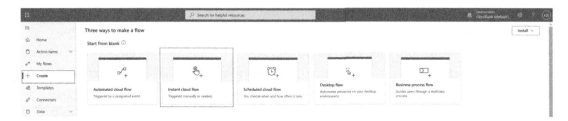

Figure 5-1. *Selecting Instant Cloud Flow*

In the screen that pops up, choose For a Selected File, give it a name, and click Create, as shown in Figure 5-2. We selected this trigger because we need it to be activated by clicking a button on a particular document. We need to provide the flow ID on the click of button, which we will see in the upcoming section.

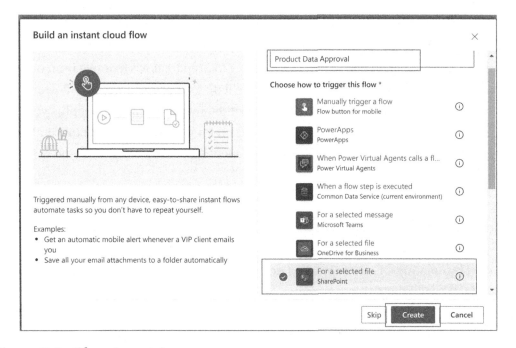

Figure 5-2. *Choosing a trigger*

When selecting the trigger, make sure the data source is SharePoint, as there is also similar trigger available for OneDrive. The flow will be created, and you will be redirected to the designer. You can add actions, conditions, and more on this screen. But before doing that, configure the trigger by providing values for Site Address and Library Name, as shown in Figure 5-3.

Click New Step and search for "Get file," then select Get File Properties. Provide values for the Site Address and Library Name, as we did in the previous step. Clicking inside the ID box, as shown in Figure 5-3, will allow you to add dynamic content in a pop-up. Select ID from the window that pops up. This dynamic ID value results from the For a Selected File action we took previously.

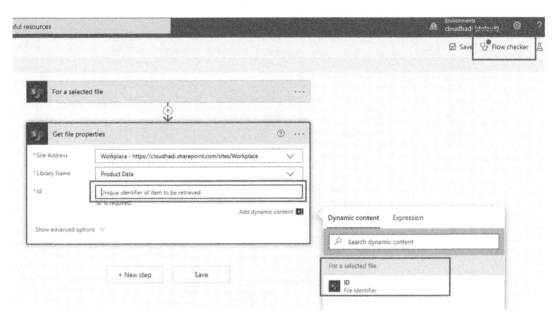

Figure 5-3. *Selecting the Dynamic Content*

As you can see in Figure 5-3, there is a warning symbol on the Flow Checker in the upper left-hand corner of the screen. You can click it to see the details. The Flow Checker instantly checks the flow and provides you with errors and warnings if there are any. As we haven't selected the ID yet, it is giving us the error that an ID is mandatory. If you click the error message, it will go away.

Get File Properties action will get you all the properties of the file. Why we use this?In the next step we need to send an approval task to the Product Lead. We need email of the Product Lead to send the approval task. The trigger For a Selected File will return only a few properties for the document, such as ID. To get all the properties of the document such as

145

Product Lead, we need to query the specified document in the library using the document's ID. Get File Properties is the built-in action that brings up all the properties of a given file. If you click Show Advanced Options, you can limit the columns to a particular view.

We now have all the properties of the document. Let's configure an approval task for the product lead. This might consist of notifying the product lead and letting the approver know the details of the document. They can act on it accordingly. To achieve this, click New Step, search for "Start and wait," and select Start and Wait for an Approval. Then click Create under Create a Connection for Approvals, in case if there is no connection. See Figure 5-4, after which I will explain the details.

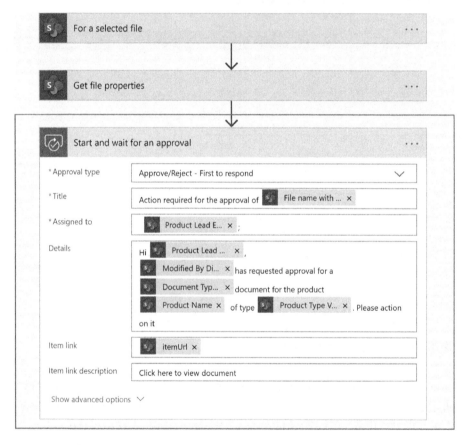

Figure 5-4. *Configuring an approval action*

The Start and Wait for an Approval action will create an approval task and wait for it to be completed before moving on to next step. For the Approval Type, select Approve/Reject — First to Respond. This means that if there are multiple approvers, once the first approver acts on a task, it will be completed. It doesn't apply in our case since we have only one approver.

For other boxes, you need to fill in the dynamic content, as you already did with the previous Get File Properties action. Click inside each text box as well as the pop-up, search for the appropriate dynamic content, and add it. For Assigned To, select Product Lead Email. When selecting Product Type in the Details section, choose Product Type Value from the dynamic content, as it is a Choice field. If you select Product Type, it will return an object instead of a value. The same goes for Document Type. For the Product Lead name, select Product Lead DisplayName.

To mention the requester name, I selected Modified By DisplayName. Finally, to provide a link to the document in the Item Link field, select itemUrl. While selecting dynamic content fields from the pop-up, make sure that they are under the right action, which in this case is Get File Properties.

In the next step, we need to figure out the outcome of the previous task and whether the approver approved or rejected it. To do this, we need to add a condition to check the result. Click New Step and search for "Condition" and add it. Once added, it will look like as in Figure 5-5.

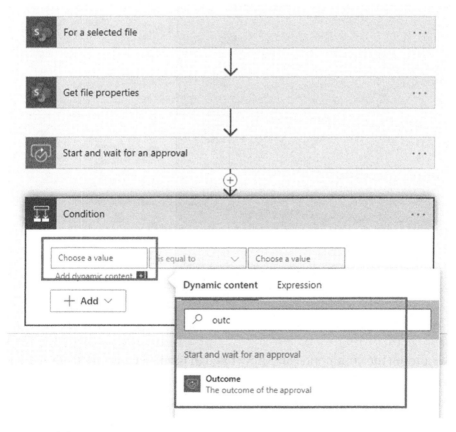

Figure 5-5. *Adding a condition to check the outcome of an approval*

Click inside the Choose a value box on the left hand side and select Outcome, as shown in Figure 5-5. In the right hand side Choose a value box, type Approve. The condition will check if the outcome is equal to Approve. We can add the desired actions inside the If Yes and If No sections.

Let's add an action in the If No section first. We'll send an email to the modified user if the outcome is rejected. To add the Send Email action inside the If No box, search and select the Send an Email(V2) action from the Dynamic content.

Next, add Dynamic content in the To, Subject, and Body sections, as shown in Figure 5-6, like we did for the approval task. When approving or rejecting, the Product Lead can provide comments. We can capture these comments using the Dynamic content Response Comments, which is added inside the body of the notification email to the modified user.

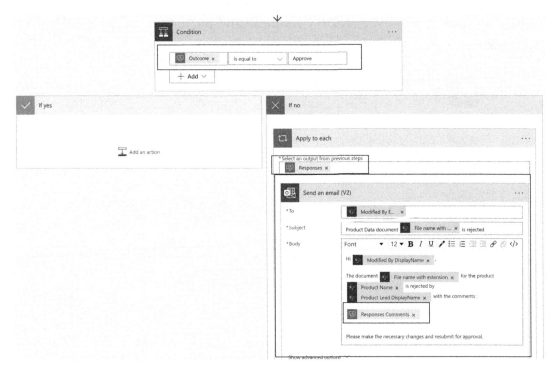

Figure 5-6. *Rejection notification*

While adding the comments, an Apply to Each loop will automatically get added and a Send an Email action will be placed inside of it. This is a known issue with Power Automate. The Approval action returns the responses in a group, even if there is only one response. Just leave that like it is for now, as it doesn't have any impact on the functionality. We'll get rid of these unnecessary Apply to Each items later in the chapter when we're learning expressions.

What we've done so far is to arrange that a notification email will get sent to the Product Executive if the Product Lead rejects the document. If the Lead approves the document, we need to publish a document and send a notification to the executive that says the document has been approved and published. To publish the document, we'll choose Approve for Set Content Approval Status of the document. We'll take a look at that next.

Next, as shown in Figure 5-7, go to the If Yes box and add an action. Search for Get File Metadata Using Path action from the Dynamic content and add it. Provide the Site Address and File Path. You can add the Dynamic contents Folder Path and File Name with Extension for the file path. The Get File Metadata step is required to get an ETag property for the document. The Etag is essential for setting the content approval status.

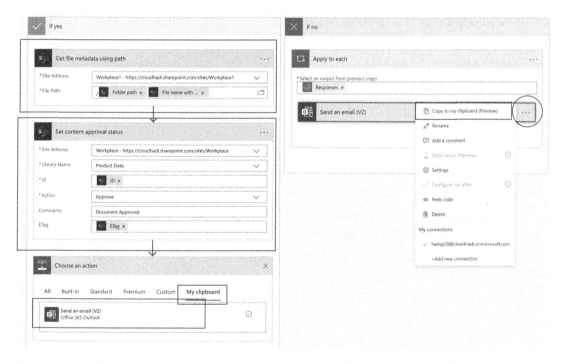

Figure 5-7. *Setting the content approval status and copying to the clipboard*

Now, search for the action Set Content Approval Status from the Dynamic content and add it. Choose values for Site Address, Library Name, and ID. Select Approve for the Action and select ETag value from the Dynamic content for the ETag label, which we created using the previous Get Metadata step. Add your comments as manual text.

Let's add the notification next. Go to the If No box, and in Send an Email (V2), click ... and then choose Copy to My Clipboard (Preview) from the drop-down. In the If Yes box, click + icon below to the Set content approval status action. Click My Clipboard tab and select Send an Email (V2). The copied action will get added below Set content approval status.

Note   The flow will refresh upon copying the action, and you'll need to click the appropriate action headings and expand it again.

Once the action is copied, make changes to its content accordingly and remove the Response Comments section from the body of the mail. We'll add the Comments section later while learning expressions. As mentioned earlier, we don't need the Apply to each action.

We could improve this process by properly naming the actions and so forth, which we'll do in the upcoming sections. Click Save at the top of the screen. This is shown in Figure 5-3 under Create Your First Flow section. You may have a warning from the Flow Checker regarding the Start and wait for approval action, as this is the first time you're using the Start and wait for approval action in your flow environment. Ignore the warning.

The flow is now ready to go. Let's test it. From the browser bar, copy the ID of the flow into a notepad. You can find the ID from the URL, where it will be in the last section right after flows/. For example, the ID for my flow is `716c40c4-3d0b-460a-bcf5-edb1345fda1a`. Let's go ahead and link this flow to the Initiate Approval column of Product Data library, which is a custom JSON-formatted column.

As shown in Figure 5-8, go to the Product Data library. Go to Initiate Approval ➤ Column Settings ➤ Format This Column. Update `action` and `actionParams` of `CustomRowAction`, as shown in Figure 5-8. Save your changes.

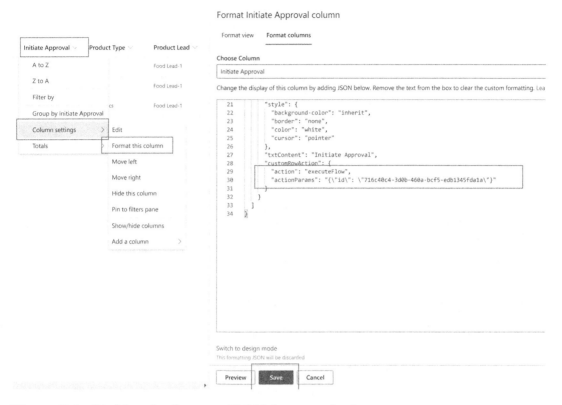

Figure 5-8. *Linking the flow to a JSON-formatted column*

The action is executeFlow and the actionParams should be followed by your flow ID, which you copied into a notepad earlier. The format is "{\"id\":\"[*flowid*]\"}". The final JSON will be as follows. Replace [*flowid*] with your flow ID.

```
{
  "$schema": "https://developer.microsoft.com/json-schemas/sp/v2/column-
  formatting.schema.json",
  "elmType": "span",
  "style": {
    "color": "white",
    "background-color": "#3d7b80",
    "border": "1px solid",
    "border-radius": "8px",
    "padding-left": "8px",
    "visibility": true
  },
```

```
"children": [
  {
    "elmType": "span",
    "attributes": {
      "iconName": "flow"
    }
  },
  {
    "elmType": "button",
    "style": {
      "background-color": "inherit",
      "border": "none",
      "color": "white",
      "cursor": "pointer"
    },
    "txtContent": "Initiate Approval",
    "customRowAction": {
      "action": "executeFlow",
      "actionParams": "{\"id\": \"[flowid]\"}"
    }
  }
]
}
```

Save your changes. By clicking Initiate Approval for one of the documents, the flow will be triggered for the selected file and a sliding panel will open on the right for running the flow. It will ask you to sign in the first time. Click Continue, then Run Flow, as shown in Figure 5-9. Note that "Food Lead-1" is the product lead for my selected document. Note the approver for your document.

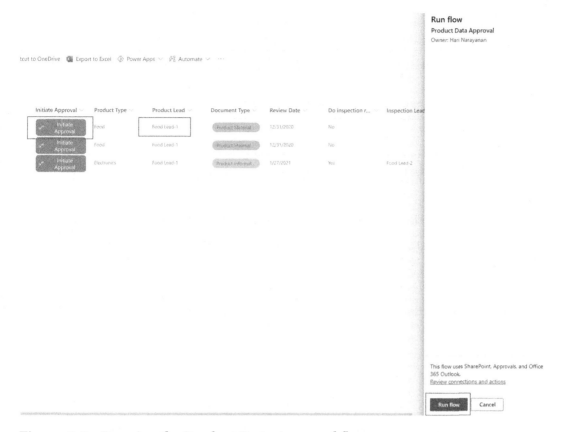

Figure 5-9. *Running the Product Data Approval flow*

The flow will now be started, and you'll get a notification in the library interface. Go back to Power Automate. My flows ➤ Product Data Approval. On this Flow Details page, you can see the 28-day run history at the bottom of the screen and click the instance of a particular flow. In this case, we have only one run instance. You can click that instance as shown in Figure 5-10.

Figure 5-10. *Flow interface and run history*

You can see the Connections panel on the right-hand side of the screen. This flow currently having three connections, Approvals, Office 365 Outlook, and SharePoint.

By clicking the run instance in the run history, it will take you to the flow designer page, where you can see that the flow is running and waiting for approval.

To check the mailbox of the approver of your document, go to `Outlook.com` and sign in with the credentials of the approver user.

Note   Users need to have a mailbox license for logging into Outlook and checking emails. You can manage licenses, reset passwords, and provide other specifications for a particular user from the Microsoft 365 admin center: `https://admin.microsoft.com/AdminPortal/Home#/users`.

In this example, Food Lead-1 is the approver of my document. If I log in with Food Lead-1's credentials, I can approve or reject in the Outlook mailbox, as shown in Figure 5-11.

Figure 5-11. *Approving and rejecting in Outlook*

As you can see, the subject and body of the mail appear according to how you have configured them in the flow. You can select Approve from the body of the mail. A comment box will expand that you can fill in. Provide some comments and then click Submit. The mail content will refresh, and it will show as "Approved."

Now go back to the flow and check the run instance again. As you can see Figure 5-12, the flow ran successfully.

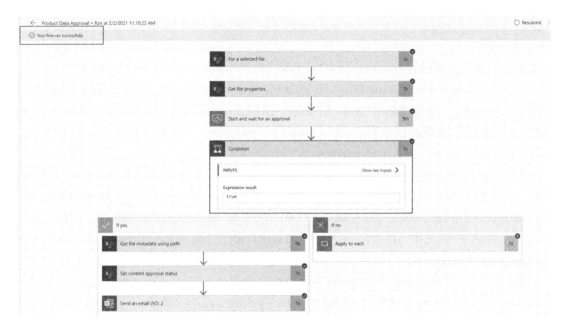

Figure 5-12. *Indication of flow running successfully*

The Set Content Approval Status shows that it was successful, and an email notification was sent. These actions got executed, as the approval outcome was Approve. If you click and expand each action title, you'll be presented with input and output details of the respective action.

Go back to the library and check the value of the Approval Status column for the document you submitted. You can see that the status has been updated to Approved. Also check your email to see the notification you received.

You successfully configured and ran your flow. The document got submitted for approval and got approved. The document will be visible to end users now.

Let's now optimize the flow now and learn some of the expressions in the process. Go back to the flow and click Edit. We should rename the condition block "Product Lead Decision" by clicking ... to the right of the Condition and updating.

Expressions

Power Automate provides us with lot of built-in expressions. We can satisfy basic operations like concatenating a string, replacing a string, and Date Time operations using expressions. You used Dynamic content in the previous section. Next to Dynamic content, you might have noticed another tab called Expression. Refer Figure 5-5 from the section Creating Your First Flow. By clicking it, you can see that there are a lot of built-in expressions available. You can select an expression and construct it from the text box with the fx symbol. Don't forget to click OK or Update once you've finalized your expression. Otherwise, your changes won't be saved.

Let's start by removing the Apply to each block which was added during the Creating Your First Flow section. Refer Figure 5-6. We can achieve this using the First expression. As the name implies, this expression will take the first value out of a collection. If there is only a single value inside the collection, it will return that value and we can avoid looping over a single item collection.

Each piece of dynamic content is built using an expression. Go to the Apply to each block, select Responses, and copy the expression into a notepad. The expression of this Dynamic content will look like the following:

```
@{outputs('Start_and_wait_for_an_approval')?['body/responses']}
```

This expression basically evaluates the outputs of the Start and Wait for an Approval action. The spaces in the action name need to be replaced by the _ character. The Start and Wait for Approval action returns a JSON object as the output. You can see this output by going to a run instance and clicking the action name and expanding and locating the body section. Following is an example of the body:

```
{
  "responses": [
    {
      "responder": {
        "id": "f2a28af6-0e40-48a9-91e1-a365a5a9cdcd",
        "displayName": "Food Lead-1",
        "email": "FoodLead-1@cloudhadi.onmicrosoft.com",
        "tenantId": "fb7cb6fd-9f0b-4c6f-8018-dc7c8634f26d",
        "userPrincipalName": "FoodLead-1@cloudhadi.onmicrosoft.com"
      },
```

```
      "requestDate": "2021-02-02T00:10:31Z",
      "responseDate": "2021-02-02T00:19:35Z",
      "approverResponse": "Approve",
      "comments": "Approved by Food Lead 1"
    }
  ],
  "responseSummary": "Approver: Food Lead-1, FoodLead-1@cloudhadi.
onmicrosoft.com\r\nResponse: Approve\r\nRequest Date: Tuesday, February 2,
2021 12:10:31 AM\r\nResponse Date: Tuesday, February 2, 2021 12:19:35 AM",
  "completionDate": "2021-02-02T00:19:35Z",
  "outcome": "Approve",
  "name": "4deae52c-562d-48b2-b417-1ac6ab35ebeb",
  "title": "Action required for the approval of Confectionary materials.
docx",
  "details": "Hi Food Lead-1,\nHari Narayananhas requested approval for a
Product Materials Informationdocument for the product Dairy Milk
of type Food. Please action on it",
  "itemLink": "https://cloudhadi.sharepoint.com/sites/Workplace/_
layouts/15/Doc.aspx?sourcedoc=%7Bd5c322f5-57db-4fc2-a375-df70a90965ed%7D&
action=edit&uid=%7BD5C322F5-57DB-4FC2-A375-DF70A90965ED%7D&ListItemId=15&
ListId=%7B9AEDD865-ECDA-41C9-A1EC-BFDDEFED3AE2%7D&odsp=1&env=prod",
  "itemLinkDescription": "Click here to view document",
  "requestDate": "2021-02-02T00:10:30Z"
}
```

You can see that the responses were returned as an array object. So, when you query "body/responses" from the outputs of the actions, it returns you an array of objects. The responses always return a collection object even if they contain only a single value.

Now, go to Send an Email (V2) action. Copy the Response Comments and put them a notepad. The expression will look like the following:

```
@{items('Apply_to_each')?['comments']}
```

So, the expression takes out Comments from the Apply to Each. Let's combine both expressions as follows. Just add the `['comments']` to the `outputs` expression.

`@{outputs('Start_and_wait_for_an_approval')?['body/responses']['comments']}`

Will this work? The answer is no, because here we are trying to take the Comments directly out of the array. We need to first get the response from the responses array before we take the comments out of it. The correct expression follows. Wrap the outputs expression with `first`.

`@{first(outputs('Start_and_wait_for_an_approval')?['body/responses'])['comments']}`

The `first` expression takes out the first response from the responses array object. Adding `['comments']` fetches the value of comments from the response.

We can add this expression to the body of Send an Email (V2). Delete Responses Comments using the x. Click the same area to open the pop-up for dynamic content, then click the Expression tab and paste the previous expression there. Remove the @ character and braces from the start and end of the expression. Click OK to save. See Figure 5-13.

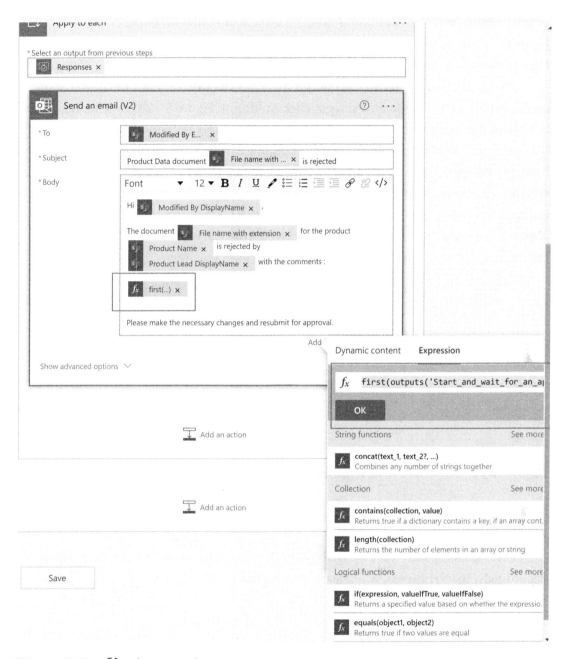

Figure 5-13. *first expression*

Once you click OK, the body of the email will be updated. Let's get rid of the Apply to each block now. Collapse Send an Email (V2) and drag it below the Apply to each loop. Click the ... icon next to Apply to each and delete it. So now we have the Send an Email action only in the If No condition. Put in the same expression for email content and inside the If Yes block as well. We haven't provided it before. Save the changes. Click the back arrow on the top left to go to the Flow Details page.

Let's see how we can rerun the flow for the same document. Click the flow instance on the details page. On the flow screen, click Resubmit. Figure 5-12 shows the Resubmit button on the completed instance page. This option is very helpful while you're debugging the flow. It enables you to run the same instance multiple times without having to retrigger the flow from the library. Once you click Resubmit, the same instance will run again with the new changes. Complete the approvals with a comment and see the approval mail in your mailbox and verify if the response comments is appearing correctly. Figure 5-14 shows the email I received from the Product Lead with the comments.

Figure 5-14. *Approval notification with comments*

You've now learned how to use expressions and used your first expression, which is `first`.

Let's look at the next use case of the Cloudhadi requirement and update the flow accordingly. In the process, you'll learn about a few more areas.

Additional Approval

We have an Inspection Lead column in the Product Data library. We need to send a document for that person to approve if Do Inspection Required is selected as Yes. (Refer back to UC-D10 and UC-D11 in Chapter 2).

Let's go back to the Product Data Approval flow, as shown in Figure 5-15, and make the changes to the Inspection Lead Approval section. Go to the Product Lead Decision/If Yes condition block. Inside the If Yes block, add a condition above Set content approval status, which you should rename "Check if inspection required." Refer Figure 5-7 under Creating Your First Flow to view Set content approval status action.

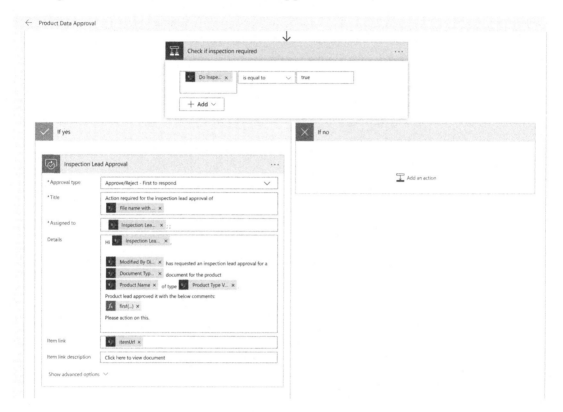

Figure 5-15. *Additional Approval for a condition*

Inside the Check if inspection required condition, select the Dynamic content Do Inspection Required on the left hand side and put true inside the right hand side box. Copy the Start and wait for an approval action from above and add it inside the If Yes block. You can refer Figure 5-5 under Creating Your First Flow section. Rename it to "Inspection Lead Approval." Modify the contents of the Inspection Lead Approval as in Figure 5-15.

Add a condition to check the value of the Outcome, like we did for the Product Lead decision. When selecting the Outcome, make sure you select the Dynamic content from the Inspection Lead Decision. There will be one more Outcome listed in the Dynamic content, which belongs to the Product Lead approval. Make sure, you select the Outcome from the Inspection Lead Decision.

Drag the Set content approval status and Send email blocks inside the If Yes block. Also add the Inspection Lead comments inside the body of the email. The expression for Inspection Lead comments will be like the following based on the name you provided in the approval action.

```
first(outputs('Inspection_Lead_Approval')?['body/responses'])['comments']
```

As shown in Figure 5-16, add an email notification for rejection by the Inspection Lead inside the If No block.

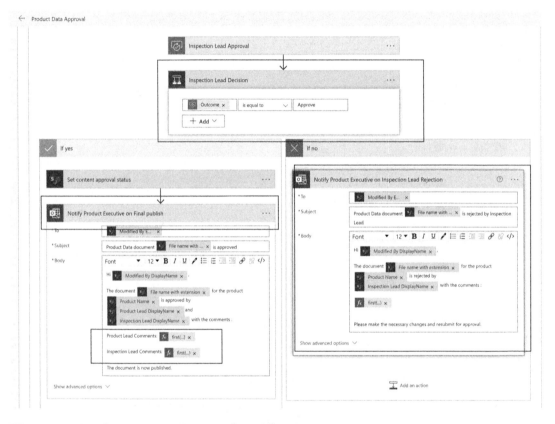

Figure 5-16. *Outcome actions and notifications*

Note   You can always rename actions to be more meaningful. For example, I renamed Send an email blocks as shown in Figure 5-16. When renaming any of the actions, make sure that if those actions are referred to anywhere in the expressions, the references are also updated. For example, if you want to rename the Start and wait for an approval action, update the expressions inside Send an email blocks for the response comments accordingly. The expression for response comments contains reference to the name of the respective approval action.

Now collapse the Inspection Lead Decision block. We also need to add actions inside the If No block for Check If Inspection Required. The execution would move to the If No block if Do Inspection Required isn't equal to true. We'd need to change the Set content approval status and notify the Product Executive in that case. We could copy the Action block from the Inspection Lead Decision/If Yes block, but doing this will result in duplicate steps. We can do it in a better way using variables.

Variables

Variables come in very handy with Power Automate flows. The Initialize Variable action is used for initializing a variable and you can use it throughout the flow by selecting it from the dynamic content. You need to specify a type of variable while initializing it. We can't initialize variables inside a condition or any other block. If you want to set a value for a variable in any of the blocks, you can do that using the Set Variable action.

There are two scenarios where we need to use the Set Content Approval and Product Executive notifications. The first is when an inspection isn't required after an approval by the product lead. The Second one is when there was an approval by the inspection lead after the one by the product lead. Let's initialize a Boolean variable and set it to true in both scenarios. Based on the value of the variable, we can set the approval status and send a notification.

To do so, collapse everything and add an Initialize Variable action just below the Start and Wait for Approval action. Name it "CanPublish." Set the Type as Boolean and the Value as False. Rename the action "Initialize bool—CanPublish." Go to the If No block of the Check Inspection Required condition and add the Set Variable action. Select CanPublish from the Name drop-down and set the Value as True. Rename the action as you wish. See Figure 5-17.

163

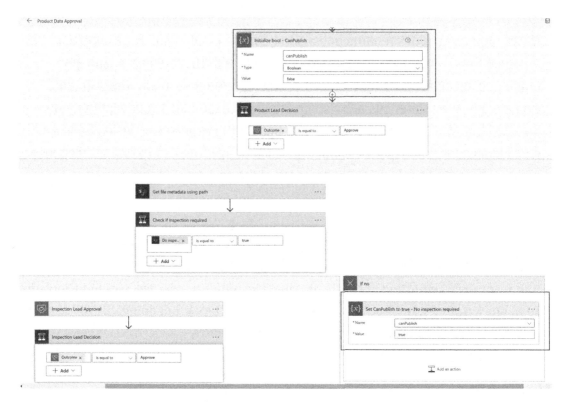

Figure 5-17. *Setting a variable*

Now, expand the Inspection Lead Decision condition and add the same Set Variable action inside the If Yes block and give it a different name.

Add a condition at the very bottom and check if can Publish is true. Rename the condition block to "Can Publish." Drag the two actions, Set content approval status and Notify Product Executive on Final publish, inside the If Yes block of the condition.

We need to take one more step before testing this. In the body of the email, we have an Inspection Lead Comments section. If Do Inspection Required isn't true, we will get an error message, as there is no Inspection Lead Approval involved.

Create a string variable to hold the Inspection comments. Initialize another variable at the top. Inside the inspection lead If Yes block, set the Approved By value to "Inspection Lead DisplayName" with the comment "Expression for the response comments of inspection lead." Choose the inspection lead display name from the Dynamic content. The expression for this is `first(outputs('Inspection_Lead_Approval')?['body/responses'])['comments']`.

Figure 5-18 shows what the set variable looks like.

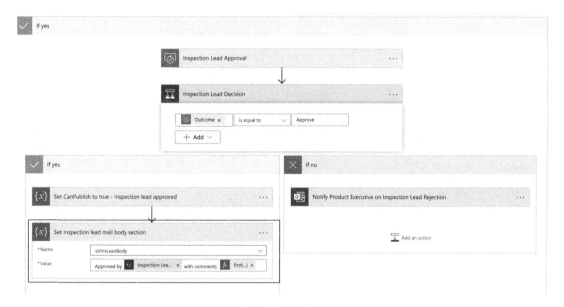

Figure 5-18. *Setting a dynamic mail body using the string variable*

Make changes to the body of the mail to accommodate this. Set the body to include only the Production Lead name and comment. Add the string variable below that. So, if the Inspection Lead is involved, the string value will be appended to the body of the mail. Otherwise, the mail will contain only the Production Lead details and comments. See Figure 5-19.

Figure 5-19. *Adding variables to body of the mail*

Save your changes and resubmit the flow by clicking the latest instance. The document will get published after the Product Lead approves it. Go back to the Product Data library and fill in the Inspection Lead value for any of the documents. Initiate the approval in the same way we did previously. The approval will go through both the leads this time. After both of them approve it, the document will be published. You can play around with different rejection scenarios as well.

Note   All the flows that we're developing in this chapter are available as exported files in the Chapter 5 folder of the GitHub repository. You can access it using `https://github.com/Apress/building-modern-workplace-sharepoint-online`. You can always import them for later use if you want to. I will cover importing and exporting the flows in the upcoming sections.

Document Generation

We have a Products List and a Product Data library. We have the use case for Cloudhadi that we'll look at later in this chapter. As soon as user enters data in the Product list, a Word document should be generated and placed inside the library with the Document Type set as "Product Information." If the user updates the information, we need to update the respective document. The document generation happens based on a template. This may seem a little vague initially, but it will become clearer when we do it using Power Automate.

Once we've finished converting this requirement to a Power Automate solution, you'll be familiar with a good number of concepts. Let's get started.

Preparing a Word Template

Let's prepare the template first. Based on the template and its product values, we will be able to generate documents. To start, open a blank Word document. Enable the Developer tab by going to File ➤ More ➤ Options ➤ Customize Ribbon, then check the tick box on the right side of the tab. In the document, enter the content as shown in Figure 5-20. The words within the light blue icons are placeholders for the values taken from the Products list inputs.

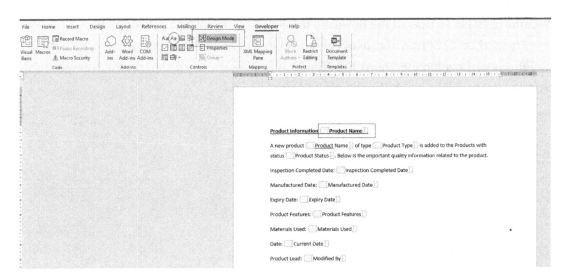

Figure 5-20. *Preparing the Word template*

If you want to create a placeholder for another feature like Product Name, you should click the Developer tab and select Design Mode. Then place your cursor next to the Product Information heading. Click the plain text icon in the top menu, as circled in Figure 5-20. A block will get created. Replace Click or Tap Here to Enter Text with Product Name as shown in the figure. Repeat these steps for all the placeholders in the content.

Once the changes are done, save the document with name Product Information Template.doc. Go to your SharePoint site ➤ Site Contents ➤ Documents and create a folder called "Templates" and upload the document there.

We now have the template ready. The next step is to create a flow that triggers adding or updating an item in the Product list.

Solutions

We can create an automated cloud flow for this purpose. Instead of creating the flow directly, let's create a solution and put the flow inside of that. Solutions allow you to bundle flows together. They improve your deployment capabilities by allowing you to export and import a set of flows together. This helps to better organize the flows as well.

In addition to this, I will introduce you to the concept of child flows. A flow can run another flow from it. To enable this to happen, both flows must be inside a solution. Keeping all this in mind, let's create a solution to satisfy the document generation requirement. Once this is done, we can move our Product Data Approval flow into this solution as well, so that all the flows are in a single place and easy to deploy.

Go to https://flow.microsoft.com and log in. As selected in Figure 5-21, click Solutions in the left pane, then click New Solution on the top menu. In the New Solutions window on the right, enter the details and click Create.

Figure 5-21. *Creating a solution*

The solution will now be created. Click it. Inside the solution view, click +New to add a flow and select Cloud Flow, as shown in Figure 5-22.

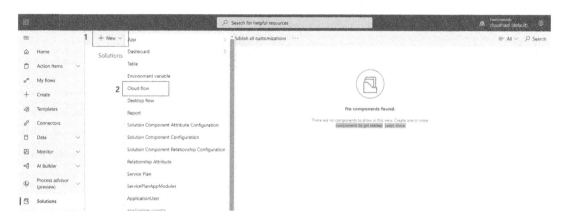

Figure 5-22. *Creating a Cloud Flow inside a solution*

A new tab will be opened. Select the When an Item Is Created Or Modified trigger, as shown in Figure 5-23.

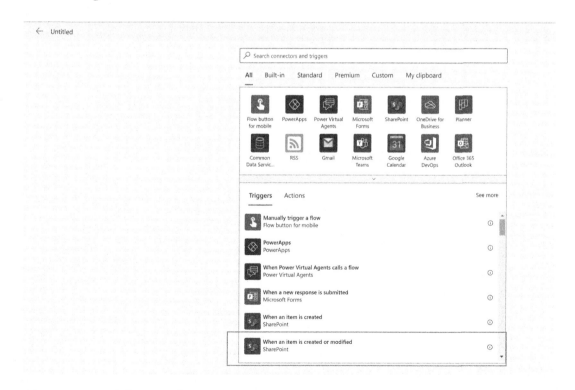

Figure 5-23. *Selecting the trigger*

The flow will be created and you can add actions. In the next section, let's see how we can generate Word content and create a document in the Product Data library based on the template and products values.

Populating and Creating a Word Document

You should still have the flow designer open from the work we did in the previous section. As shown in Figure 5-24, select Site Address and List Name, then add a new step and search for Populate a Microsoft Word template. Choose this action, as selected in the figure. This is a premium action, so you'll be asked to sign up the first time you select it. You can sign up for a 90-day free trial of the program.

Figure 5-24. *Populating a Microsoft Word template*

The action will be added. As shown in Figure 5-25, select your site for the Location. In the Document Library section, choose "Documents," where you uploaded the template. Browse the File section and select the Product Information Template.docx. All the placeholders we added in the template will be populated. Fill in the appropriate Dynamic content for each of them. For example, select Expiry Date from Dynamic content to the right side box against the label Expiry Date.

Figure 5-25. *Populating the placeholders with dynamic content*

This step creates Word content using the dynamic values. We need to make use of this content to create a document inside SharePoint. Add a new step, search, and select Create Product Info File, as shown in Figure 5-26. Fill in the Site Address section. For the Folder Path, choose /ProductData. Let's make the file name "Product Name." For the File Content, search for "Microsoft Word document" in the dynamic content pop-up. The Word content we created in the previous step will come up. Select it.

This will create a file inside the Product Data library. Rename the step "Create Product Info file."

After creating the document, we need to set its metadata accordingly. To do that, use the Update File Properties action. Select Site Address and Library Name, and choose "ItemId" as the ID. For the other properties, select the dynamic content accordingly. Set the review date as "Expiry Date" and set Product Lead claims as "Modified By Display Name," as shown in the figure. Select Cloudhadi Document for the Content Type at the bottom.

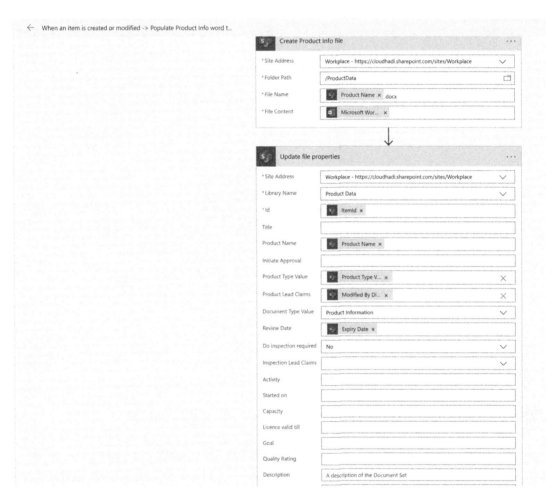

Figure 5-26. *Creating a file and updating the file properties*

Save your changes and click the back arrow. As shown in Figure 5-27, rename the flow "Product Info Generation," provide a description, and save. To rename, go to Edit ➤ Details.

Figure 5-27. *Renaming the flow and providing a description*

Now go back to the products list and create a new item. The flow will be triggered. You can check the flow status from the run history, as we did earlier. In a few minutes, the document will be generated and get created inside Product Data library. The properties of the document will also be updated.

If you open the document, you can see that the placeholders in the content are now populated with the data from the products list. Figure 5-28 shows the document that was generated for the item I created.

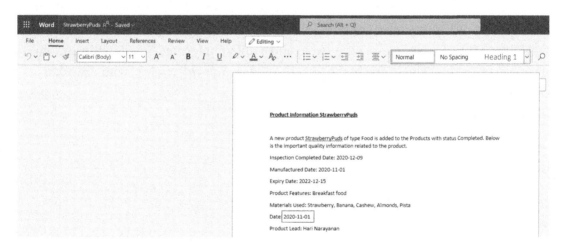

Figure 5-28. *Generated Word document*

One mistake you'll notice is that the Date is populated with the manufactured date, which is supposed to be the current date. Let's go back to the flow and see how we can calculate the current date by making sure we have the right time zone. After that, we can update the Populate a Product Info word template action with the current date value for the Date placeholder. Along with that, we'll see how to handle Update document scenarios, as we have only covered the Create document scenario for document generation up until now.

Date and Time Expressions

Power Automate date expressions are very useful when automating business processes with the help of flows. We can get the current date by using a built-in expression. We can add seconds, minutes, hours, and days to a specific date. Go to expressions in the pop-up. Scroll to date and time and click See More. In Figure 5-29, you can see that there are a large number of built-in expressions available for date time operations.

Let's calculate the current date and update it in Populate Product Info Word Template. Go back to the Product Info Generation flow we created for the Cloudhadi Workplace solution and add a new action called "Convert time zone" just below the trigger condition. In the Base Time box, add an expression utcNow(), as shown in Figure 5-29. This will get you the Coordinated Universal Time (UTC). Select Source Time Zone as the UTC and select your time zone as the Destination. Unless you complete this step, the flow will always give you the UTC. In the format string, there are few formats available to select. In this case, we need to add a different format. Scroll to the bottom and select Custom Value. Type in the format as [*yyyy-MM-dd*] to align with the other dates we have set up. Save your changes.

Figure 5-29. *Getting, converting, and formatting Current Date*

If you go back to the Flow Details page and try to rerun the same instance from run history, you will end up getting an error message at the Create Product Info File step. This is because the file has already been created there. You may need to go to the library and delete or rename the previous file to test whether the current date is populated. This is because we added only the Create File step. We need to identify whether the flow was triggered for Create or Modify. If it was triggered for Create, we need to include a step for creating the file. If it was triggered for Modify, the action needs to be for updating the file. We'll see how to handle that in the next section.

Creating and Updating the Document

There are few work-arounds for distinguishing between a created trigger and a modified trigger. The best one for our scenario is to compare the modified time with the created time. For instance, if the modified time is less than created time plus 30 seconds, the trigger occurred when an item is created. Otherwise, the flow is triggered when an item is updated. There is only a rare chance that a user will modify the product within 30 seconds of creating it.

Go back to the flow, add a new condition below Populate a Product Info word template action, and rename it to "Create or Update." Inside the condition, check that Modified is greater than addSeconds(triggerBody()?['Created'],30). In the If Yes block, we need to add update actions. Add a new action called "Update file." In the File Identifier, add /ProductData/ProductName.docx, where Product Name is a Dynamic content. Put in the same file content as you did for Create File. The Update File action identifies the document with the path and updates the file content of it. Rename the action like you did for Create File.

Let's arrange the Create section now, which is in If No block, as shown in Figure 5-30. Drag the Create Product Info File icon inside of the If No box.

For the next step, which is Update File Properties, we had configured the ItemId Dynamic content from the Create File action. But that will no longer work. If update section is executed, we should have the ItemId from the Update Product Info File and not from the Create Product Info File. So, we must create a variable and set its value in both Create and Update scenarios. Create an integer variable one step before the Create or Update condition. Give it a name; say "itemID." Add the Set Variable action inside both the If Yes and If No blocks. In the If No block, which is for Create, set the value to ItemId by using the Create Product Info File action.

We need to add an extra action in the If Yes block, as the Update Product Info File action will not return ItemId. Add a new action next to it called Get File Metadata Using Path. Provide the Site Address and File Path. In the next step, set the Dynamic content ItemId resulted from the Get file metadata using path action to the variable itemID.

Finally, go to Update File Properties and update the ID to the variable ItemId. Save the changes. Figure 5-30 shows how the flow will look with the Create or Update condition.

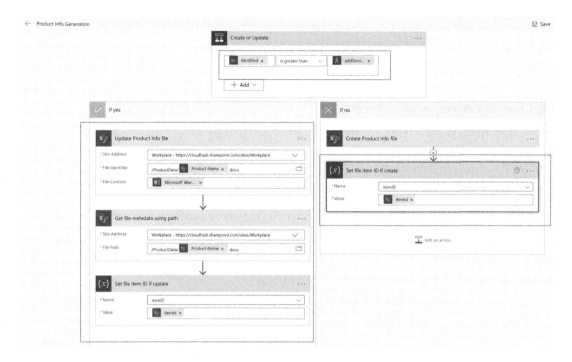

Figure 5-30. *Flow with the Create or Update condition*

Now if you go back to the Products list and update any of the products for which you previously generated a document, the flow will update the file with the new information inside the Product Data library. You can play around with this by creating and updating few items.

In the last few sections, we went over solutions, Word document generation, and some of the file operations. In the next section, we'll learn about child flows and how they can satisfy one of the business requirements.

Child Flows

As you know, we have three product types in Cloudhadi: Food, Electronics, and Furniture. We created a flow for document generation using a single template for all three types. However, let's assume that the requirement is to have three different templates, and based on the type, we need to generate different document.

Let's also assume that there is a requirement to run several actions based on the product type after generating the Word documents and to push it to Product Data library. If the product type is Food, the flow needs to interact with the service portal to check all the existing service requests created for the Food type. Based on that, we need to do a cost estimate for the product. Finally, we need to post a message to a Teams channel. There is a similar process for the other Product types as well. We will cover all of these actions in chapters 6 and 8 while we discuss about SharePoint Framework(SPFx) and Teams. Let's not worry about them for now. In short, what I want to convey is that when a product is created or modified in the list, we need to do several operations, which are similar for different product types.

It's not advisable to create all these actions in the Product Info Generation flow, as they could end up growing into hundreds of steps and the flow would become cumbersome to manage. In addition, there will be similar actions for each product type and we may want to reuse the actions. So, for better maintenance and management, we'll use child flows. A child flow can be called from the parent flow and, in turn, respond back to the parent flow.

We can understand child flows better by creating flows for the previous requirements. Let's create three different flows, which we'll connect to the parent flow to generate different documents. Once we're through looking at the SPFx and Teams, we'll update these flows to include the cost estimation requirement. This will happen in Chapter 8.

To start with, let's make two additional copies of the Product Information Template, Food Info Template.docx, and name them "Electronics Info Template.docx" and "Manufacturing Info Template.docx." We should also modify the content heading with the appropriate product type; for example, "Food Product Information for [*Product Name*]." Leave the other contents as is. Upload all the three documents to the same location, which is Site Contents ➤ Documents ➤ Templates.

Now, let's create a child flow for the Food type. In the child flow, we'll add some inputs and then create actions based on the inputs. When we add the action to call a child flow from a parent flow, we'll supply the values for these inputs from the parent flow. So, inputs are basically the parameters that receive values from the parent flow.

Go to Solutions ➤ Cloudhadi Workplace and then create a new cloud flow. Select the trigger Manually Trigger a Flow and new flow will be created. Open the trigger Manually trigger a flow as show in Figure 5-31 and then click + Add an Input. Add Product ID as an input and set the Number and Product Type types as Text. Add the current date as the date input. These are the inputs expected by the flow. When you call this flow from the parent flow, you'll need to supply these inputs. You can make each input mandatory or optional using the ... symbol after it. By default, the inputs are mandatory, and let's keep it that way. We're adding the current date to avoid having to convert the time zone for each of the child flows. We can keep it in the parent flow and pass it to child flows.

In the next step, let's add a new Get Products Item action to get the item's properties from the Products list based on the Product ID. Remember, the ProductID needs to be supplied by the parent flow, which will get it in the input field 'Product ID' which we provided. As shown in Figure 5-31, select the ProductID input from Dynamic content against the Id field of Get Product Item. For the Populate a Microsoft Word Template action, select Food Info Template.docx against the File field and fill in the placeholders with the Dynamic content from the previous step. For Current Date, select "currentDate."

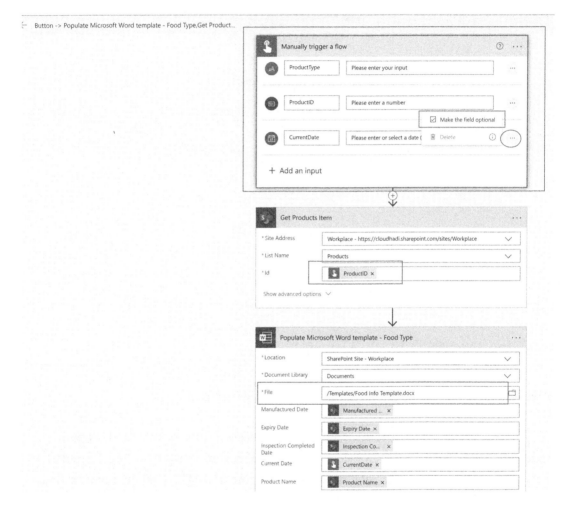

Figure 5-31. *Child flow inputs*

Copy the Create or Update condition block and Update File Properties from the Product Info Generation flow. You can do this by opening both flows side by side and clicking the ... icon next to both actions in the Product Info Generation flow and copying

179

them to the clipboard. If you copy a parent action, such as the Create or Update action, all the child actions inside of it will also be copied. Then you can go back to the child flow and just add the actions from the clipboard.

If the connections was not copied, just expand each SharePoint action and click the SharePoint connection to restore the respective connection. See Figure 5-32. Also copy the Initialize Variable for ItemID to the child flow from the Product Info flow.

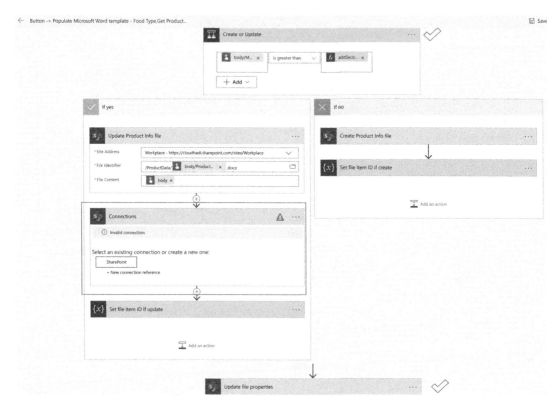

Figure 5-32.   *Copying actions and restoring connections*

Next let's update the dynamic content inside each action. Start by updating the right side of the Create or Update condition to `addSeconds(outputs('Get_Products_Item')?['body/Created'], 30)`, as shown in Figure 5-33. The Created must be read from the outputs of Get Products Item. Update the Modified, Product Name, and Microsoft Word content with the respective Dynamic content. Make sure you update the Dynamic contents of Update File Properties as well.

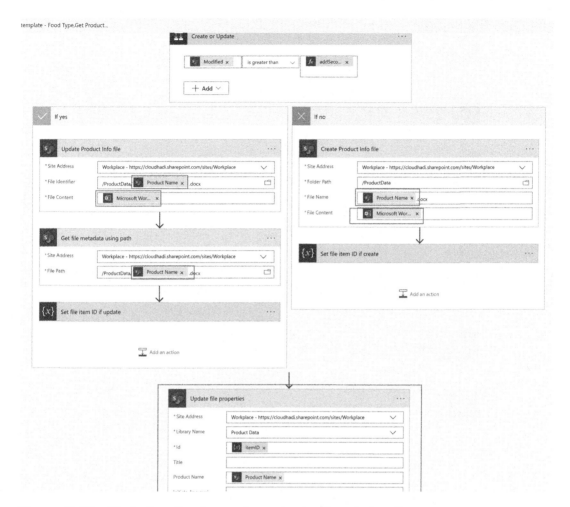

Figure 5-33. *Updating the dynamic contents of copied actions*

Then collapse all the actions and add new step at the bottom of the screen, as shown in Figure 5-34. Select Respond to a PowerApp or Flow. Without this step, the child flow can't return the execution to the parent flow. Save your changes. The flow will look like the one in the figure now.

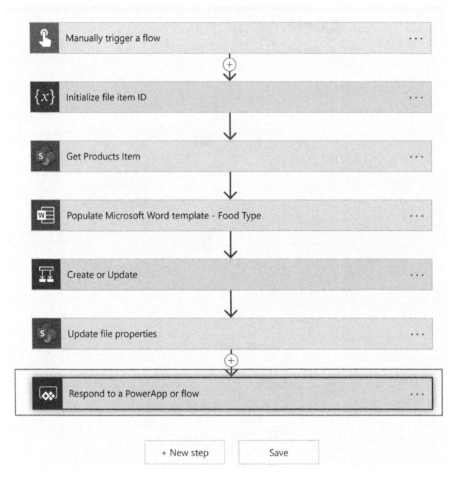

Figure 5-34. *Child flow initial design*

Now go back to the Details page for the flow and rename the flow "Food Product Operations" and provide a description, as shown in Figure 5-35. Click Edit next to Run Only Users on the right side of the screen, and under Connections Used update the connections for Word Online and SharePoint to your email address using the drop-down menu. Click OK on any pop-ups that appear. Save your changes.

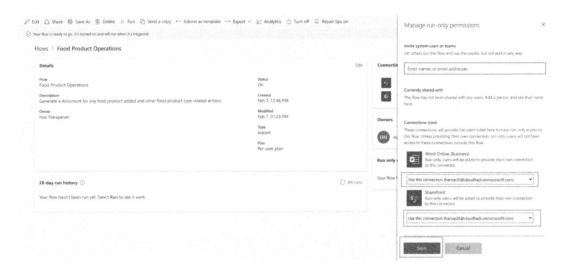

Figure 5-35. *Updating run-only permissions*

This is an essential step, as child flows can't run in run-only user mode. The child flows support only embedded connections. If you leave it set to run-only user, you'll get an error from the flow checker in the parent flow. This is because in run-only user mode, the child flow expects the connection to be passed from parent flow, which isn't supported.

Our child flow for Food type should be ready to go now. Go back to the Product Info Generation flow, add a Switch Condition in the Convert Time Zone action, and fill in the Product Type Value, as shown in Figure 5-36. In the Equals box at the top, enter "Food." Then, add a Run a Child Flow action, and select Food Product Operations from the drop-down menu. Select the values for child flow inputs as shown in Figure 5-36.

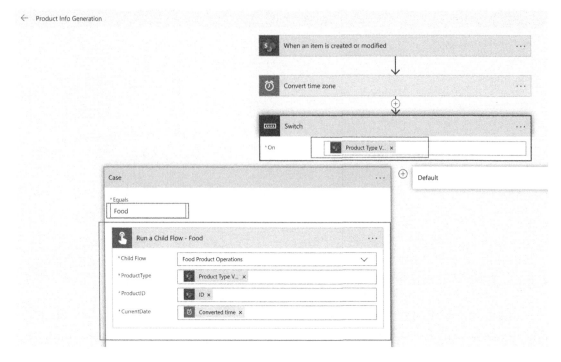

Figure 5-36. *Calling a child flow from the parent flow*

Delete all other actions below Switch. The parent flow will now look compact and quite easy to manage.

Let's run a test to see if everything works as expected. The parent flow will call the child flow and you can see the run history from the child flow details page. The execution will return to the parent flow and it will get executed successfully.

In a similar way, we can create child flows for Electronics and Manufacturing. You can create a copy of the flow, but you may not be able to add manually triggered flows to the solution. We need the flows to be in the same solution. So, a better way to do this would be to create flows within the solutions. Copy the steps from the existing flow with the help of clipboard and make the necessary modifications. At this stage, the only modifications would be done in the populate template step. You need to browse a different template and fill in the dynamic content. Don't forget to update the Run Only Users settings for each flow.

Figure 5-37 shows how to create a copy a flow, just for your understanding. When you create a copy of a flow from a solution, it will get created outside the solution. As the trigger is manual, you won't be able to add it back to the solution. You must create manually triggered flows as new flows from the solution. So, we can't use this feature for creating duplicate flows for our solution. However, we can use the copying feature for supported flows in the solution or for all flows created outside solutions. To copy the flow, go to the flow details page and click Save As. Update the title for the flow and save.

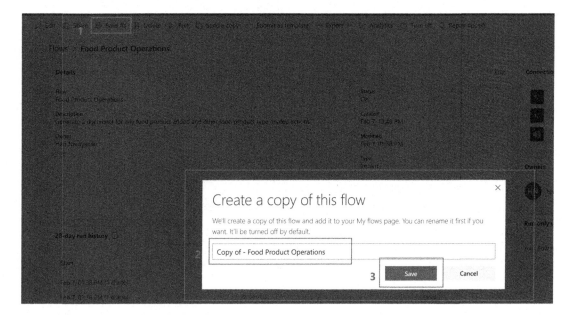

Figure 5-37. *Copying a flow*

Once you've created the two flows, go back to the parent flow and add two more cases to Switch. Select each flow from the drop-down and supply the inputs. See Figure 5-38.

Figure 5-38. *Adding cases to Switch in the parent flow*

If you go to the Cloudhadi Workplace solution page, you can see all the flows in one place. In the next section, we'll learn about exporting and importing solutions and flows.

Exporting and Importing Solutions

Before getting into importing and exporting, let's add the first flow we created, Product Data Approval, to the same solution. Go to Solutions ➤ Cloudhadi Workplace ➤ Add Existing ➤ Cloud Flow. Select Outside Solutions, then Product Data Approval, and click Add, as shown in Figure 5-39.

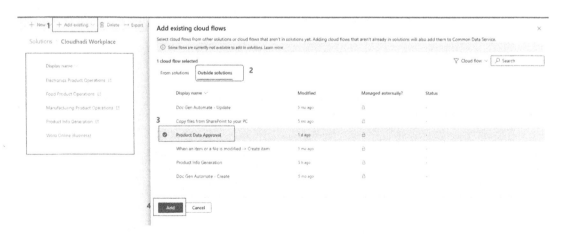

Figure 5-39. *Adding existing cloud flows to the solution*

The flow will be added to the solution in a few seconds. Let's try to export the solution now. The Export option is available on the top menu, as shown in Figure 5-40. Click it. Publish all the changes in the sliding window on the right. Run Check for Issues. Then click Next.

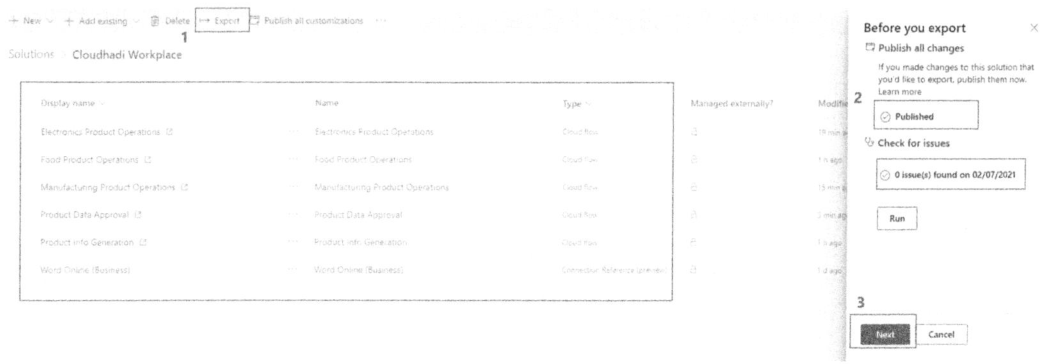

Figure 5-40. *Checking and publishing the solution*

You'll get the option to export as either managed or unmanaged. Doing it unmanaged means that you can still edit the flow after importing it into the next environment. Doing it managed allows the flow to be distributed and installed to nondevelopment environments. For our usual scenario of moving the development to a testing or production environment, we can use the unmanaged option. Select Unmanaged and click Export. It will take few minutes for the export to be completed.

Now extract the downloaded ZIP file and let's take a look inside. Inside the workflow folder, you'll see five JSON files, one for each workflow. Open and format any of these files using Visual Studio Code or online. You can see connectionReferences and definition under Properties. All the connections, actions, triggers, and so forth are defined in the JSON. You can make some changes to the JSON before importing into another environment if you need to. When you make changes to the workflow files and import them, you may need to recheck all the connections as we did in Child Flows section Figure 5-32.

Let's see how we can import a solution. If you're importing to the same environment, you can change the version number in the solution.xml. You can find this file under the root folder. After making the changes, compress the files into a ZIP file. To compress, select the files inside the root folder and compress. For example, select the Workflows folder and the other three XML files, and then compress. If you right-click and compress the root folder, the import won't work. Once the ZIP file is ready, you can go to the flow environment. To import, go to Solutions and then click import, as shown in Figure 5-41.

Browse the ZIP file and click Next. Click Import at the next step. If there is an existing solution, it will be updated; otherwise, it will be created. If an existing solution is being updated, a warning will be displayed.

Figure 5-41. *Importing a solution*

This is how to export and import a solution between environments. Similarly, you can export and import individual flows outside solutions. You can see the export option in the flow details page of a flow. The import option will be available upon selecting My Flows from the left navigation bar. On selecting import, you'll get an option to upload the flow package. Upload the ZIP file and click Import. Once the import is completed, you'll be asked to choose the connections. You'll also have the option to choose between creating a new flow and updating an old one. Once the import and connections are successful, you can open the flow.

So far, we've covered some of the aspects of Power Automate and satisfied a few requirements of the Cloudhadi project. We'll get further into this in Chapter 8 when we integrate Teams with Power Automate. In the remainder of this chapter, let's learn more about the Power Automate capabilities. We'll start with handling general errors.

Error Handling

Let me explain the error-handling scenario with an example. Go to your solution and open the Food Product Operations flow. Expand the Create or Update condition. We added an Update Product Info File action there inside the If Yes block. This update will happen if there is an update to any product item that has already been created. This assumes that the document named ProductName.docx is already there. But what happens if we change the product name during an update? For example, if we added a product called "Banana Pud," a document named Banana Pud.docx would be created in the Product Data library. But let's say, the next day you modified the product details and changed the name to "Banana Rose Pud." The Food Product Operations flow would see that as an update and try to update Banana Rose Pud.docx, which doesn't exist. So, the update would fail, resulting in a flow failure. We need to make sure that in case an update action fails, it executes a Create action for the document instead. We'll see how to do that next.

As shown in Figure 5-42, click the + symbol following the Update Product Info File step in the flow, then click Add a Parallel Branch. Copy the Create Product Info File action from the If No block to the parallel branch. Rename the action "Create Product Info File if update fails." Click the ... icon to the right of the action and then click Configure run after in the drop-down. Using Configure run after, you can define when the action should take place. You can define it to be take place after the previous action gets succeeded, failed, skipped, timed out or combination of any of these.

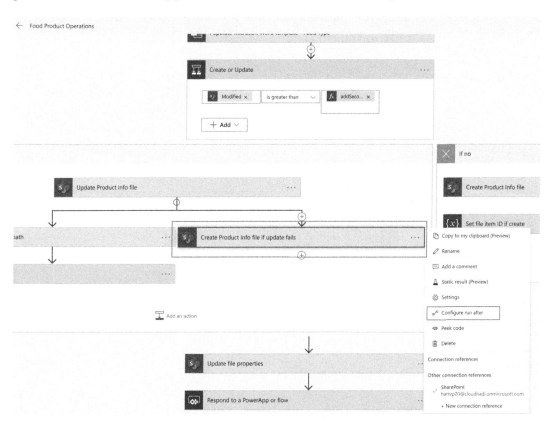

Figure 5-42. *Adding a parallel branch and configuring run after*

In the resulting pop-up, tick off the check box for Has Failed, as done in Figure 5-43.

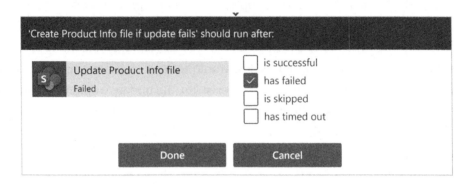

Figure 5-43. *Configuring run after*

Clicking Done will ensure that the action will execute if Update Product Info File fails. If it is successful, it will continue the execution with the normal operations. We need to add one more step, which is to set the item ID variable. Copy the step Set file item ID if create from If No and add it the following step and rename to Set file item ID if update. The final flow will look like the one in Figure 5-44. Save your changes.

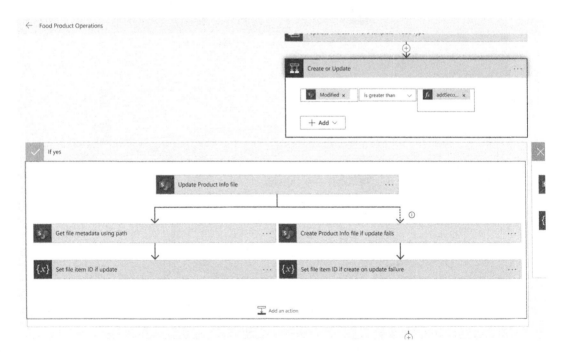

Figure 5-44. *Error handling on action failure*

This is one of the scenarios where Power Automate helps you to handle errors well. Let's look at Timeout next.

Timeout

You may have seen a "has timed out" option in the Configure run after pop-up. For example, there may have been some scenarios where you called a web service with one of your actions and the service didn't respond for five minutes. You can configure an action upon the time-out of this action. Also, you need to specify the time-out as five minutes in the settings for the action.

Let's take a look at a Timeout scenario with the Product Data Approval flow. Open the flow from the solution. The requirement is to time out the approval block after seven days and send an email to the product executive saying the approval request has expired and the document needs to be submitted for approval again.

Click the ... symbol after the 'Start and Wait for an Approval' section and then Settings. For the Timeout option, specify the Duration as "P7D," as shown in Figure 5-45.

This ensures that the action will be timed out after seven days. The value we provided is in the standard date/time format. *P* denotes the duration of the period and *D* denotes the days. If you want to set the time-out for ten minutes, you would need to specify "PT10M," where *T* denotes time and *M* denotes minutes. If you instead entered "P10M," that would indicate ten months.

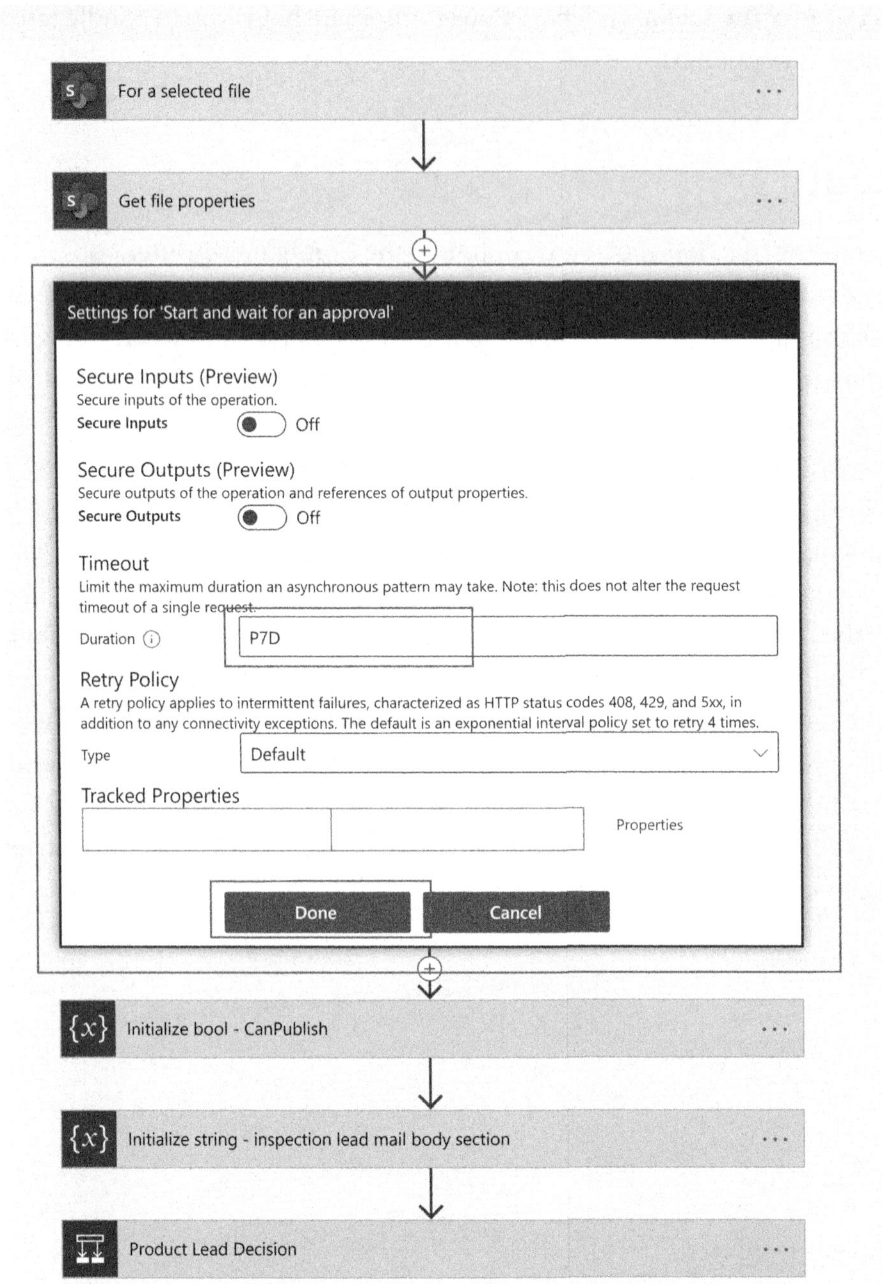

Figure 5-45. *Timeout settings*

When you're finished, click Done to save the changes. Now the approval is set to time out after seven days, but what will happen after the time-out? We can add a parallel branch. Here, you can add Send an Email (V2) and set Configure run after to "has timed out" like you did for "has failed" in the previous section. Then, you can add contents to the email and rename the action. See Figure 5-46.

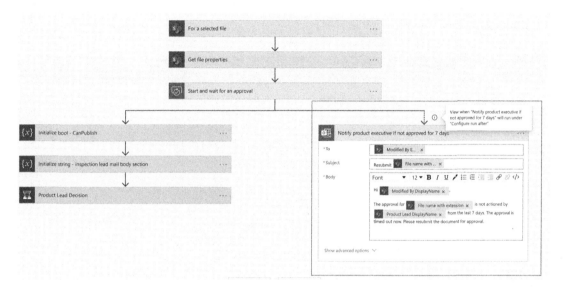

Figure 5-46. *Adding an action after the time-out*

Then, save your changes to the flow. So now, if the approver doesn't act on the request for seven days, the request will be timed out and the Product Executive will get an email asking them to submit the document for approval again.

There are many other topics to explore within Power Automate. Why not click each item in the left navigation pane and go through them? In the next section, we will see how Power Automate can interact with Power Apps.

Power Talk

We learned about Power Apps in Chapter 4. In this section, I'll introduce you to how to connect Power Automate with Power Apps. We can see how to do this with a simple example.

In the last chapter, we created a Products App using Power Apps. Now let's modify that app to include a button called "Report an Issue." By clicking the button, the service desk will be notified. For now, this just needs to be done with an email that goes to service desk saying, "An issue has been reported with Products App" accompanied by the email of the person who reported the issue.

We can start the process by going to `https://make.powerapps.com` and then Apps ➤ Products App, as shown in Figure 5-47.

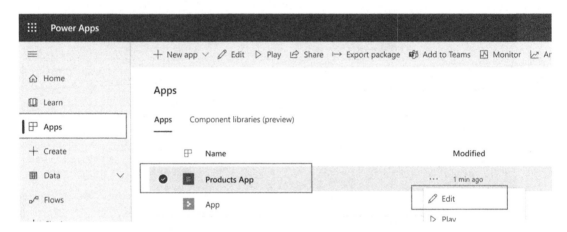

Figure 5-47. *Editing a canvas app in Power Apps*

In the canvas app, select BrowseGallery1, click + insert a Button, and then place the button below BrowseGallery1 at the bottom center. Rename it to Report an issue. See Figure 5-48.

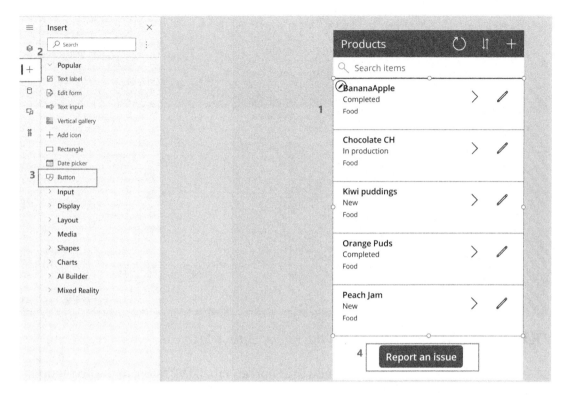

Figure 5-48. *Adding a button*

Now save your changes and let's go back to `https://flow.microsoft.com` and create a flow. As shown in Figure 5-49, select Create, then Instant Cloud Flow, and choose PowerApps as a trigger. Give it a name and click Create.

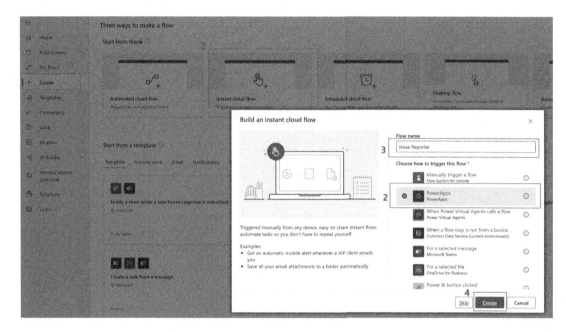

Figure 5-49. *Creating a flow with the Power Apps trigger*

Once the flow has been created, add the Send an Email (V2) step. In the To section, provide your email ID for now. Once the service portal is ready, we can configure it to the service desk. Fill in the Subject and Body, as done in Figure 5-50. Click inside the body of the email, and then select Ask in PowerApps from the dynamic content. When you're linking this flow to Power Apps, it will expect a parameter.

Figure 5-50. *Configuring a Power Apps parameter*

By clicking Ask in PowerApps, a parameter will be added to the body. Save the changes to the flow.

Now go back to the Products app and click the Report an Issue button. Select Power Automate from the top menu. The Issue Reporter flow will be available for you select. Click it, and the flow will get linked to the button. See Figure 5-51.

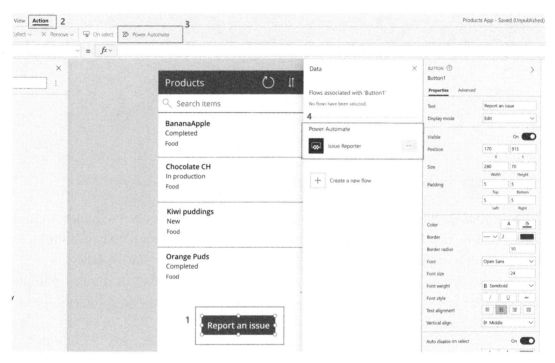

Figure 5-51. *Associating the flow with a Power Apps button*

Now you have associated the Issue Reporter flow to the button. Select the button and set the value to the OnSelect property. Give User().Email as the parameter. The flow will expect this parameter to be passed. The expression will look like this: IssueReporter.Run(User().Email). See Figure 5-52.

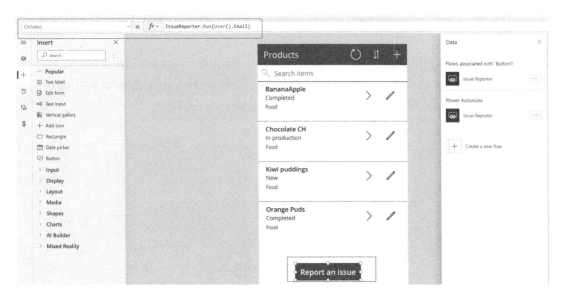

Figure 5-52. *Supplying a parameter to the associated flow*

Save your changes and publish like you did in the previous chapter 4 Connecting the Screens section Figure 4-22. Preview the app and click the Report an issue button. The flow will be triggered and you will get an email. Note that for now we have not configured any alert or disabling effect for the button. So, if you click the button multiple times, you'll receive multiple emails. If you go to the Issue Reporter flow, you can see run instance details there as well.

Note   The flows developed in this chapter are available as ZIP packages in the Chapter 5 folder of the GitHub repository: `https://github.com/ Apress/building-modern-workplace-sharepoint-online/tree/ main/Chapter%205`. The final Products App is available in the Chapter 4 folder: `https://github.com/Apress/building-modern-workplace- sharepoint-online/tree/main/Chapter%204`.

This was a quick preview of how to link Power Apps with Power Automate. We'll do more work on this flow in the upcoming chapters.

Summary

This chapter has been all about using Power Automate with SharePoint. You got a glimpse of how powerful Power Automate can be when it comes to automating business processes. With respect to Power Automate as an automation tool, what we covered is only the tip of the iceberg. There are many other connectors, templates, actions, and data sources available within the platform. In addition to this, you can build Artificial Intelligence(AI) models using Power Automate.

You learned about how to use Power Automate with SharePoint Online in this chapter. You mastered the basics of how to use triggers, actions, parallel branches, and more. You saw how easily you can interact with SharePoint items with Power Automate. You learned about expressions and how to construct them. You learned about solutions and child flows. Now you know how to link flows together. You learned about handling errors using the Configure Run After feature. You practiced implementing Timeout actions. Finally, you connected Power Apps with Power Automate. In the process of learning, you implemented some of the process automation for Cloudhadi workplace, the project behind our learning.

I hope you're now in a strong position to explore more and more with Power Automate. Keep practicing, and when we cover Teams, we'll come back to Power Automate again. In the next chapter, we'll move along and develop custom forms using SPFx. See you there. We'll start with some hands-on coding with React.

CHAPTER 6

SharePoint Framework

In the first three chapters, we looked at the basics of SharePoint Online and then a case study. Based on the case study, we developed forms and formatted columns and views using JSON. We learned how to provision sites using Patterns and Practices (PnP). In Chapters 4 or 5, we went over Power Apps and Power Automate. You found out how to create forms using Power Apps and how to automate business processes using Power Automate. In this chapter, we'll learn a full code-based approach for customizing SharePoint Online and satisfying complex business requirements.

The SharePoint Framework (SPFx) is a development model that uses the context of the current user and the browser connection. SPFx is the most modern way of customizing SharePoint solutions. You can use any JavaScript framework for developing SPFx solutions.

In this chapter, we'll continue to take a learning-by-doing approach. We'll develop a SPFx web part step by step. In the process, you'll learn the concepts of custom developement using SPFx and find out how to implement business requirements.

We'll use React, a JavaScript library, for our development. You'll become familiar with the concepts involved in React when we develop a web part, which we'll use the Service Portal requirement from Cloudhadi to build. At the end, you'll deploy the app to a SharePoint App Catalog and host it in the workplace home page. At the end of this chapter, you'll get an overview on SPFx extensions. Then in the next chapter, I'll give you an example of one of the extensions.

App Catalog

Before we develop an SPFx web part, we need a place where we can upload and deploy it. We'll create an App Catalog site for that purpose. It'll be like what we created for the communication site in Chapter 1.

© Harinarayanan V P 2021
Harinarayanan V P, *Building the Modern Workplace with SharePoint Online*,
https://doi.org/10.1007/978-1-4842-6945-9_6

To start creating the App Catalog site, go to `https://admin.microsoft.com` and then Show All ➤ SharePoint. Click More Features on the left navigation bar, go to the Apps section, and click Open, as shown in Figure 6-1.

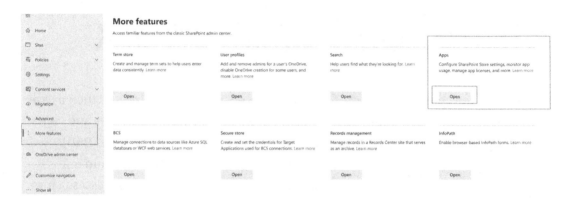

Figure 6-1. *Creating the App Catalog site*

On the page that comes up, select App Catalog and click OK to create an App Catalog site. For the Title, enter "App Catalog," and provide URL as "AppCatalog." Add yourself as the administrator. Click OK and the App Catalog site will be created. If you go to the Contents screen for the created site, you'll see Apps for SharePoint, as shown in Figure 6-2. We'll upload and deploy our SPFx web parts here once they're created.

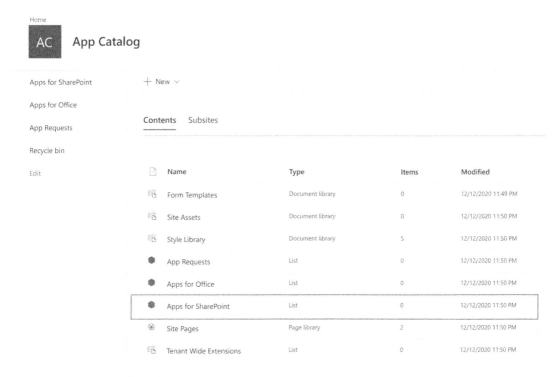

Figure 6-2. *Apps for SharePoint screen*

Development Environment

Before we start developing our first web part, we need to set up our development environment. Download and install the following open-source software in your machine:

- *Node.js*: Node.js is the runtime platform on which the SPFx web part is going to run. We need to use Node.js v10.x for SharePoint Online. To get it, go to `https://nodejs.org/dist/latest-v10.x` and download the package based on your machine's operating system. If you have a 64-bit version of Windows, you can select `node-v10.23.3-x64.msi`.

- *Visual Studio Code*: We also need a code editor; I recommend using Visual Studio Code. You might already have it installed from the previous chapters. If not, you can download it here: `https://code.visualstudio.com/`.

- *Gulp, Yeoman, and Yeoman SharePoint Generator*: Gulp helps us to build the web part, bundle it, and package it. We can upload this package to the App Catalog. Yeoman generates files for your application based on the configuration you requested. The Yeoman SharePoint Generator does this job specifically for your SharePoint client-side web part.

Let's see how to install these things. First, ensure that Node.js v10.x is installed on your computer. Open the command prompt and run `node -v`, which should give you a version starting with v10. In the next line, navigate to a folder where you'll place the SPFx web part. For example, I navigated to `C:\Projects\SPFx`. Now, run the following command to install Gulp, Yeoman, and SharePoint Generator:

```
npm install gulp yo @microsoft/generator-sharepoint --global
```

NPM, or Node Package Manager, is the package manager for JavaScript. It gets installed automatically when installing Node.js. You can install and use various packages using NPM during our development. `--global` will help you to install the tools globally on your machine. This will take some time to complete.

Service Portal Web Part

Let's get straight into action by creating the Service Portal web part, which is one of the key requirements of Cloudhadi modern workplace project. In the process, you'll learn about TypeScript, and React as well.

Go back to the command prompt and run `yo @microsoft/sharepoint`. You'll be prompted with the questions you see in Figure 6-3. Answer them as shown.

```
C:\Projects\SPFx>yo @microsoft/sharepoint
```

```
           ------
          |      |                --------------------------------
          | (o)--|               |           Welcome to the       |
          `------'               |      SharePoint Client-side     |
         (  _`U`_ )              |         Solution Generator      |
         /___A___\               |                                 |
          |   ~   |               --------------------------------
        , _____ ._
        `   o   Y `
```

```
Let's create a new SharePoint solution.
? What is your solution name? cloudhadi-ServicePortal
? Which baseline packages do you want to target for your component(s)? SharePoint Online only (latest)
? Where do you want to place the files? Create a subfolder with solution name
Found npm version 6.4.1
? Do you want to allow the tenant admin the choice of being able to deploy the solution to all sites No
? Will the components in the solution require permissions to access web APIs that are unique and not
? Which type of client-side component to create? WebPart                                           No
Add new Web part to solution cloudhadi-service-portal.
? What is your Web part name? cloudhadi-ServicePortal
? What is your Web part description? Service portal web part for cloudhadi modern workplace
? Which framework would you like to use?
  No JavaScript framework
> React
  Knockout
```

Figure 6-3. *Creating a SPFx web part using React*

After entering all the information and selecting the framework, the web part will be created. It will take a few minutes to complete. Once this is done, change the directory to the solution path by typing in "cd Cloudhadi-ServicePortal." Next, enter Code. in the command prompt. This will open the solution in Visual Studio Code. Alternatively, you can go to the solution directory and open the solution file in Visual Studio Code.

Let's try to understand some of the files in the solution before previewing the web part. All the files in the solution are generated by the Yeoman generator for SharePoint.

SPFx Solution Files

The important files and folders follow.

CloudhadiServicePortalWebPart.ts

CloudhadiServicePortalWebPart.ts is the entry point of the web part. The file name always ends with WebPart.ts. The .ts denotes that it is a TypeScript file. TypeScript is the primary language used in SPFx web parts. The web part file is located in src ➤ web parts ➤ cloudhadiServicePortal.

Open the file in the Visual Studio Code solution, and let's read through it. You can see that React and ReactDOM are imported. As we're developing this web part in React, we need to inherit those. You can also see that BaseClientSideWebPart, IPropertyPaneConfiguration, and PropertyPaneTextField are imported. BaseClientSideWebPart provides the basic functioning for the web part. The other two help to provide the property pane configuration. We'll come back those two in a later section.

CloudhadiServicePortalWebPart.manifest.json

There are some properties configured in the `CloudhadiServicePortalWebPart.manifest.json` file, such as the title, icon, description, and more. This is in the same path as that for the webpart.ts file.

Components

The Components folder contains the React (.tsx) files. You selected React as the framework for your web part. When you're creating a React solution, components are the individual building blocks of it. All the React components go inside this folder. We'll take a deeper look at the React files in upcoming sections.

Config

The Config folder contains the configuration files for your web part. `Config.json` defines the entry point for your web part. You can see that it is pointing to CloudhadiServicePortalWebPart.js by default. The .ts file gets compiled into `.js`, hence the path points to .js. Package-solution.json contains the packaging information such as the name of the web part, the ID, and the version. `serve.json` contains server configurations. We can run and test the web part in a workbench before deploying to the App Catalog. We specify the workbench URL in the `serve.json`.

This is a general overview of some important files to get started. You'll get familiar with remaining files and code while we're building the solution. Let's run this solution in SharePoint Workbench before we start developing.

Running the Web Part

The SPFx uses Hypertext Transfer Protocol Secure (HTTPS) and it is implemented using a development self-signed Secure Sockets Layer (SSL) certificate. We must make our development environment trust the certificate before testing the web part. We can do this with the help of a gulp command. Go back to the command prompt and run

```
gulp trust-dev-cert
```

You'll get a pop-up. Read through it and click Yes. Once you've done that, run `gulp build` to build the solution. It will take few seconds. Make sure there are no errors.

Note   To clear the console, use the CLS (Clear Screen) command. To stop running a command, press Ctrl+C and enter "Y" for the confirmation message.

To preview your web part, run gulp serve. This command will do the build as well before opening the preview. The preview will open in your local workbench. The SharePoint Workbench is a developer design surface that enables you to quickly preview and test web parts without deploying them in SharePoint. SharePoint Workbench includes the client-side page and the client-side canvas in which you can add, delete, and test your web parts in development. Click + and add the "cloudhadi-ServicePortal" web part. See Figure 6-4.

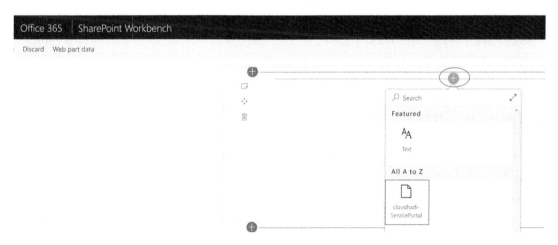

Figure 6-4. *Adding a web part in your local workbench*

Once the web part is added, you can see some of its content. If you go to your solution, src ➤ components ➤ CloudhadiServicePortal.tsx, you can see that this content is coming from this React file. So, we start our development from this .tsx file. The ClouhadiServicePortalWebPart.ts is the entry point of the web part, which will render this React file upon loading the web part. If we need to some property configuration for the web part, we will do it in the ClouhadiServicePortalWebPart.ts file.

In the next section, we'll plan our solution for the Service Portal. After that, we can make changes to the solution accordingly.

Planning the Solution

As per the Service Portal use cases, we need to have the option to submit a request and view the existing requests. (See the use cases in the "Service Portal Use Cases" section of Chapter 2). We'll provide a live chat option for now, and in Chapter 8, we'll integrate it with Power Virtual Agents. We'll connect the web part to the Service Portal list to store and update request information.

We need an interface with four buttons: Submit Request, View My Requests, FAQs, and Live Chat. "Submit Request" should take the user to a form where they can enter the request information and submit. "View My Requests" should take the user to page where they can see their previous requests as a list; by clicking each request, they can find out more details about that request. "FAQs" should take the user to a page where they can see common queries. The "Live Chat" option we can keep only as a button for now.

Let me get you started with React and explain how we can design this solution in the library. Once the solution is designed, we can go to the code for the web part and start coding.

Introduction to React

To put it simply, React is a JavaScript library for building user interfaces (UIs). React uses pieces of code called components to construct complex UIs. So when we're designing the solution for our web part, we can imagine how it can be built using components.

A component is basically a JavaScript file, but we develop it in TypeScript, which will later get converted into JavaScript. We can divide components into two types: the parent component and the child component. A child component is a component that stays inside another component. A parent component is the component that holds the child component. So, all the components maintain a parent and child relationship. You can also have a single component web part. Go to your Solution ➤ src ➤ Webparts ➤ CloudhadiServicePortal.tsx file to understand this better.

Let's clean up the code in CloudhadiServicePortal.tsx as follows and save by pressing Ctrl+S:

```
import * as React from 'react';
import styles from './CloudhadiServicePortal.module.scss';
import { ICloudhadiServicePortalProps } from './
ICloudhadiServicePortalProps';
export default class CloudhadiServicePortal extends React.Component<ICloudh
adiServicePortalProps, {}> {
  public render(): React.ReactElement<ICloudhadiServicePortalProps> {
    return (
      <div className={ styles.title }>
        Service Portal
      </div>
    );
  }
}
```

CloudhadiServicePortal.tsx is your TypeScript class file for the component CloudhadiServicePortal. I'll explain later why the file extension is .tsx. import is for external reference to this file. We are importing React, scss, and Props files. To use the React features, we need to import React. The scss file sets the style here. You can refer to CloudhadiServicePortal.module.scss in the same folder and view some default classes defined there. ICloudhadiServicePortalProps is defining an interface for our class file. We'll get more into that while creating other properties.

You can see that the class ClouhadiServicePortal extends React.Component. React. Component is the base class for all components. The first step in creating a component is to extend it from React.Component. export default is used so that you can import this class from any other class. When you export the class, you can name it whatever you like, as the default is specified with export.

You can see the render() and return() methods inside the CloudhadiServicePortal.tsx file. These two methods help to render the content into the Document Object Model (DOM). The DOM represents the UI of your web part. This means that if you wrap a <div> element inside return() using the render() method, you can see the div in your browser.

The div that you're seeing inside the return is not HTML but JSX. JSX is a syntax extension to JavaScript. It basically creates React elements. So, when you add a `<div>ServicePortal</div>`, it creates a React element, div. The `className` denotes the style of the element. You can refer to styles in the .scss file using the `ClassName ={ styles.nameoftheClass}` syntax.

When we implement the solution, I'll explain each of the concepts involved in React. You'll learn by building. Let's start designing the solution.

Service Portal Design

In a nutshell, we need three components. The Home component, CloudhadiservicePortal, is the home of the Service Portal, where we have four buttons: Create a New Request, View Existing Requests, FAQs, and Live Chat. We will have four additional components for all these four pages. In addition, from the View Existing Requests component, the user should be able to click each request and redirect to that request. Let's make an additional component for that. So, in total we have six components. Figure 6-5 is a visual representation of our design.

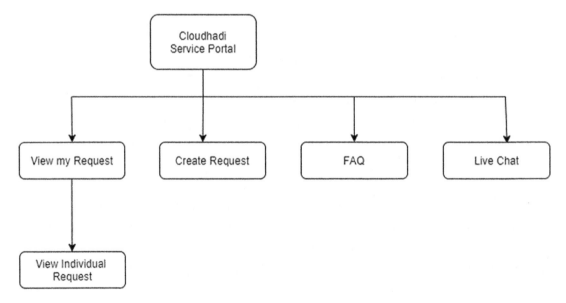

Figure 6-5. *Service Portal design*

We already have the Home component in our solution. Let's now create the remaining five components. But before we di that, let me introduce you to the two base concepts of React: Props and State.

Props and State

Props are variables passed to a component by its parent component. For example, if we want to include the `ViewRequests` component from the Home component to view the requests in the home page, we can use the following tag:

```
<ViewRequests />
```

If we want to specify that only five requests should be displayed, we can include the following tag:

```
<ViewRequests reqCount=5 />
```

This means that the parent component is passing a prop called `reqCount` to the child component. We can access this prop from the child component. We'll see that in action after creating the components.

State is like a local. You can create a variable and set its state inside a component. You can't access or modify this state from outside the component. We'll look at various ways of setting a state.

There are two ways of writing a React component. One uses a function and the other uses a class. A functional component accepts props and returns a React element output. A stateful component is a component that can change its own state. Usually, we write a stateless component as a functional component. We can have stateful components also act as functional components if we introduce React Hooks. In our application, we'll have only functional components. We'll manage state with the help of the `useState` hook.

In the next section, we'll start designing the solution by creating the functional components.

Creating the Request Component

To start creating the Request component, go to your solution ➤ src ➤ Webparts ➤ CloudhadiServicePortal ➤ components. Then, click New File and name it CreateRequest.tsx. See Figure 6-6.

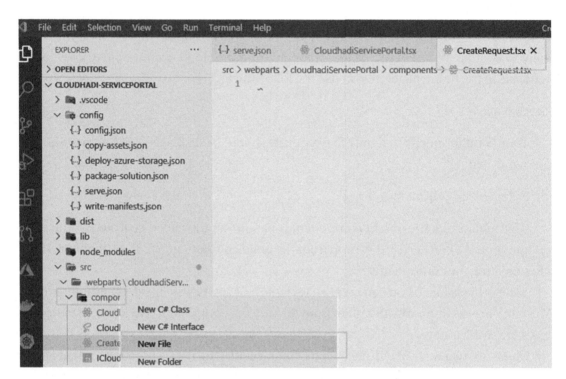

Figure 6-6. *Creating a component*

In this component, we need to create a form for the user to submit the service request. Once the form logic is ready, we can connect it to the home component and manage state. We need to have fields like the request title and description in the form. For that, let's import NPM packages for fluent UI controls so that we can create a good-looking form.

Go back to command prompt and if any command is running, stop it using Ctrl+C. Make sure you're in the Project folder. Run the command `npm install @fluentui/react`.

Then, modify the CreateRequest.tsx with the following code. This will set up the UI for the Create Request form.

```
import * as React from 'react';
import styles from './CloudhadiServicePortal.module.scss';
import { TextField, Dropdown, Stack, IStackTokens, PrimaryButton,
DefaultButton } from '@fluentui/react';

const stackTokens: IStackTokens = { childrenGap: 30 };
function CreateRequest() {
    return (
        <div className={styles.cloudhadiServicePortal}>
            <div className={styles.container}>
                <div className={styles.row}>
                    <div className={styles.column}>
                        <span className={styles.title}>New Service
                        Request</span>
                        <div id="requestForm">
                            <div className={styles.formGrid}>
                                <div className={styles.formGridRow}>

                                    <TextField label="Request Title"
                                    required></TextField>
                                    <TextField label="Request Description"
                                    multiline rows={4} required></TextField>
                                    <Dropdown
                                        placeholder="Select an option"
                                        label="Related to"
                                        options={[
                                            { key: 'Access', text: 'Access'
                                            },
                                            { key: 'Materials', text:
                                            'Materials' },
                                            { key: 'Equipemnts', text:
                                            'Equipments' },
                                            { key: 'General', text:
                                            'General' }
                                        ]}
                                        required
                                    />
```

```
                                    <Stack horizontal tokens={stackTokens}
                                    className={styles.buttonStack}>
                                        <PrimaryButton className={styles.
                                        button} text="Submit" />
                                        <DefaultButton text="Cancel" />
                                    </Stack>
                                </div>
                            </div>
                        </div>
                    </div>
                </div>
            </div>
    );
}
export default CreateRequest;
```

Let's get deeper into the code. In the CreateRequest.tsx, we created the UI structure for a new request form. The component was created as a functional component.

In the UI, I used fluent UI controls, including TextField and DropDown to fit the request title and description. The buttons are wrapped inside a Stack. The Stack helps us to provide a gap between the two the buttons using the childrenGap property. I defined a const variable and configured the Gap property. And, in the Stack, I set the tokens property of the variable. Note that required property is added to the form fields.

Next, let's update CloudhadiServicePortal.module.scss with the following styles:

```
@import '~office-ui-fabric-react/dist/sass/References.scss';
.cloudhadiServicePortal {
  .formGrid
  {
    @include ms-Grid;
  }
  .formGridRow
  {
```

```
  @include ms-Grid-row;
  padding-top: 5px;
  padding-bottom: 5px;
  font-weight:600;
  font-size:12px;

}
.labelCol
{
  @include ms-Grid-col;
  @include ms-lg2;
  @include ms-sm6;
  @include ms-md4;
  color:white;
}
.textCol
{
  @include ms-Grid-col;
  @include ms-lg10;
  @include ms-sm6;
  @include ms-md4;
  color:white;
}
.container {

  max-width: 700px;
  margin: 0px auto;
  box-shadow: 0 2px 4px 0 rgba(0, 0, 0, 0.2), 0 25px 50px 0
  rgba(0, 0, 0, 0.1);
}

.row {
  @include ms-Grid-row;
  @include ms-fontColor-white;
  background-color: $ms-color-white;
  padding: 20px;
}
```

```scss
.column {

  @include ms-Grid-col;
  @include ms-lg10;
  @include ms-xl8;
  @include ms-xlPush2;
  @include ms-lgPush1;
}

.title {
  @include ms-font-xl;
  @include ms-fontColor-black;
  padding-bottom: 10px;
  font-weight:600;
  font-size:18px;
  height:24px;

}

.subTitle {
  @include ms-font-l;
  @include ms-fontColor-white;
}

.description {
  @include ms-font-l;
  @include ms-fontColor-white;
}

.buttonStack {
  padding-top:20px;
  padding-bottom:20px;
}
.button {
  // Our button
  text-decoration: none;
  height: 32px;
```

```
// Primary button
min-width: 80px;
background-color: rgb(3, 120, 124);
padding-top:10px;

border-color: $ms-color-themePrimary;
color: $ms-color-white;

// Basic button
outline: transparent;
position: relative;
font-family: "Segoe UI WestEuropean","Segoe UI",-apple-system,BlinkMac
SystemFont,Roboto,"Helvetica Neue",sans-serif;
-webkit-font-smoothing: antialiased;
font-size: $ms-font-size-m;
font-weight: $ms-font-weight-regular;
border-width: 0;
text-align: center;
cursor: pointer;
display: inline-block;
padding: 0 16px;

.label {
  font-weight: $ms-font-weight-semibold;
  font-size: $ms-font-size-m;
  height: 32px;
  line-height: 32px;
  margin: 0 4px;
  vertical-align: top;
  display: inline-block;
  }
 }
}
```

Here, I modified some of the classes in the .scss module and added some new classes to prepare the UI for the form. The grid classes are helpful in having a responsive form. Try to correlate between the styles and the .tsx file.

Note   To explore fluent UI controls further, you can go to `https://developer.`
`microsoft.com/en-us/fluentui#/controls/web/`.

In the last line of the code that follows, I'm exporting the component using the export default `CreateRequest`. This enables any other component to include this component by importing the component reference and using the `<CreateRequest />` tag.

Let's add a Create New Request button to our home component and link the Create Request form. To do so, go to CloudhadiServicePortal.tsx and modify the code as follows:

```
import * as React from 'react';
import styles from './CloudhadiServicePortal.module.scss';
import { ICloudhadiServicePortalProps } from './
ICloudhadiServicePortalProps';
import CreateRequest from './CreateRequest';
export default class CloudhadiServicePortal extends React.Component<ICloudh
adiServicePortalProps, {}> {

  public render(): React.ReactElement<ICloudhadiServicePortalProps> {
    return (
      <CreateRequest />
    );
  }
}
```

What we just did is to include the `CreateRequest` component in the home component. Now, let's go back to the command prompt and run gulp serve. Once the workbench is loaded, add the CloudhadiServicePortal web part in the same way we did before. A form will appear like the one in Figure 6-7.

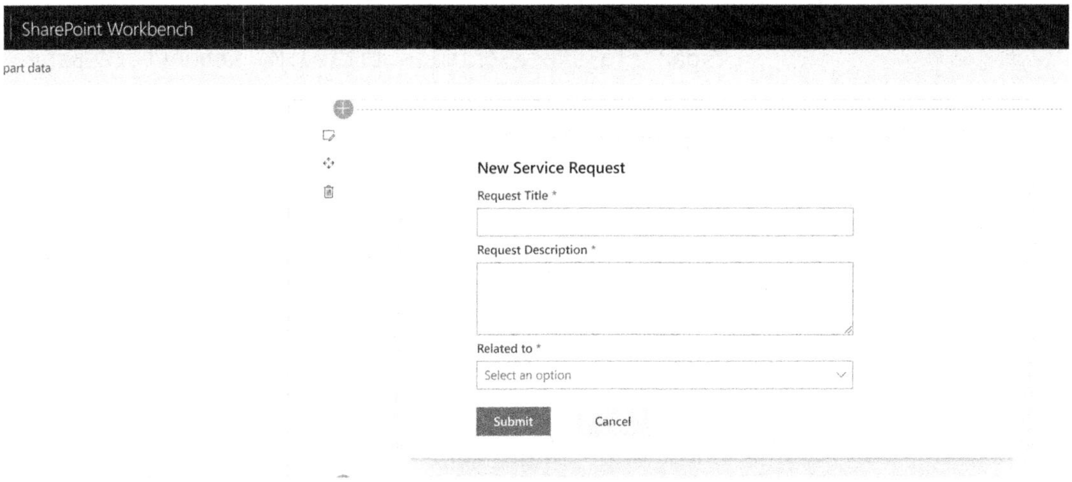

Figure 6-7. *New Service Request form in Workbench*

In the next step, we'll add a Create a New Request button in the home component. The Create Request form will appear only if that button is clicked. We'll see how to do that next with the help of a state variable.

I'll also introduce you to the useState() hook. We can convert the home component into a function component, which was previously a class component.

Working with Multiple Components

Before we link the Create Request to the home component, let's create the base template for three more components so that we can link those as well. Right-click CreateRequests. tsx and click Copy. Then, right-click the Components folder and click Paste. You can right-click the appropriate file and rename it or use the F2 key on a keyboard to do so.

Then, go to ViewMyRequests.tsx and replace the contents of the file with the following code. For now, we're just renaming the component and cleaning up the new request content.

```
import * as React from 'react';
import styles from './CloudhadiServicePortal.module.scss';
function ViewMyRequests() {
    return (
        <div className={styles.cloudhadiServicePortal}>
            <div className={styles.container}>
                <div className={styles.row}>
```

```
                    <div className={styles.column}>
                        <span className={styles.title}>My Requests</span>
                        <div id="viewForm">
                        </div>
                    </div>
                </div>
            </div>
        );
}
export default ViewMyRequests;
```

Like you did before, copy and paste `ViewMyRequests` two times. Rename the two new files "FAQs.tsx" and "LiveChat.tsx." Update the code inside these files by changing the component name, ID of the `div`, and titles to "Frequently Asked Questions" and "Chat with a Virtual Agent," respectively. The highlighted items in the previous code are those that require changes.

Now we have templates for the three components ready in addition to the Create Request form. Go to the home component CloudhadiServicePortal.tsx and replace the code with that which follows. I will explain each section of code in detail to follow.

Note   Before working on the home component, make sure you update the CompilerOptions in the file tsconfig.json, which can be found in the root directory. Also update the target to "es6" and the lib to "es5," "es6," "dom," or "dom.iterable." Add the allowSyntheticDefaultImports `true` property in the CompilerOptions. This will allow us to import the specified namespaces from React. Also, while developing SPFx, always try to use the latest version of tools and libraries. As of June 2021, 1.12.1 is the latest SPFx version available and it supports Node 14.x. Refer the below Microsoft page for updates on versions. `https://docs.microsoft.com/en-us/sharepoint/dev/spfx/compatibility`.

```
import React, { useState } from 'react';
import styles from './CloudhadiServicePortal.module.scss';
import {CommandBar, ICommandBarItemProps} from 'office-ui-fabric-react/lib/
CommandBar';
```

```
import CreateRequest from './CreateRequest';
import ViewMyRequests from './ViewMyRequests';
import FAQ from './FAQ';
import LiveChat from './LiveChat';

function CloudhadiServicePortal() {
  const [selectedForm, setSelectedForm] = useState(<CreateRequest />);
  const onMenuClick = (form) => {
    setSelectedForm(form);
  }
  const _items: ICommandBarItemProps[] = [
    {
      key: 'New',
      text: 'New Request',
      iconProps: { iconName: 'Add' },
      onClick: () => onMenuClick(<CreateRequest />)
    },
    {
      key: 'View',
      text: 'View My Requests',
      iconProps: { iconName: 'GroupedList' },
      onClick: () => onMenuClick(<ViewMyRequests />)
    },
    {
      key: 'FAQ',
      text: 'FAQ',
      iconProps: { iconName: 'Questionnaire' },
      onClick: () => onMenuClick(<FAQ />)
    },
    {
      key: 'Chat',
      text: 'Live Chat',
      iconProps: { iconName: 'Chat' },
      onClick: () => onMenuClick(<LiveChat />)
    }
  ];
```

```
  return (
    <div>
      <CommandBar
        items={_items}
      />
      <div>
        {selectedForm}
      </div>
    </div>
  );
}
export default CloudhadiServicePortal;
```

As you can see in the code, the home component is now a functional component. The statement `const [selectedForm, setSelectedForm] = useState(<CreateRequest />)` declares a state variable called `selectedForm`. The argument for `useState()` is based on the initial value of this state variable. This means the variable `selectedForm` is initiated with the value `<CreateRequest />`, which is of type of JSX object. If we want to update the value of the `selectedForm` variable, we can call `setSelectedForm` with the new value. This will change the state of the component by adding a new value to the variable.

One question that might come to mind is why we use `const` for this statement. We use `const` for declaring a variable that isn't going to be reassigned with a new value. And we use let for variables that can be reassigned. You may also wonder why we use `const` here as the value indicating that `selectedForm` will be reassigned. This is where you need to understand what a state change does. When you change the state of a variable, the component will be rendered again. That means that the `selectedForm` variable will become a new variable in a new scope with a new value. So we can use `const` while declaring a state variable with the `useState` hook.

If you go back to the code, you'll see that we've imported all the components, `CreateRequest`, `ViewMyRequest`, `FAQ`, and `LiveChat`. In addition, we imported `CommandBar` from the fluent UI so that we could create a command bar to redirect us between the components.

`const _items` initializes an object with four keys, one for each component. Each object is configured with a key, icon, and name. In the `onClick` of each key, we're invoking the `onMenuClick` function with the JSX of the respective component. The `onMenuClick` function sets the value of the `selectedForm` variable to the passed JSX object.

In the return function, we have the command bar and the selectedForm variable to render. The command bar items are set to the _items variable. The command bar will have four items. By clicking New Request, it will pass <CreateRequest /> to the onMenuClick function. The function will set the state variable selectedForm to the passed JSX. The component will now render <CreateRequest /> along with the command bar. The <CreateRequest /> JSX will load the CreateRequest component into the parent component. Similarly, clicking on any of the other three components will pass the respective JSX into the state variable and will render the respective component into the parent component.

As the initial value of the state variable is set to <CreateRequest/ >, the Create Request form will be loaded first.

Now go back to the command prompt and run gulp serve if you're not doing so already. Figure 6-8 shows how the form will look. Click each item in the command bar to see how it appears. As we have only title added for the other components, we can only see that one for now.

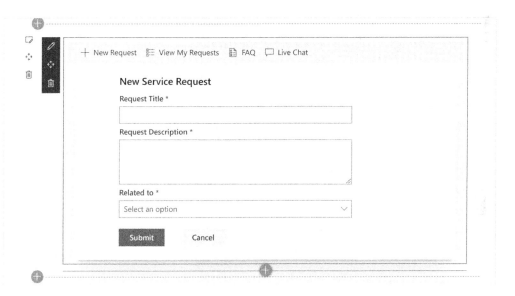

Figure 6-8. *Command bar for all the components*

Let's do a quick recap of what we've learned so far. We created a React-based SPFx web part for our Service Portal. We created multiple components and linked multiple child components with the parent component. We implemented conditional rendering of the components with the help of the useState() React hook. In the process, we learned a few important concepts about React.

In the next section, we'll connect the Create Request form to SharePoint.

Communicating with SharePoint

We already created the UI for the Create Request form. When a user submits data, we need to save that into a back-end list in SharePoint. To set this up, go to the Service Portal library from Site Contents, edit the default view in the Service Portal list, click the Add Column drop-down, and select Show/hide. Then, select the columns as shown in Figure 6-9 and click Apply.

Figure 6-9. *Configuring the Service Portal list view*

We also need to make use of PnPjs (Patterns and Practices client-side libraries) for connecting to SharePoint. PnPjs is a collection of libraries for consuming SharePoint, Graph, and Microsoft 365 APIs. First, let's install PnPjs using npm install @pnp/sp. Execute this command in the Visual Studio Code terminal. To get the SharePoint context to our web part, we need to do the setup using the onInit method within CloudhadiServicePortalWebPart.ts. This will ensure that the context is set before any other code runs. Go to src ➤ web parts ➤ ClouhadiServicePortal ➤ ClouhadiServicePortalWebPart.ts. Add an import { sp } from "@pnp/sp"; line in the import section. Then add the following onInit method above the render() method:

```
public onInit(): Promise<void> {
    return super.onInit().then(_ => {
    sp.setup({
        spfxContext: this.context
      });
    });
  }
```

Replace your code for CreateRequests.tsx with the following code. After the code, I'll provide an explanation of it.

```
import React, { useState, useEffect } from 'react';
import styles from './CloudhadiServicePortal.module.scss';
import { Label, TextField, Dropdown, Stack, IStackTokens, PrimaryButton,
DefaultButton, concatStyleSets } from '@fluentui/react';
import { MessageBar, MessageBarType } from 'office-ui-fabric-react';
import { ICreateRequestProps } from './ICreateRequestProps';
import { ICreateRequestState } from './ICreateRequestState';
import { sp } from "@pnp/sp";
import "@pnp/sp/webs";
import "@pnp/sp/lists";
import "@pnp/sp/items";
import { IItemAddResult } from "@pnp/sp/items";
const stackTokens: IStackTokens = { childrenGap: 30 };
let csrNumber = "CSR" + Math.floor(Math.random() * (99999));
function CreateRequest() {
    // States variables for form fields
    const [reqTitle, setReqTitle] = useState("");
    const [reqDesc, setReqDesc] = useState("");
    const [relatedTo, setRelatedTo] = useState("");
    const [success, setSuccess] = useState(false);
    // Creates a Cloudhadi Service Request upon clicking of the Submit button
    const createCSR = async () => {
        try {
            csrNumber = "CSR" + Math.floor(Math.random() * (99999));
            const iar: IItemAddResult = await sp.web.lists.
            getByTitle("Service Portal").items.add({
                Title: csrNumber,
                RequestTitle: reqTitle,
                RequestDescription: reqDesc,
                Relatedto: relatedTo,
            });
            setSuccess(true);
        }
```

```
        catch (error) {
            throw (error);
        }
    }
    // Set field values on change–Text fields
    const handleChange = (event, setFieldValue) => {
        setFieldValue(event.target.value);
        console.log(event.target.value);

    }
    // Set field values on change–Dropdown fields
    const handleDropDownChange = (selOption, setFieldValue) => {
        setFieldValue(selOption.text);
        console.log(selOption.text)
    }
    // Render form
    return (
        <div className={styles.cloudhadiServicePortal}>
            <div className={styles.container}>
                <div className={styles.row}>
                    <div className={styles.column}>
                        <span className={styles.title}>New Service
                        Request</span>
                        <div id="requestForm">
                            <div className={styles.formGrid}>
                                <div className={styles.formGridRow}>
                                    <TextField label="Request
                                    Title" onChange={(event) =>
                                    handleChange(event, setReqTitle)}
                                    required></TextField>
                                    <TextField label="Request
                                    Description" onChange={(event) =>
                                    handleChange(event, setReqDesc)}
                                    multiline rows={4} required></
                                    TextField>
                                    <Dropdown
```

```
            placeholder="Select an option"
            label="Related to"
            options={[
                { key: 'Access', text:
                'Access' },
                { key: 'Materials', text:
                'Materials' },
                { key: 'Equipments', text:
                'Equipments' },
                { key: 'General', text:
                'General' }
            ]}
            onChanged={(selOption) => {
            handleDropDownChange(selOption,
            setRelatedTo); }}
            required
        />
        <Stack horizontal tokens={stackTokens}
        className={styles.buttonStack}>
            <PrimaryButton className={styles.
            button} text="Submit" onClick={()
            => createCSR()} />
            <DefaultButton text="Cancel" />
        </Stack>
        {success === true &&
            <MessageBar messageBarType=
            {MessageBarType.success}
            isMultiline={false} >Successfully
            created Service Request. Reference
            no:{csrNumber}</MessageBar>
        }
      </div>
    </div>
  </div>
</div>
```

```
            </div>
        </div>
    </div>
  );
}
export default CreateRequest;
```

Let's take a deep look at this code. We can import PnP modules and `ItemAddResult`, as you can see from the code. These are required for us to communicate with SharePoint. In addition, we can import `MessageBar` and `MessageBarType` for the purpose of displaying a success message.

I declared three pairs of state variables with the `useState` hook. Each pair is for each of the three fields in our form. One pair of variables declared to set success with the initial value as `false`.

Let's look at the `return` method next. You can see that I added the `onChange` property for both of the text fields. `onChange` calls the `handleChange` method with `event` and `setReqTitle` as parameters. The `handleChange` method just described is expecting the event and the `set` variable. For example, for the `request title` field, we pass `setReqTitle` as the parameter. The `handleChange` method will use that and set the value to `reqTitle`. `event.target.value` will give you the text box value. For the drop-down field, it is slightly different. We used the `OnChanged` method for capturing drop-down change. Also, we are passing the option as a parameter to get the selected option text.

So, what we're exactly doing here is to set the value for the corresponding state variable whenever there is a change in an input field. The state variables will always have the latest value of the input fields. When we're clicking the Submit button, we just need to pass these state variables. We have a message bar that will display only if the success of the variable equals `true`.

By clicking the Submit button, we're calling the `CreateCSR()` method. This is an `async` function, which is making use of the `await` expression. This helps to run the code asynchronously, ensuring that no two lines of code are running at the same time.

In the `CreateCSR()` method, we're accessing the Service Portal list with the help of PnP. In the `add` call, all the field values are passed. The field values are represented in the Internal Name: Value format. We can get the value of form fields from the corresponding state variable. For the `Title`, I'm setting a random number. This can act like a ticket number. If the item is created successfully, the variable's `success` will be set to `true` and the message bar will display.

Now go back to the command prompt, make sure you're in the Web Part folder, and run gulp serve. The local workbench will be loaded, but this time we need to access the SharePoint Workbench, as we're interacting with the list. Go to `{yoursiteURL}/_layouts/15/workbench.aspx` and enter data, and you'll get a success message saying, "Successfully created Service Request…. ,' as shown in Figure 6-10.

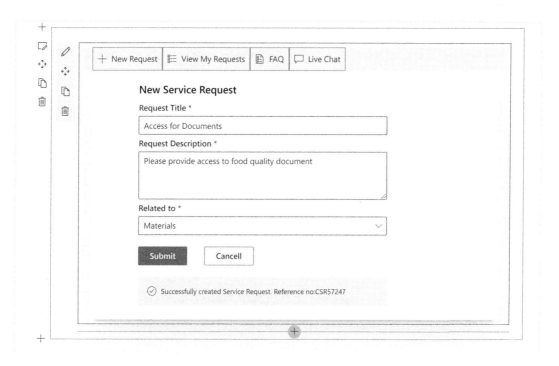

Figure 6-10. *Creating a request in SharePoint Workbench*

If you go to the Service Portal list, you'll see that an item has been created and all the details have been entered. See Figure 6-11.

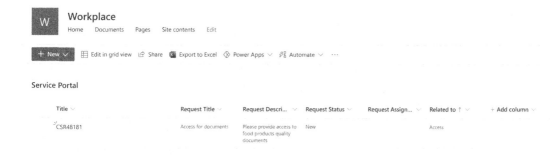

Figure 6-11. *Service Portal list item*

Try creating multiple items and also create items from different user logins. Next, let's go to ViewMyRequests.tsx and see how we can display a list of requests specific to the user.

Reading Multiple Items

On the View Requests page, we need to pull all the requests specific to the user from the Service Portal list. First, let's create a state interface by making a IViewRequestsState.ts file and updating the code as follows:

```
export interface IViewRequestsState {
    ID:number;
    Title: any;
    RequestTitle:string;
    RequestStatus:string;
 }
```

Then, we'll update the ViewRequests.tsx with the following code. I'll explain the details after the code.

```
import React, { useState, useEffect } from 'react';
import { sp } from "@pnp/sp";
import "@pnp/sp/webs";
import "@pnp/sp/lists";
import "@pnp/sp/items";
import "@pnp/sp/site-users/web";
import { IViewRequestsState } from './IViewRequestsState';
import { DetailsList, DetailsListLayoutMode, IColumn } from 'office-ui-
fabric-react/lib/DetailsList';
import { Link } from '@fluentui/react';
// Column headers
const columns = [
    { key: 'Title', name: 'Request No.', fieldName: 'Title', minWidth: 70,
    maxWidth: 200, isResizable: true },
    { key: 'RequestTitle', name: 'Request Title', fieldName:
    'RequestTitle', minWidth: 160, maxWidth: 200, isResizable: true },
```

```
    { key: 'RequestStatus', name: 'Status', fieldName: 'RequestStatus',
    minWidth: 70, maxWidth: 200, isResizable: true }];
];
// Render list of requests
function ViewMyRequests() {
    // On component mount
    useEffect(() => {
        loadMyRequests();

    }, [])
    // State variables for request items
    const [myItems, setMyItems] = useState([]);
    // Load Service requests
    const loadMyRequests = async () => {
        let currentUser = await sp.web.currentUser();
        await sp.web.lists.getByTitle("Service Portal").items
            .filter(`Author/EMail eq '${currentUser.Email}'`)
            .select('ID', 'Title', 'RequestTitle', 'RequestStatus')
            .get().then((items) => {
                let result: IViewRequestsState[] = [];
                items.forEach(element => {
                    result.push({
                        ID: element.Id, Title: <Link href="#">{element.
                        Title}</Link>, RequestTitle: element.RequestTitle,
                        RequestStatus: element.RequestStatus
                    });
                });
                return result;
            }).then(resultdata => setMyItems(resultdata));
    };
    // On click of item
    const _onItemInvoked = (item: any): void => {
        // Call child component with ID
        console.log(`Call with '${item.ID}' to see individual request`)
        };
```

```
    return (
  <div className={styles.cloudhadiServicePortal}>
             <div className={styles.container}>
                 <div className={styles.row}>
                     <div className={styles.column}>
                         <span className={styles.title}>My Service
                         Requests</span>
                         <DetailsList
                             items={myItems}
                             columns={columns}
                             layoutMode={DetailsListLayoutMode.
                             justified}
                             onItemInvoked={_onItemInvoked}
                         />
                     </div>
                 </div>
             </div>
         </div>    );
}
export default ViewMyRequests;
```

On the View Requests page, the first step we'll take is to load the requests specific to a user. You can refer to the loadMyRequests declaration here. The import "@pnp/sp/site-users/web" statement will import the modules that we need in order to retrieve the user who is currently logged in. Our next step is to make a PnPjs call to the Service Portal list. Using the *filter* keyword, the items are filtered with that of current user. We specify the columns using the *select* keyword. Then, we'll define an array object result that inherits the IViewRequestsState interface. We defined the interface earlier, and we're importing it in this component. Each of the values is stored in this array. For the Title, we'll add it as a Link so that we can view it as such while clicking each item. The Link is imported from the @fluentui/react library. We defined Title as the any type earlier in the interface specifications in the IViewRequestsState.ts file. Finally, let's set this array object to a myItems state variable by calling setMyItems(resultdata).

We need to call loadMyRequests upon loading the component. We'll make use of the useEffect hook for this purpose. Functions passed to useEffect are executed on every component rendering unless you pass a second argument to them. To make sure that loadMyRequests will be called only while the component initially loads, we need to pass an empty array variable. What we've done so far is to load the service requests of the current user into an object array when the component renders for the first time.

The next step is to display all these items in a list. We can make use of the DetailList control from the Fabric UI. We imported the DetailsList and DetailsListLayoutMode modules. In the control, we passed items, columns, layoutMode, and onItemInvoked parameters. The columns are defined above with key, name, styles, and more. We have three columns: Title, RequestTitle, and RequestStatus. Title is named Request No. myItems is passed to the items parameter. We set the value for myItems earlier. We also stored ID in myItems, but it won't be displayed here as we aren't specifying it in columns. But we'll need it later on when we invoke the individual request.

We're calling the onItemInvoked function a method. In this method, we're currently passing on the ID and writing to the console. In the next section, we'll link to the individual request.

Let's save the code and run gulp serve. If you Refresh SharePoint Workbench, you should now be able to see all the requests you created in the View Existing Requests tab. If you double-click Request No., you can see that the ID of the clicked item is logged into the console, as shown in Figure 6-12. Press the F12 key and click Console. Then, go ahead and double-click any request and the message "Call with 'ID' to see individual request" will come up in the console. Try logging in with other user accounts to see the various request details. The figure shows the requests I created.

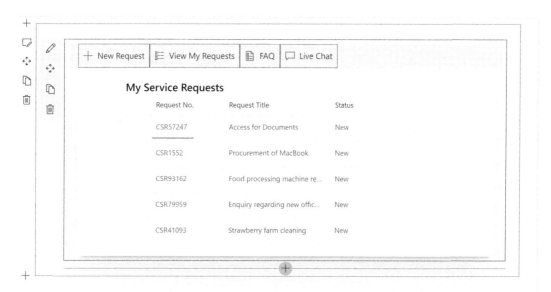

Figure 6-12. *The set of data read and displayed in the SharePoint list*

In the next section, we'll set up the redirection to individual request details with the help of another pair of state variables and conditional rendering.

Component Interaction

In this section, you'll learn how props can be passed from parent component to the child component and vice versa. We have the View Requests component. Upon clicking the Request No., we need to be redirected to the Service Request Details page. We can make use of the CreateRequest.tsx page to render the request details.

First, we need to update the IViewRequestsState.ts file to include a few more details such as a description of the request. This will help in using the same interface in the CreateRequest.tsx file.

Update the IViewRequestsState.ts file as follows:

```
export interface IViewRequestsState {
    ID:number;
    Title: any;
    RequestTitle:string;
    RequestStatus:string;
    RequestDesc?:string;
    RequestAssignedTo?:string;
    RelatedTo?:string;
}
```

Here, we marked a few more fields as optional by using ?. Now, we can use the same interface for both the ViewRequests.tsx and CreateRequest.tsx files while retrieving items from the SharePoint list and storing it in state variables. We're already using this state in the ViewRequests.tsx file.

We need to add a property interface for the CreateRequests.tsx file in order to establish communication with the ViewRequests.tsx file. Let's create a new file called "IViewRequestsProps.ts" and update it as follows:

```
export interface ICreateRequestProps {
    ID?:number;
    resetView?:any;
}
```

The next step is to replace the _onItemInvoked method to redirect to the CreateRequest page. For that, we need to pass the props between the components. We should update ViewMyRequests.tsx with the following code. I'll provide an explanation at the end.

```
import React, { useState, useEffect } from 'react';
import { sp } from "@pnp/sp";
import "@pnp/sp/webs";
import "@pnp/sp/lists";
import "@pnp/sp/items";
import "@pnp/sp/site-users/web";
import { IViewRequestsState } from './IViewRequestsState';
import { DetailsList, DetailsListLayoutMode } from 'office-ui-fabric-react/
lib/DetailsList';
import { Link } from '@fluentui/react';
import CreateRequest from './CreateRequest';
// Column headers
const columns = [
    { key: 'Title', name: 'Request No.', fieldName: 'Title', minWidth: 100,
    maxWidth: 200, isResizable: true },
    { key: 'RequestTitle', name: 'Request Title', fieldName:
    'RequestTitle', minWidth: 100, maxWidth: 200, isResizable: true },
    { key: 'RequestStatus', name: 'Request Status', fieldName:
    'RequestStatus', minWidth: 100, maxWidth: 200, isResizable: true }
];
// Render list of requests
function ViewMyRequests() {
    // On component mount
    useEffect(() => {
        loadMyRequests();
    }, [])
    // Reset to view requests
    const resetViewRequest = () => {
        setDoViewRequest(false);
    };
```

```
    // State variables for request items
    const [myItems, setMyItems] = useState([]);
    // State variables for viewing an individual request
    const [doViewRequest, setDoViewRequest] = useState(false);
    const [requestID, setRequestID] = useState(0);
    // Load Service requests
    const loadMyRequests = async () => {
        let currentUser = await sp.web.currentUser();
        await sp.web.lists.getByTitle("Service Portal").items
            .filter(`Author/EMail eq '${currentUser.Email}'`)
            .select('ID', 'Title', 'RequestTitle', 'RequestStatus')
            .get().then((items) => {
                let result: IViewRequestsState[] = [];
                items.forEach(element => {
                    result.push({
                        ID: element.Id, Title: <Link href="#">{element.
                        Title}</Link>, RequestTitle: element.RequestTitle,
                        RequestStatus: element.RequestStatus
                    });
                });
                return result;
            }).then(resultdata => setMyItems(resultdata));

    };
    // On click of item
    const _onItemInvoked = (item: any): void => {
        // Call child component with ID
        setRequestID(item.ID);
        setDoViewRequest(true);
    };

    // Load all requests
    if (!doViewRequest) {
        return (
            <DetailsList
                items={myItems}
```

```
            columns={columns}
            layoutMode={DetailsListLayoutMode.justified}
            onItemInvoked={_onItemInvoked}
        />
    );
}
// Call to load individual request
else {
    return (
        <CreateRequest ID={requestID} resetView={resetViewRequest} />
    );
}
}
export default ViewMyRequests;
```

In the ViewMyRequests.tsx file, let's create two new pairs of state variables. The first pair, doViewRequest and setDoViewRequest, identifies whether we need to view the individual request details or to view all our requests. In the initial render, we have doViewRequest set as false. This means that all our requests will be displayed, as we saw earlier. The second pair of variables is for holding a request ID while clicking the request number of an item. In the _onItemInvoked method, we're setting this request ID and doViewRequest as true.

Whenever you click an item, the doViewRequest becomes true. I added an If Else condition before the return call. If doViewRequest is false, we'll load all of our requests. If it isn't, the individual request will be loaded by calling the CreateRequest component. While calling the CreateRequest component, I'm passing the requestID through the ID property. The CreateRequest component can receive this property.

There is another property, resetView, with which I'm passing a function call. The function resetView is setting the doViewRequest to false. So, in the CreateRequest component, I can make use of this property and invoke this function. We'll see how it works in the CreateRequest component.

What we've done so far is to introduce two pairs of state variables. View All My Requests will be loaded as before unless Request No. is clicked, doing which sets the variable values. Once the variable values are set, the same component will load the individual request details by calling the CreateRequest component. The CreateRequest component expects some parameters to load the details, which are supplied via props.

Next, let's see how the CreateRequest component handles the display. To start, replace the code with the following. I'll explain the changes afterward.

```
// Import section
import React, { useState, useEffect } from 'react';
import styles from './CloudhadiServicePortal.module.scss';
import { TextField, Dropdown, Stack, IStackTokens, PrimaryButton,
DefaultButton, concatStyleSets } from '@fluentui/react';
import { MessageBar, MessageBarType } from 'office-ui-fabric-react';
import { ICreateRequestProps } from './ICreateRequestProps';
import { sp } from "@pnp/sp";
import "@pnp/sp/webs";
import "@pnp/sp/lists";
import "@pnp/sp/items";
import { IItemAddResult } from "@pnp/sp/items";
import { IViewRequestsState } from './IViewRequestsState';
const stackTokens: IStackTokens = { childrenGap: 30 };
let csrNumber = "CSR" + Math.floor(Math.random() * (99999));

function CreateRequest(props: ICreateRequestProps) {
    // Initiate form element and Title
    let formTitle = "New Service Request";
    let formStructure = <div className=""></div>;

    // Create New Service Request
    if (!props.ID) {
        // State variables for form fields
        const [reqTitle, setReqTitle] = useState("");
        const [reqDesc, setReqDesc] = useState("");
        const [relatedTo, setRelatedTo] = useState("");
        const [success, setSuccess] = useState(false);

        // Create a Cloudhadi Service Request upon clicking the Submit button
        const createCSR = async () => {
            try {
                csrNumber = "CSR" + Math.floor(Math.random() * (99999));
```

```
        const iar: IItemAddResult = await sp.web.lists.
        getByTitle("Service Portal").items.add({
            Title: csrNumber,
            RequestTitle: reqTitle,
            RequestDescription: reqDesc,
            Relatedto: relatedTo,

        });
        setSuccess(true);
    }
    catch (error) {
        throw (error);
    }

}
// Set field values on change–Text fields
const handleChange = (event, setFieldValue) => {
    setFieldValue(event.target.value);
}

// Set field values on change–Dropdown fields
const handleDropDownChange = (selOption, setFieldValue) => {
    setFieldValue(selOption.text);
}
formStructure = <div className={styles.formGridRow}>

    <TextField label="Request Title" onChange={(event) =>
    handleChange(event, setReqTitle)} required></TextField>
    <TextField label="Request Description" onChange={(event) =>
    handleChange(event, setReqDesc)} multiline rows={4} required>
    </TextField>
    <Dropdown
        placeholder="Select an option"
        label="Related to"
        options={[
            { key: 'Access', text: 'Access' },
            { key: 'Materials', text: 'Materials' },
```

```
                    { key: 'Equipments', text: 'Equipments' },
                    { key: 'General', text: 'General' }

                ]}
                onChanged={(selOption) => { handleDropDownChange(selOption,
                setRelatedTo); }}
                required
            />
            <Stack horizontal tokens={stackTokens} className={styles.
            buttonStack}>
                <PrimaryButton className={styles.button} text="Submit"
                onClick={() => createCSR()} />
            </Stack>
            {success === true &&
                <MessageBar messageBarType={MessageBarType.success}
                isMultiline={false} >Successfully created Service Request.
                Reference no:{csrNumber}</MessageBar>
            }
        </div>;
    }
    // Display service request
    else {
        // On component mount
        useEffect(() => {
                loadRequest(props.ID);
        }, [])
        // State variable for Item
        const [currentItem, setCurrentItem] = useState<IViewRequestsState>({
            ID: 0, Title: "", RequestTitle: "", RelatedTo: "",
            RequestStatus: "", RequestAssignedTo: ""
        });

        // Load current item
        const loadRequest = async (reqID) => {
            await sp.web.lists.getByTitle("Service Portal").items
                .getById(reqID)
```

```
            .select('ID', 'Title', 'RequestTitle',
            'RequestDescription', 'Relatedto', 'RequestStatus',
            'RequestAssignedTo/EMail')
            .expand('RequestAssignedTo')
            .get().then((item: any) => {
                let result: IViewRequestsState = {
                    ID: item.Id, Title: item.Title, RequestTitle: item.
                    RequestTitle, RequestDesc: item.RequestDescription,
                    RelatedTo: item.Relatedto,
                    RequestStatus: item.RequestStatus,
                    RequestAssignedTo: (typeof item.RequestAssignedTo
                    !== "undefined") ? item.RequestAssignedTo.EMail :
                    ""                            }
                return result;
            }).then(resultdata => setCurrentItem(resultdata));
    };
    formTitle = `Service Request ${currentItem.Title}`
    formStructure = <div className={styles.formGridRow}>

        <TextField label="Request Title" disabled value={currentItem.
        RequestTitle} ></TextField>
        <TextField label="Request Description" disabled value=
        {currentItem.RequestDesc} multiline rows={4} ></TextField>
        <TextField label="Related to" disabled value={currentItem.
        RelatedTo} ></TextField>
        <TextField label="Request Assigned To" disabled
        value={currentItem.RequestAssignedTo} ></TextField>
        <TextField label="Request Status" disabled value={currentItem.
        RequestStatus} ></TextField>
        <Stack horizontal tokens={stackTokens} className={styles.
        buttonStack}>
            <PrimaryButton className={styles.button} text="Back to My
            Requests" onClick={props.resetView} />
        </Stack>

    </div>
}
```

241

```
    // Render form
    return (
        <div className={styles.cloudhadiServicePortal}>
            <div className={styles.container}>
                <div className={styles.row}>
                    <div className={styles.column}>
                        <span className={styles.title}>{formTitle}</span>
                        <div id="requestForm">
                            <div className={styles.formGrid}>
                                {formStructure}
                            </div>
                        </div>
                    </div>
                </div>
            </div>
        </div>
    );
}
export default CreateRequest;
```

The first change you need to make is to import IViewRequestsState and ICreateRequestProps into the CreateRequest.tsx file. Then, pass the props as a variable into the function called CreateRequest with props as the alias: (props: ICreateRequestProps). Now we'll be able to access the property values using props inside the component.

We're splitting the component into two sections using an If Else condition. If props.ID isn't defined, that means we need to display the New Service Request form. If props.ID has a value, that means it was called from ViewRequests.tsx with an ID.

Initiate the formTitle and formStructure variables outside of If Else condition. Move all the previous declarations for CreateRequest inside the if(!props.ID) condition. Take out the div form and assign it to the formStructure variable. Remove the Cancel button, as we don't need it.

In the If Else condition, I added the logic for `Display Service Request`. Define `useEffect` and call the `loadRequest` method inside that. This is same as we did for the View Requests component, except that this time we're querying a single item instead of multiple items. We're using ID to query the Service Portal list to retrieve all the field values. I defined a pair of state variables. The `currentItem` variable is an object variable that stores the property values of the item. The result is stored in this variable.

The `formTitle` is set to the title of the current item. All the other fields are defined as `disabled` text fields that will display different item values. The values are retrieved from the `currentItem` object.

Finally, there is a `Back to My Requests` button. Clicking the button invokes `props.resetView`. This will call the parent component function `resetViewRequest`. While calling the Create Request Component form, we passed this function as a prop. Upon calling the `resetViewRequest` function, the state variable `doViewRequest` will set to `false` and all my requests will be loaded back. This is how we establish the communication from child to parent.

To summarize, in the Create Request component, what we did is a conditional rendering based on the props value. If a prop value for ID is passed, the component will render an existing request. The request details are queried based on the passed ID. If it isn't passed, the component will render a form to submit a new service request as we have previously seen. So, the same component behaves as a new or display form using conditional rendering. To go back to the called component, we will again make use of a prop.

Run gulp serve. If you click a request in View My Requests, you'll see an individual request detail loaded in disabled mode, as shown in Figure 6-13. By clicking the Back to My Requests button, you can go back and view all of your requests.

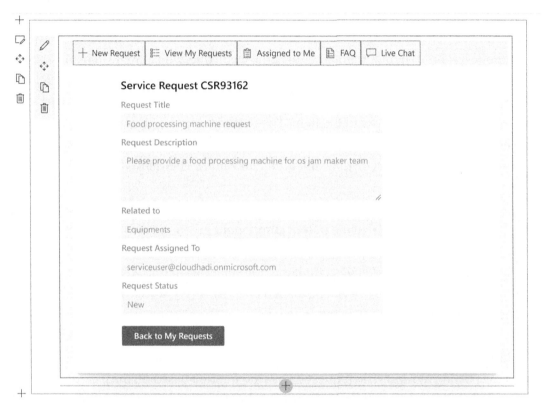

Figure 6-13. *Component communication using props*

We now have the options to create a service request, view all the service requests of a specific user, and view the details of an individual request. What we're missing is being able to assign the service request to a user, a view for service requests assigned to the user, and an option to change the request status.

Personalized Components

Whenever a new service request is created, I'm assigning it to a specific user: serviceuser@cloudhadi.onmicrosoft.com. I configured a Power Automate flow and linked to the Service Portal for this purpose. The flow is shared in the Github repository. Refer to the AssignServiceRequest folder inside Chapter 6 folder in the GitHub repository (`https://github.com/Apress/building-modern-workplace-sharepoint-online/tree/main/Chapter%206/AssignServiceRequest`). The flow name is Assign Service Request. If I log in as this service user, I should be able to see request assigned to me. You can use any account for this purpose. Later on, we'll see how to add this user to site and list.

But before we get to that, let's copy the ViewMyRequests.tsx component, paste it under Components, and rename it "AssignedRequests.tsx." Replace the code with the following. After we're done doing that, we'll get into the details.

```
import React, { useState, useEffect } from 'react';
import { sp } from "@pnp/sp";
import "@pnp/sp/webs";
import "@pnp/sp/lists";
import "@pnp/sp/items";
import "@pnp/sp/site-users/web";
import { IViewRequestsState } from './IViewRequestsState';
import styles from './CloudhadiServicePortal.module.scss';
import { DetailsList, DetailsListLayoutMode } from 'office-ui-fabric-react/
lib/DetailsList';
import { Link, VerticalDivider } from '@fluentui/react';
import CreateRequest from './CreateRequest';
// Column headers
const columns = [
    { key: 'Title', name: 'Request No.', fieldName: 'Title', minWidth: 70,
    maxWidth: 200, isResizable: true },
    { key: 'RequestTitle', name: 'Request Title', fieldName:
    'RequestTitle', minWidth: 160, maxWidth: 200, isResizable: true },
    { key: 'RequestStatus', name: 'Status', fieldName: 'RequestStatus',
    minWidth: 70, maxWidth: 200, isResizable: true }];
// Render list of requests
function AssignedRequests() {
    // On component mount
    useEffect(() => {
        loadMyRequests();
    }, [])
    // Reset to view requests
    const resetViewRequest = () => {
        setDoViewRequest(false);
    };
    // State variables for request items
    const [myItems, setMyItems] = useState([]);
```

245

```
// State variables for viewing individual requests
const [doViewRequest, setDoViewRequest] = useState(false);
const [requestID, setRequestID] = useState(0);
// Load Service requests
const loadMyRequests = async () => {
    let currentUser = await sp.web.currentUser();
    await sp.web.lists.getByTitle("Service Portal").items
        .filter(`RequestAssignedTo/EMail eq '${currentUser.Email}'`)
        .select('ID', 'Title', 'RequestTitle', 'RequestStatus')
        .get().then((items) => {
            let result: IViewRequestsState[] = [];
            items.forEach(element => {
                result.push({
                    ID: element.Id, Title: <Link href="#">{element.
                    Title}</Link>, RequestTitle: element.RequestTitle,
                    RequestStatus: element.RequestStatus
                });
            });
            return result;
        }).then(resultdata => setMyItems(resultdata));
};
// On click of item
const _onItemInvoked = (item: any): void => {
    // Call child component with ID
    setRequestID(item.ID);
    setDoViewRequest(true);
};

// Load all requests
if (!doViewRequest) {
    return (
<div className={styles.cloudhadiServicePortal}>
            <div className={styles.container}>
                <div className={styles.row}>
                    <div className={styles.column}>
```

```
                    <span className={styles.title}>Requests
                    Assigned to me</span>
                    <DetailsList
                        items={myItems}
                        columns={columns}
                        layoutMode={DetailsListLayoutMode.
                        justified}
                        onItemInvoked={_onItemInvoked}
                    />
                </div>
            </div>
        </div>
    </div>
    );
  }
  // Call to load individual request
  else {
      return (
          <CreateRequest ID={requestID} resetView={resetViewRequest} />
      );
  }
}
}
export default AssignedRequests;
```

This code is very similar to that of ViewRequests.tsx. The only difference is that to change the name of the function, you need to change the name in the export and update `Author/Email` to `RequestAssignedTo/Email`. This will ensure that all requests assigned to the current user are displayed. The changes are highlighted in the code.

We now have the `AssignedRequests` component ready. We need to link it to our home component command bar by adding one more tab. We also need to make sure that only the service account user can view that. But we need to do a few more things before editing the home component.

Go to your workplace site ➤ site contents ➤ permissions. Then, as shown in Figure 6-14, choose the Service Executives group, click New, then click Service User, and hit Share. I added serviceuser@cloudhadi.onmicrosoft.com as the service user here. This user will be added to the group.

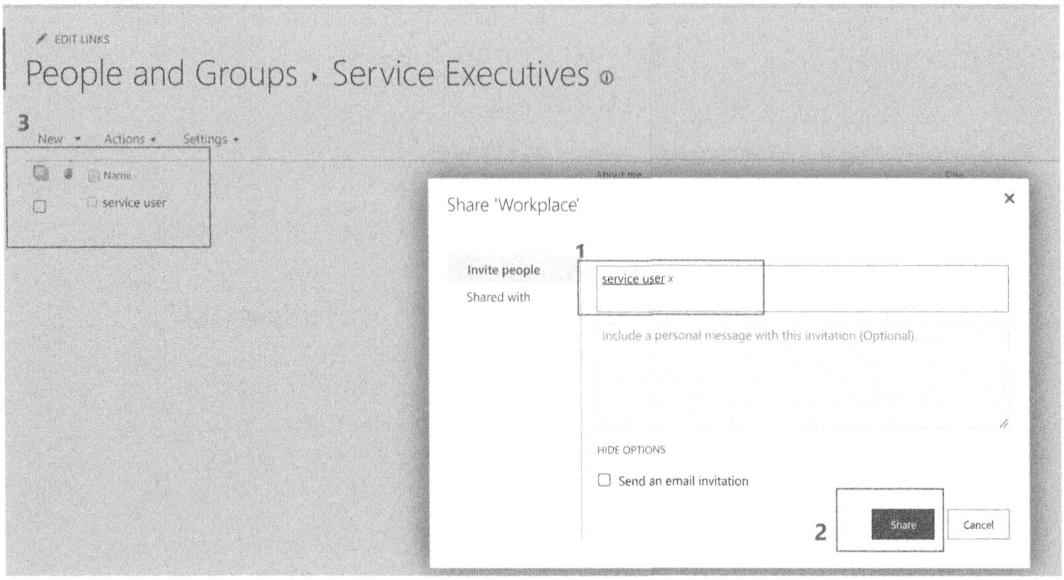

Figure 6-14. *Adding a service user to the Service Executives group*

You might have noticed that this group only has Read permission for the site. But we need to provide Full Control permissions to the group. Once the user is added, go to the Service Portal list and then List Settings using the Settings button on the top right. Then, click Permissions for this List. On the permissions page, click Stop Inheriting Permissions, and when you get a pop-up, click OK. Select Service Executives and click Edit User Permissions on the ribbon. Check off Full Control Permission and click OK. Now, the service account executives have Full Control permission on the list, even though they have only Read access to the site. See Figure 6-15.

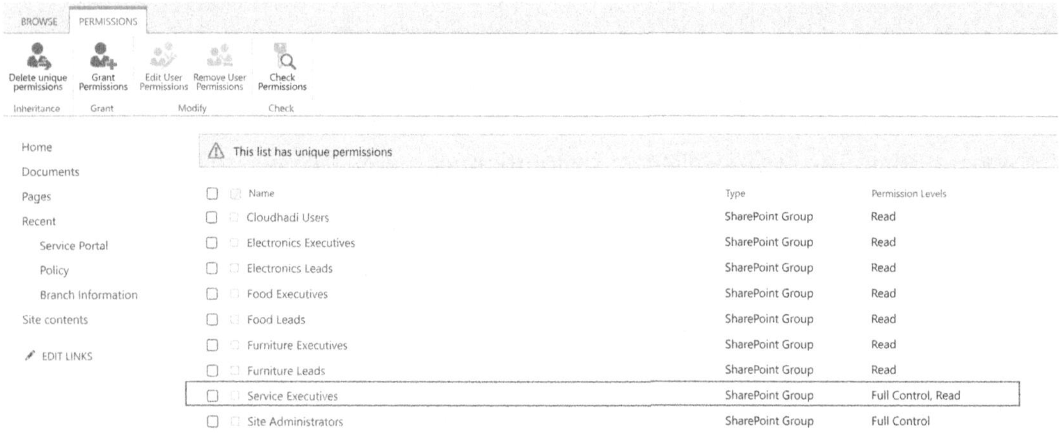

Figure 6-15. *Setting unique permissions in the Service Portal list*

Let's now go back to the code and modify the home component, CloudhadiServicePortal.tsx, with the following code. This will add a new menu item in the command bar if the logged-in user belongs to the Service Executives group.

```
// Import section
import React, { useState, useEffect } from 'react';
import styles from './CloudhadiServicePortal.module.scss';
import { CommandBar, ICommandBarItemProps } from 'office-ui-fabric-react/
lib/CommandBar';
import CreateRequest from './CreateRequest';
import ViewMyRequests from './ViewMyRequests';
import FAQ from './FAQ';
import LiveChat from './LiveChat';
import AssignedRequests from './AssignedRequests';
import { sp } from "@pnp/sp";
import "@pnp/sp/site-users/web";
function CloudhadiServicePortal() {
  // Declare state variable and function for setting form
  const [selectedForm, setSelectedForm] = useState(<CreateRequest />);
  // Declare state variable and function for group check
  const [serviceExecutive, setServiceExecutive] = useState(false);
  // Set form upon click of the command bar menu
  const onMenuClick = (form) => {
    setSelectedForm(form);
  }
  // Command bar items
  let _items: ICommandBarItemProps[] = [
    {
      key: 'New',
      text: 'New Request',
      iconProps: { iconName: 'Add' },
      onClick: () => onMenuClick(<CreateRequest />)
    },
    {
      key: 'View',
      text: 'View My Requests',
```

```
      iconProps: { iconName: 'GroupedList' },
      onClick: () => onMenuClick(<ViewMyRequests />)
    },

    {
      key: 'FAQ',
      text: 'FAQ',
      iconProps: { iconName: 'Questionnaire' },
      onClick: () => onMenuClick(<FAQ />)
    },
    {
      key: 'Chat',
      text: 'Live Chat',

      iconProps: { iconName: 'Chat' },
      onClick: () => onMenuClick(<LiveChat />)
    }

];
// On component mount
useEffect(() => {
    // Set as service executive if the logged-in user belongs to the group
    checkServiceExecutive();
}, []);
// Check if current user belongs to the Service Executives group and set
    the user as Service Executive if belongs to the group
const checkServiceExecutive = async () => {
    let groups: any = await sp.web.currentUser.groups();
    await groups.forEach(group => {
      if (group.LoginName == 'Service Executives') {
        setServiceExecutive(true);
        return;
      }
    }
    );
}
// Add 'Assigned to Me' tab if the user is a service executive
```

```
if (serviceExecutive) {
  _items.splice(2, 0, {
    key: 'Assigned',
    text: 'Assigned to Me',
    iconProps: { iconName: 'ClipboardList' },
    onClick: () => onMenuClick(<AssignedRequests />)
  });
}
return (
  <div>
    <CommandBar
      items={_items}
    />
    <div>
      {selectedForm}
    </div>
  </div>

);
}
```

In the previous code, we first need to import the AssignedRequests component and
the useEffect and pnp sp modules and then create a pair of state variables for setting
true or false based on the logged-in user. In the useEffect, I'm calling a method that
loops through the logged-in user groups. If the Service Executives group is found,
it sets the serviceExecutive variable to true and return. If the group isn't found, the
variable remains as false, which is its initial value.

Next, add an if condition just above the return section. If the serviceExecutive
variable is true, insert the Assigned to Me menu item to the command bar in position 3;
that is, index 2.

Then, run gulp serve-deprecated and open Workbench from the service user
account. Now, as shown in Figure 6-16, you can see the Assigned to Me tab next to
View My Requests. Make sure you assign some of the requests to the service user
manually if you haven't set up the flow to assign them automatically. If you check from
a non–service executive user workbench, you won't see the tab. Please note that the
gulp serve task has been deprecated and renamed to serve-deprecated. To address
this, the gulpfile.js in new SPFx v1.12.1 projects has been updated to add an alias serve

for the renamed serve-deprecated task. If you are using SPFx v1.12.1, you can use gulp serve command. Else use gulp serve-deprecated.

Figure 6-16. *Conditional command bar menu*

You can click any of the assigned requests to view their details. The service executive needs to update the request status here. So, we need to make some changes to the Create Request and Assigned Requests components to accommodate this.

Handling Updates

We need to distinguish the call from the View Requests and Assigned Requests components. Start by adding a new optional property, `isAssigned?:boolean;`, to the ICreateRequestProps.ts file. Then, modify AssignedRequests.tsx by adding the new prop. Replace `<CreateRequest ID={requestID} resetView={resetViewRequest}/>` with `<CreateRequest ID={requestID} resetView={resetViewRequest} isAssigned={true}/>` in the call to load individual request.

Next, replace the contents inside the CreateRequests.tsx with the following code:

```
// Import Section
import React, { useState, useEffect } from 'react';
import styles from './CloudhadiServicePortal.module.scss';
import { TextField, Dropdown, Stack, IStackTokens, PrimaryButton } from
'@fluentui/react';
```

```
import { MessageBar, MessageBarType } from 'office-ui-fabric-react';
import { ICreateRequestProps } from './ICreateRequestProps';
import { sp } from "@pnp/sp";
import "@pnp/sp/webs";
import "@pnp/sp/lists";
import "@pnp/sp/items";
import { IItemAddResult } from "@pnp/sp/items";
import { IViewRequestsState } from './IViewRequestsState';
const stackTokens: IStackTokens = { childrenGap: 30 };
let csrNumber = "CSR" + Math.floor(Math.random() * (99999));

function CreateRequest(props: ICreateRequestProps) {

    // Initiate form element and Title
    let formTitle = "New Service Request";
    let formStructure = <div className=""></div>;

    // State variable for request status and success
    const [reqStatus, setReqStatus] = useState("New");
    const [success, setSuccess] = useState(false);

    // Set field values on change of the respective Dropdown fields
    const handleDropDownChange = (selOption, setFieldValue) => {
        setFieldValue(selOption.text);
    }
    // Create New service request
    if (!props.ID) {
        // State variables for form fields
        const [reqTitle, setReqTitle] = useState("");
        const [reqDesc, setReqDesc] = useState("");
        const [relatedTo, setRelatedTo] = useState("");

        // Create a Cloudhadi Service Request upon click of the Submit button
        const createCSR = async () => {
            try {
                csrNumber = "CSR" + Math.floor(Math.random() * (99999));
                const iar: IItemAddResult = await sp.web.lists.
                getByTitle("Service Portal").items.add({
```

```
                Title: csrNumber,
                RequestTitle: reqTitle,
                RequestDescription: reqDesc,
                Relatedto: relatedTo,

        });

        setSuccess(true);
    }
    catch (error) {
        throw (error);
    }
}
// Set field values ontext fields on change of respective Text fields
const handleChange = (event, setFieldValue) => {
    setFieldValue(event.target.value);
}
formStructure = <div className={styles.formGridRow}>

    <TextField label="Request Title" onChange={(event) =>
    handleChange(event, setReqTitle)} required></TextField>
    <TextField label="Request Description" onChange={(event) =>
    handleChange(event, setReqDesc)} multiline rows={4} required>
    </TextField>
    <Dropdown
        placeholder="Select an option"
        label="Related to"
        options={[
            { key: 'Access', text: 'Access' },
            { key: 'Materials', text: 'Materials' },
            { key: 'Equipments', text: 'Equipments' },
            { key: 'General', text: 'General' }

        ]}
        onChanged={(selOption) => { handleDropDownChange(selOption,
        setRelatedTo); }}
        required
    />
```

```
    <Stack horizontal tokens={stackTokens} className={styles.
    buttonStack}>
        <PrimaryButton className={styles.button} text="Submit"
        onClick={() => createCSR()} />
    </Stack>
    {success === true &&
        <MessageBar messageBarType={MessageBarType.success}
        isMultiline={false} >Successfully created Service Request.
        Reference no:{csrNumber}</MessageBar>
    }
    </div>;
}
// Display service request
else {
    // On component mount
    useEffect(() => {
        loadRequest(props.ID);
    }, [])
    // State variable for Item
    const [currentItem, setCurrentItem] = useState<IViewRequestsState>({
        ID: 0, Title: "", RequestTitle: "", RelatedTo: "",
        RequestStatus: "", RequestAssignedTo: ""
    });
    // Load current item
    const loadRequest = async (reqID) => {
        await sp.web.lists.getByTitle("Service Portal").items
            .getById(reqID)
            .select('ID', 'Title', 'RequestTitle',
            'RequestDescription', 'Relatedto', 'RequestStatus',
            'RequestAssignedTo/EMail')
            .expand('RequestAssignedTo')
            .get().then((item: any) => {
                let result: IViewRequestsState = {
```

```
                    ID: item.Id, Title: item.Title, RequestTitle: item.
                    RequestTitle, RequestDesc: item.RequestDescription,
                    RelatedTo: item.Relatedto,
                    RequestStatus: item.RequestStatus,
                    RequestAssignedTo: (typeof item.RequestAssignedTo
                    !== "undefined") ? item.RequestAssignedTo.EMail : ""
                }
                return result;
            }).then(resultdata => setCurrentItem(resultdata));
    };
    formTitle = `Service Request ${currentItem.Title}`;
    if (!props.isAssigned) {
        formStructure = <div className={styles.formGridRow}>

            <TextField label="Request Title" disabled
            value={currentItem.RequestTitle} ></TextField>
            <TextField label="Request Description" disabled
            value={currentItem.RequestDesc} multiline rows={4} >
            </TextField>
            <TextField label="Related to" disabled value={currentItem.
            RelatedTo} ></TextField>
            <TextField label="Request Assigned To" disabled
            value={currentItem.RequestAssignedTo} ></TextField>
            <TextField label="Request Status" disabled
            value={currentItem.RequestStatus} ></TextField>
            <Stack horizontal tokens={stackTokens} className={styles.
            buttonStack}>
                <PrimaryButton className={styles.button} text="Back to
                My Requests" onClick={props.resetView} />
            </Stack>
        </div>
    }
    else {
        // Update status of current item
        const updateRequestStatus = async () => {
            try {
```

```
        await sp.web.lists.getByTitle("Service Portal").items
            .getById(currentItem.ID)
            .update({
                RequestStatus: reqStatus
            });
        currentItem.RequestStatus = reqStatus;
        setSuccess(true);
    }
    catch (error) {
        throw (error);
    }
};
formStructure = <div className={styles.formGridRow}>
    <TextField label="Request Title" disabled
    value={currentItem.RequestTitle} ></TextField>
    <TextField label="Request Description" disabled
    value={currentItem.RequestDesc} multiline rows={4} >
    </TextField>
    <TextField label="Related to" disabled value={currentItem.
    RelatedTo} ></TextField>
    <TextField label="Request Assigned To" disabled
    value={currentItem.RequestAssignedTo} ></TextField>
    <Dropdown
        defaultSelectedKey={currentItem.RequestStatus}
        placeholder="Select an option"
        label="Request Status"
        options={[
            { key: 'New', text: 'New' },
            { key: 'In Progress', text: 'In Progress' },
            { key: 'Completed', text: 'Completed' },
            { key: 'Rejected', text: 'Rejected' }
        ]}
        onChanged={(selOption) => { handleDropDownChange
        (selOption, setReqStatus); }}
        required
    />
```

```
            <Stack horizontal tokens={stackTokens} className={styles.
            buttonStack}>
                {currentItem.RequestStatus != "Completed"
                && <PrimaryButton className={styles.button}
                text="Update" onClick={() => updateRequestStatus()}/>}
                <PrimaryButton className={styles.button} text="Back to
                Assigned Requests" onClick={props.resetView} />
            </Stack>
            {success === true &&
                <MessageBar messageBarType={MessageBarType.success}
                isMultiline={false} >Successfully updated Service
                Request :{currentItem.Title}</MessageBar>
            }
        </div>
    }
}
// Render form
return (
    <div className={styles.cloudhadiServicePortal}>
        <div className={styles.container}>
            <div className={styles.row}>
                <div className={styles.column}>
                    <span className={styles.title}>{formTitle}</span>
                    <div id="requestForm">
                        <div className={styles.formGrid}>
                            {formStructure}
                        </div>
                    </div>
                </div>
            </div>
        </div>
    </div>
);
}
export default CreateRequest;
```

The first step is to move the handleDropDownChange method and success message state variable to the top, above the if(!props.ID) condition. This will make it available for the else condition as well. This will also create a new pair of variables for request status. In the else condition (Display service request), add another If Else block that checks the value of props.isAssigned. Move the form structure declaration for View Requests inside that block. If isAssigned isn't passed or isn't true, the form structure is assigned with the previous View Requests form.

In the else block, add a PnP method for updating the RequestStatus. For the form structure, add a drop-down for the RequestStatus. Keep the other fields as disabled. For the dropdown, set defaultSelectedKey as currentItem.RequestStatus. In the onChanged method, pass setReqStatus to update the state variable. By clicking the Update button, the updateRequestStatus method will be called and the status will be updated. The success message will be displayed, and the dropdown will get updated with the status value. When the status value is completed, the Update button won't be displayed, as there are no further updates expected. The Back to Assigned Requests button will take you back to the assigned requests, like it did for View Requests.

Try clicking Assigned Requests and update the status. Figure 6-17 shows one of my assigned requests from the service user account. While changing the status, keep in mind that sometimes you might need to click twice on the value in the Fabric UI drop-down.

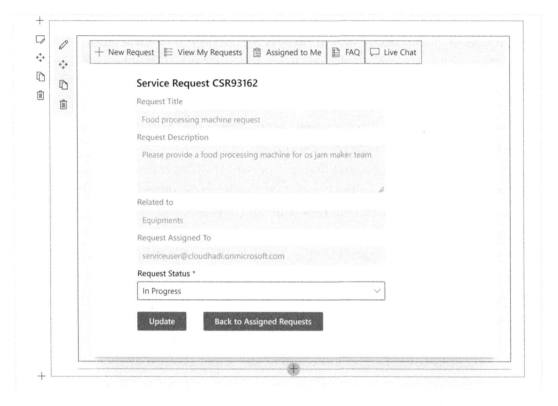

Figure 6-17. *Actioning a request*

The new status will be reflected in the `Assigned Requests` component. You could add a logic to avoid displaying the `Completed` requests, by modifying the filter condition in the AssignedRequests.tsx file to `filter(`RequestAssignedTo/EMail eq '${currentUser.Email}' and RequestStatus ne 'Completed'`)`

I hope you now feel familiar with the React concepts PnPjs and SPFx. Next, let's package this web part and deploy it to SharePoint.

App Deployment

Go to the command prompt, stop running `gulp serve-deprecated`. Run `gulp bundle --ship`. This will build and minify your source code. Once completed, run `gulp package-solution --ship`. The web part will be packaged. Go to your project folder ➤ solution, and locate CloudhadiWebPart.sppkg.

Go to the App Catalog site we created in the "App Catalog" section at the beginning of the chapter, then go to Apps for SharePoint and upload the .sppkg file. Click Deploy on the pop-up. See Figure 6-18.

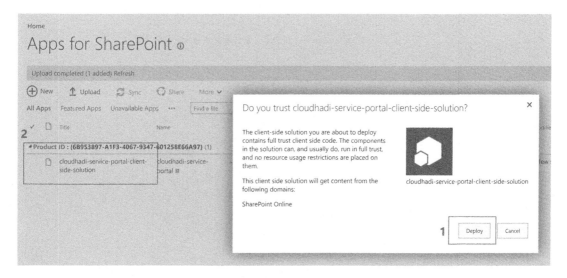

Figure 6-18. *Deploying the SPFx web part*

Now go back to the Workplace site. Go to Settings icon on the top right side, click Add an App. Select cloudhadi-service-portal-client-side-solution from the list of Apps to choose from. Wait a few minutes for the App to be added and then refresh the page.

Once the app is added, go to the home page and edit. Add a new two-column section. Click +, search for cloudhadi-ServicePortal and add it to the first section. The Service Portal will now be added to the home page. (We will rearrange this later.) Publish the page. Figure 6-19 shows the home page with the Service Portal.

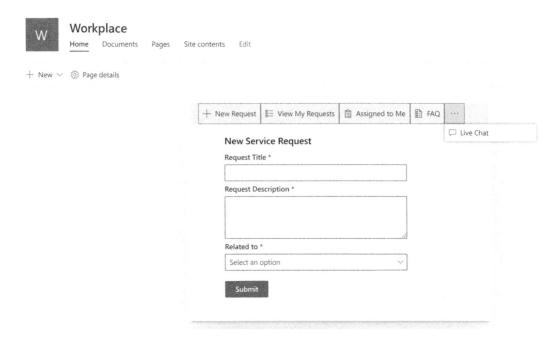

Figure 6-19. *SPFx web part in the SharePoint page*

Overview of SPFx Extensions

In this chapter, you've learned about SPFx web parts. SPFx extensions help you to extend the SharePoint user experience. For example, we can add a new context menu to the Product Data library using the SPFx command set extension. We can also create a customized view for a column inside a library using Field Customizer extensions. If you want to modify the header or footer section of a page, you can make use of the Application Customizer extension. Creating an extension is like creating a web part: You need to select Extension and the type of extension while creating it from the command prompt.

In Chapter 8, we'll create an extension when dealing with Teams.

Note   All the items this chapter—including the web part code, package, and assignment flow—are available in the Chapter 6 folder of the GitHub repository: `https://github.com/Apress/building-modern-workplace-sharepoint-online/tree/main/Chapter%206`. In addition to this, latest development news and respective URLs in the SPFx space also shared there.

Summary

The aim of this chapter has been to get you started with SPFx and ensure that you're using the latest recommended concepts during development. You learned about creating an App Catalog and an SPFx web part, as well as packaging and deploying the app to the catalog.

We reviewed the basic concepts of React. We discussed about hooks and how to create a solution where only hooks are used to manage the state. We took a look at components and how to have an interaction between the components using props. We touched upon conditional rendering and using PnP operations with SharePoint. In the process, we created a Cloudhadi service portal where users can submit and view requests, and service executives can act on the requests. In the next chapter, we'll learn about the modern search capabilities available in SharePoint Online.

CHAPTER 7

Modern Search

The topic we'll look at in this chapter is slightly different than the ones in the previous chapters. *Search* is a term that we're all familiar with in our day-to-day lives. In our Cloudhadi portal, we may have thousands of documents and pieces of production information flowing in. How can we find the information we need quickly and easily? SharePoint Search can help us do that.

SharePoint offers both a classic and modern search experience. The modern search, named Microsoft Search, brings together results from different data sources, including SharePoint, OneDrive, and Exchange Server. The focus of this chapter will be limited to SharePoint Search.

On the top of every page of our workplace site, there is a Search Box. If you search for something from the home page using the Search Box, it will pull out all of its results from the workplace site. The results are displayed in a default page named search.aspx.

Using the SharePoint Framework (SPFx) model of modern development, Patterns and Practices (PnP) Modern Search web parts were introduced in 2017. With PnP Search web parts, you can configure and customize your search in SharePoint Online sites. PnP v4 is the latest-available version that makes use of Microsoft Graph application programming interfaces (APIs).

My goal in this chapter is to take you through out-of-the-box (OOB) search configurations and introduce you to PnP Modern Search customizations. By the end of this chapter, you'll be familiar with Modern Search concepts and customizations. Let's get going!

Out-of-the-Box Searches

Let's start with the search box that comes OOB. Go to your workplace site home page and type in "food," as shown in Figure 7-1.

© Harinarayanan V P 2021
Harinarayanan V P, *Building the Modern Workplace with SharePoint Online*,
https://doi.org/10.1007/978-1-4842-6945-9_7

Figure 7-1. *SharePoint search box*

When you type in something, the search box will show you the results. If you immediately find what you're looking for, you can directly click the result. If you want to view more results, click the right arrow or Show More Results to go to the search page. See Figure 7-2 for search page.

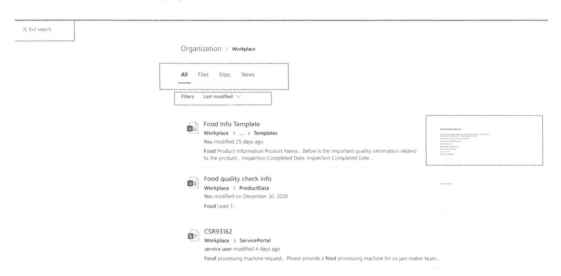

Figure 7-2. *Default search page*

In the default search page, all the results that match the *food* keyword will come up, with a filter option at the top. If you click the filter drop-down, you can filter based on the last modified date. For some of the results, you can see a preview of the file. There are also four tabs above the results that specify different types of search results. You can exit the search results using Exit Search, which will take you back to the home page.

Go to the Service Portal list, Products list, or Product Data library. Now, if you search in the top Search Box, you'll be given the results from the respective list of libraries that you just chose. The watermark on the Search Box indicates which scope the search is going to execute in.

As you can see, the OOB search box is quite limited in terms of having an enhanced search experience. The PnP Modern Search solution helps to build enhanced search-based solutions in SharePoint Modern Experience. We'll get more into that next.

Search Objective

As per the Cloudhadi requirements, our objective is to search for all Product Data documents. In addition to this, we should be able to filter these documents using Product Type, Document Type, and Modified.

PnP Modern Search

The PnP Modern Search is an open-source solution. To get it, we need to go to the GitHub repository of Modern Search and download the SPFx package. Once it is downloaded, we can integrate it into our workplace site and work with the different features of the web parts involved.

Let's start by downloading "pnp-modern-search-parts-v4.sppkg" at `https://github.com/microsoft-search/pnp-modern-search/releases/download/4.0.0/pnp-modern-search-parts-v4.sppkg`. After that, we'll go to the App Catalog site, upload the .sppkg file under Apps for SharePoint, and deploy. Click Make This Solution Available to All Sites in the Organization while deploying it, as shown in Figure 7-3.

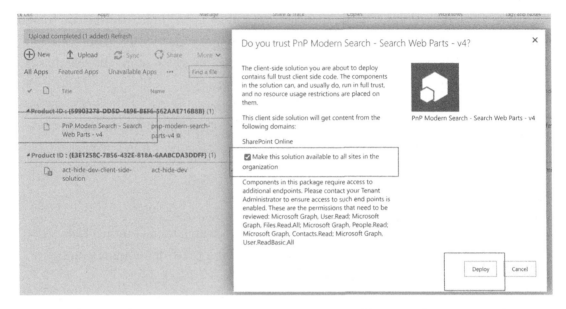

Figure 7-3. *Deploying PnP Modern Search package file in to the App Catalog*

Next, we'll download the extensibility package from `https://github.com/ microsoft-search/pnp-modern-search/releases/download/4.0.0/ pnp-modern-search-extensibility.sppkg`, and deploy it to the App Catalog using the same steps we took for uploading the previous .sppkg.

Let's now add a custom search page for the workplace site by going back to the workplace site, clicking Settings, and then selecting Add a Page, as shown in Figure 7-4.

Figure 7-4. *Adding a page in Settings*

Then, select the Blank template and click Create Page, as done in Figure 7-5.

Figure 7-5. *Choosing a template and creating a page*

Once the page is created, you'll be redirected to a screen where you can edit the page. Type in "ModernSearch" and add the One-Third Left Column section to the page, as selected in Figure 7-6.

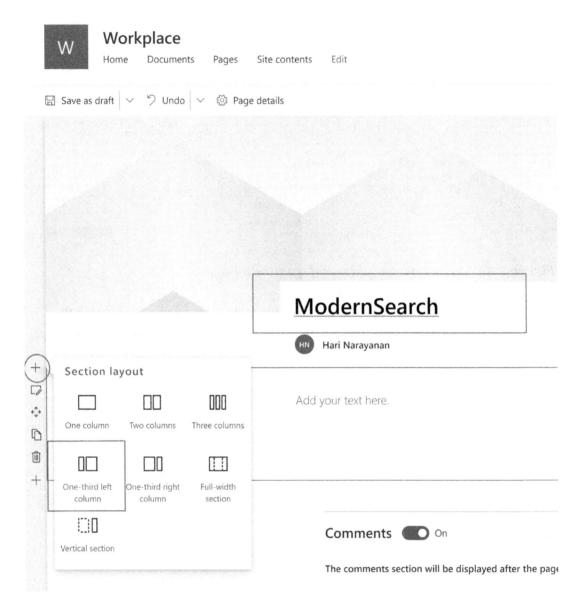

Figure 7-6. Setting the layout

Once the section is added, add the PnP—Search Results web part on the right side of the screen, as shown in Figure 7-7.

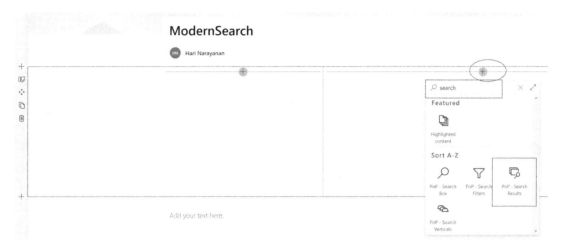

Figure 7-7. *Adding the PnP—Search Results web part*

Repeat the same steps for the section on the left side of the screen, but this time choose the PnP-Search-Filters web part. As soon as both web parts are added, we can configure them. Click the Configure button for the Search Results web part. Figure 7-8 shows the initial configuration of the Search Results web part.

Figure 7-8. *PnP—Search results: query and result source*

Now, select SharePoint Search and update the query text to "{searchTerms}*." This will display the results across all the local SharePoint sites. Our aim is to restrict the search results to all Product Data documents. Select Result Source ID for Documents. This will set the scope to all documents in the site. We need to further refine our search by setting the refinement filters to Path: "[*yourSiteURL*]/ProductData*. Now, you'll be able to see all the approved Product Data documents in your search results. Note that to appear in the search, the documents must be approved, as we have the content approval set in the library. If you want to have more documents to play around with in the search, you can upload more documents into the Product Data library and get them approved.

If you click Next from the bottom of the web part properties panel, you can change the layout, show results count, and more. Change the web part title to "Product Data Documents" from Webpart title.

Next, click Configure for the Filter web part and select the data from the Search Results web part. Also set the operator to AND. This will ensure that all the filter conditions match while we're applying the filters. See Figure 7-9.

Figure 7-9. *Connecting the Filter web part to the search results*

If you click Edit, you can see options for adding fields to the filter in the pop-up. Our objective is to filter using Product Type, Document Type, and Modified date. Before setting up the filter, we need to learn about managed properties. Let's save and publish the page for now. We'll get back to adding filters after going through the search schema in the next section.

Search Schema

The search function works based on the search index. When users try to find information by interacting with the search pages, the returned results are determined by the contents of a search index. The content is collected in and retrieved from the search index using a search schema. In this way, the schema controls the search. The schema contains crawled properties, crawled property categories, the crawled to managed property mapping, and the managed property settings. Managed property settings define what you can search for and how.

We must crawl content to build up the search index. In SharePoint Online, crawling happens automatically on a defined crawl schedule. When the Product Data library gets crawled, the contents and the metadata of the documents are represented as crawled properties. Let's find out the crawled properties for the Product Type, Document Type, and Modified by going to our workplace site, then Site Settings ➤ Site Collection Administration ➤ Search schema, as shown in Figure 7-10.

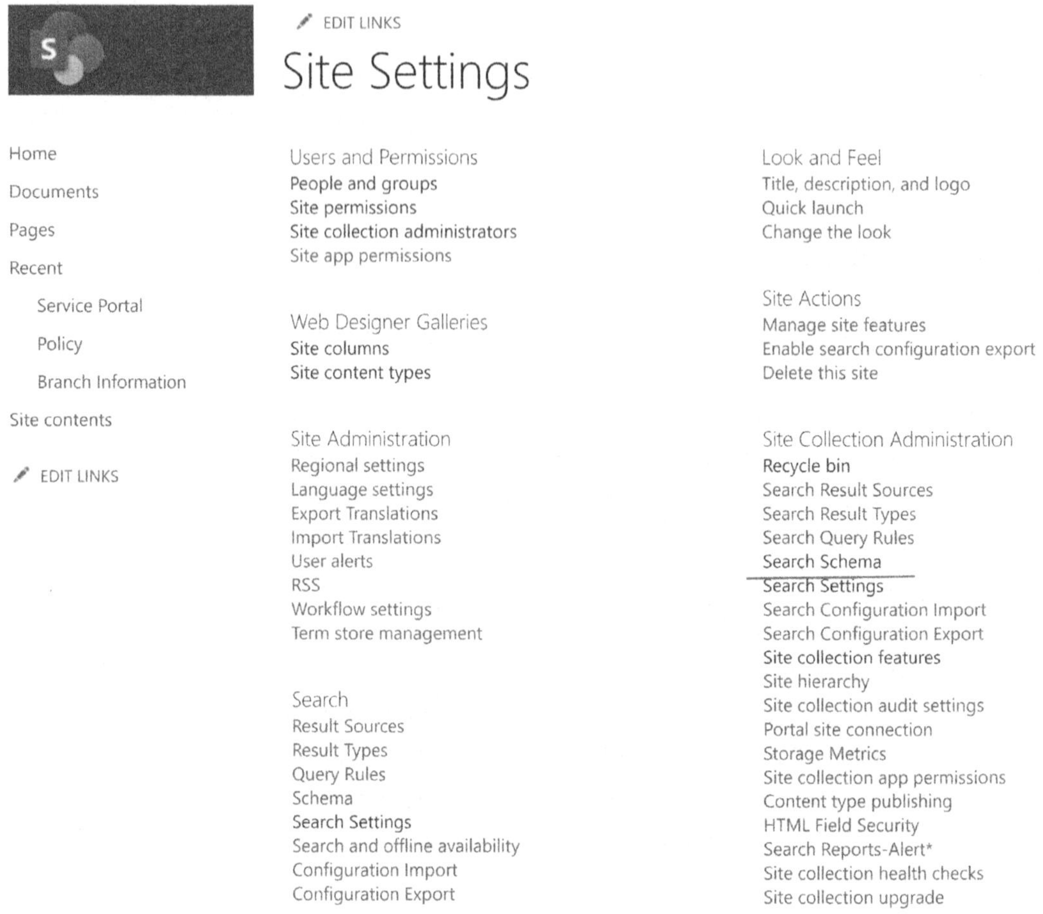

Site Settings

/ EDIT LINKS

Home

Documents

Pages

Recent

   Service Portal

   Policy

   Branch Information

Site contents

/ EDIT LINKS

Users and Permissions
People and groups
Site permissions
Site collection administrators
Site app permissions

Web Designer Galleries
Site columns
Site content types

Site Administration
Regional settings
Language settings
Export Translations
Import Translations
User alerts
RSS
Workflow settings
Term store management

Search
Result Sources
Result Types
Query Rules
Schema
Search Settings
Search and offline availability
Configuration Import
Configuration Export

Look and Feel
Title, description, and logo
Quick launch
Change the look

Site Actions
Manage site features
Enable search configuration export
Delete this site

Site Collection Administration
Recycle bin
Search Result Sources
Search Result Types
Search Query Rules
Search Schema
Search Settings
Search Configuration Import
Search Configuration Export
Site collection features
Site hierarchy
Site collection audit settings
Portal site connection
Storage Metrics
Site collection app permissions
Content type publishing
HTML Field Security
Search Reports-Alert*
Site collection health checks
Site collection upgrade

Figure 7-10. *Navigating to Search Schema*

On the page that comes up, click Crawled Properties and search for "producttype," as shown in Figure 7-11.

Figure 7-11. *Crawled Properties page*

In the Property Name section, you can see two properties, one of which is ows_ ProductType. The metadata product type will be represented by this crawled property. Similarly, for the Document Type and Modified date, you can search and find ows_ Modified and ows_DocumentType.

So, the crawled properties do contain the content and metadata of items. But to include these contents and metadata in the search index, you must map the crawled properties to the managed properties. Only managed properties are written to the search index.

Let's quickly recap what we just covered: To search your content and metadata, it must be crawled. The crawling creates/updates the crawled properties, which represent the metadata and content of the crawled items. But the search index looks for managed properties. So, we must map the crawled properties to the managed properties. Finally, the search index returns the search results on a search query.

Managed properties are defined by many settings. These settings define how the contents are shown in results and how users can search for them. For example, if you want users to filter results by Product Type, the Managed Property product type must be refinable. For our requirements, we need to have three refinable properties: Product Type, Document Type, and Modified date.

We can create a new managed property or we can make use of the existing managed properties that have already been created OOB. If you go to search schema and search for "refinable," you can see the large number of managed properties available. Let's map three of these properties to the crawled properties for Product Type, Document Type, and Modified date. Start by searching for "refinablestring," as shown on Figure 7-12.

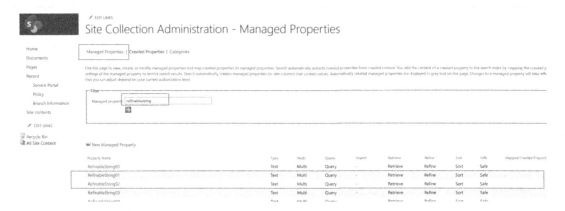

Figure 7-12. *Refinable managed properties*

Then click RefinableString01. Note that you can't edit most of the properties. You can see the type of the property is Text and Refinable is Yes—Active. Scroll down to the bottom of the page and click Add a Mapping, next to Mappings to Crawled Properties. Then, search for "producttype," select ows_ProductType, and click OK, as shown in Figure 7-13.

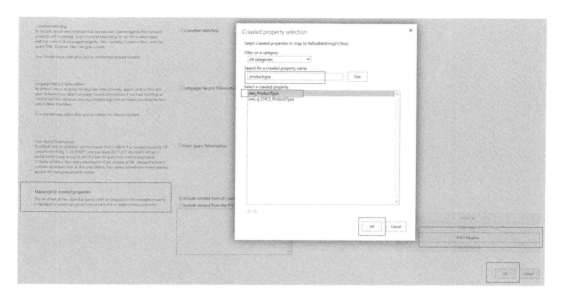

Figure 7-13. *Mapping to crawled properties*

Now the crawled property for Product Type is mapped to RefinableString01. Repeat the same steps for RefinableString02 and RefinableDate01 for Document Type and Modified date, respectively. Choose the crawled properties accordingly.

Once you complete these changes, you need to reindex the product data list. Doing this will ensure that the mapping to the search index gets updated during the next scheduled crawl. Go to the product data list ➤ list settings ➤ advanced settings. See Figure 7-14.

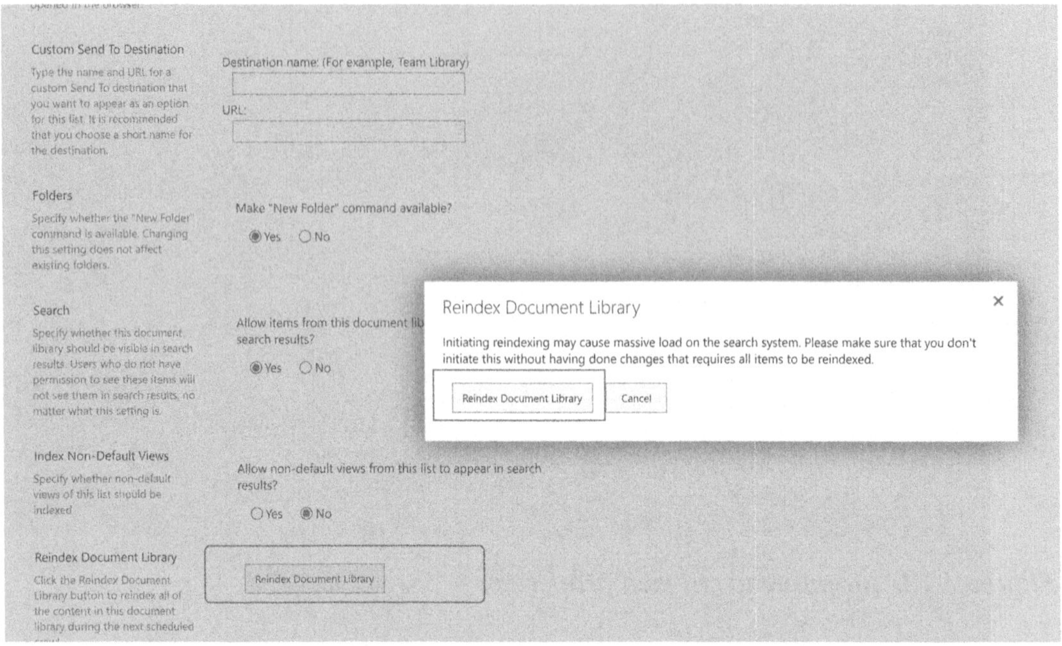

Figure 7-14. *Reindexing the document library*

As shown in Figure 7-14, click Reindex Document Library and click the same on the pop-up. Don't forget to scroll down and hit OK at the bottom of the screen when you're finished. It will take no longer than 15 minutes for the search index to get updated.

Filters

We have already connected the Filter web part to the Search Results web part from the Filter web part properties. To make the filters work, we also need to update the managed metadata properties in the web parts. In addition, we need to connect the Search Results web part to the Filter web part from the Search Result web part properties. This means that two-way connections need to be established.

Once you're done with the reindexing, wait 15 minutes and then go back to the search page and edit the page. Then, take the following steps to achieve the filter functionality:

1. Edit the Search Results web part properties and add the three managed properties to Selected Properties. Click the Selected Properties drop-down; scroll down; and check off the boxes for

RefinableDate01, RefinableString01, and RefinableString02, as
shown in Figure 7-15. This ensures that Product Type, Document
Type, and Modified will be available in the results.

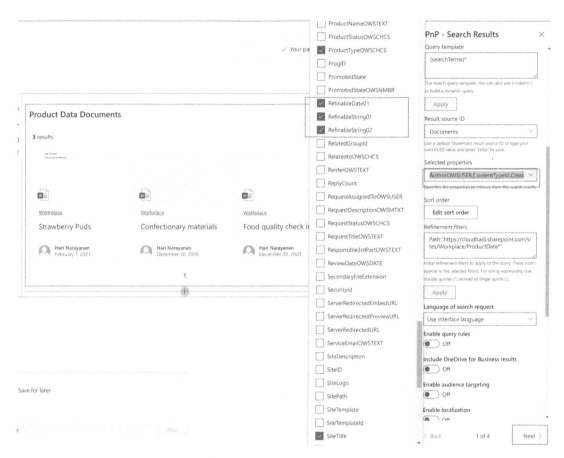

Figure 7-15. *Adding the three managed properties to Selected Properties*

2. Close the drop-down and click Next in the properties window. On
    the page that follows, select Details List for the layout instead of
    Cards. The layout will be updated as shown in Figure 7-16. Scroll
    down and click the Manage columns button on the right side of
    the screen. This will allow you to define which columns appear in
    the results.

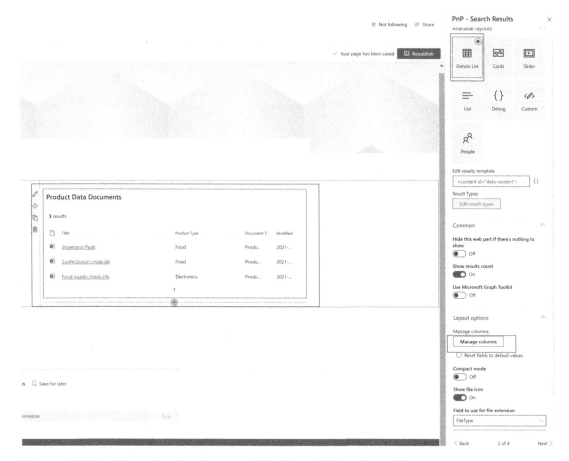

Figure 7-16. *Changing the layout of the Search Results web part*

3. On the Manage columns pop-up, add the columns shown in
    Figure 7-17. Set the minimum and maximum width as per the
    figure. The width is set according to probable width of these
    properties. Also check all the boxes in the Sortable and Resizable
    columns. This will ensure that you can resize the columns by
    dragging and dropping from the results.

Manage columns

Add, update or remove columns for the details list layout. You can use either property values in the list directly without any transformation or use an Handlebars expression in the value field. HTML is supported for all fields as well.

	Column display name *	Column value *	Use Handlebars expression	Minimum width (px)	Maximum width (px)	Sortable	Resizable	Multiline		
1 ∨	Title	`<a href="{{slot ite..` ✎	☑	30	200	☑	☑	☐	ⓘ ✕
2 ∨	Product Type	RefinableString01 ∨	☐	30	100	☑	☑	☐	ⓘ ✕
3 ∨	Document Type	RefinableString02 ∨	☐	150	400	☑	☑	☐	ⓘ ✕
4 ∨	Modified	`{{getDate Refinable..` ✎	☑	100	400	☑	☑	☐	ⓘ ✕
	Column display name	Select property ∨	☐	50	310	☐	☐	☐	ⓘ +

Save   Cancel

Figure 7-17. *Managing columns*

Check off Use Handlebars expression for the Modified property. We also need to format Modified, as it is a date field. We'll use the handlebar expression for that. Handlebars is a templating language, which we use for formatting the columns in Search web parts. A pencil icon will appear when you check off the Use Handlebars check box. Click it and update the handlebars expression to "{{getDate RefinableDate01 "MMM DD, YYYY"}}," then click Save. See Figure 7-18. Save the Managed columns when you're finished.

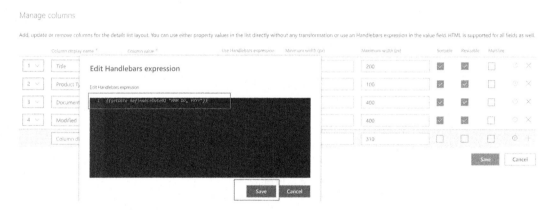

Manage columns

Add, update or remove columns for the details list layout. You can use either property values in the list directly without any transformation or use an Handlebars expression in the value field. HTML is supported for all fields as well.

Figure 7-18. *Edit Handlebars Expression*

The Results web part for Product Type, Document Type, and Modified date will be ready now. The modified date will be in the [*MMM, DD, YYYY*] format. Next, we need to make the connection to the Filters web part.

4. Click Next in the properties window. Switch the toggle in the
    Connect to a Filters Web Part to On. Select the Filters web part
    from the Use Filters from this component drop-down, as shown in
    Figure 7-19.

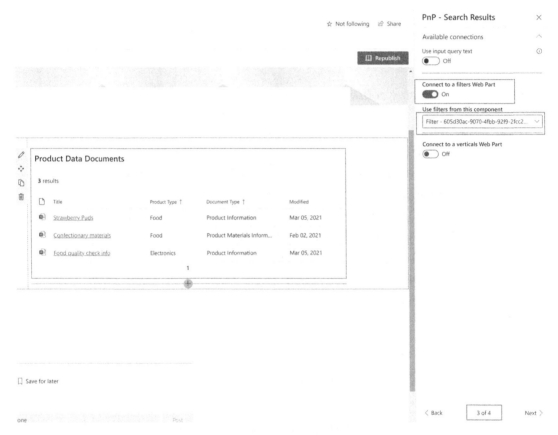

Figure 7-19. *Turning on Connect to a Filters Web Part*

We're now done configuring the Search Results web part. In the
next step, we'll edit the Filter web part.

5. You can edit the Filter web part by using the pencil icon and
    clicking Edit in customize filters, as you did earlier. See Figure 7-9
    under section PnP Modern Search. On the Edit Filters pop-up,
    add the Product Type, Document Type, and Modified columns,
    as shown in Figure 7-20. Choose the filter fields in each column.
    Choose the Check Box template for Product Type and Document

Type, and check off Show Count. For the Modified, choose the Date Range template. Check off Expand by Default for all the columns. Leave the Sort settings as is. You can try different configurations for all these settings if you'd like. Once you're done, click Save.

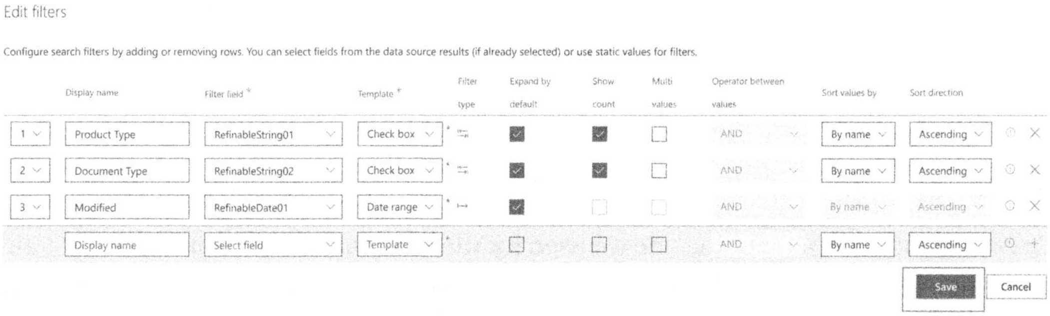

Edit filters

Configure search filters by adding or removing rows. You can select fields from the data source results (if already selected) or use static values for filters.

	Display name	Filter field *	Template *	Filter type	Expand by default	Show count	Multi values	Operator between values	Sort values by	Sort direction		
1 ∨	Product Type	RefinableString01	Check box ∨		☑	☑	☐	AND ∨	By name ∨	Ascending ∨	ⓘ	✕
2 ∨	Document Type	RefinableString02	Check box ∨		☑	☑	☐	AND ∨	By name ∨	Ascending ∨	ⓘ	✕
3 ∨	Modified	RefinableDate01	Date range ∨		☑	☐	☐	AND ∨	By name ∨	Ascending ∨	ⓘ	✕
	Display name	Select field ∨	Template ∨		☐	☐	☐	AND ∨	By name ∨	Ascending ∨	ⓘ	+

Save   Cancel

Figure 7-20. *Edit Filters screen*

This completes all the required settings. Close the properties window now and publish the page. The search page will now look like in the one in Figure 7-21.

Before you're done, try filtering with Product Type, Document Type, and different date ranges. Add as many contents as possible from the Product Data library. All documents must be approved.

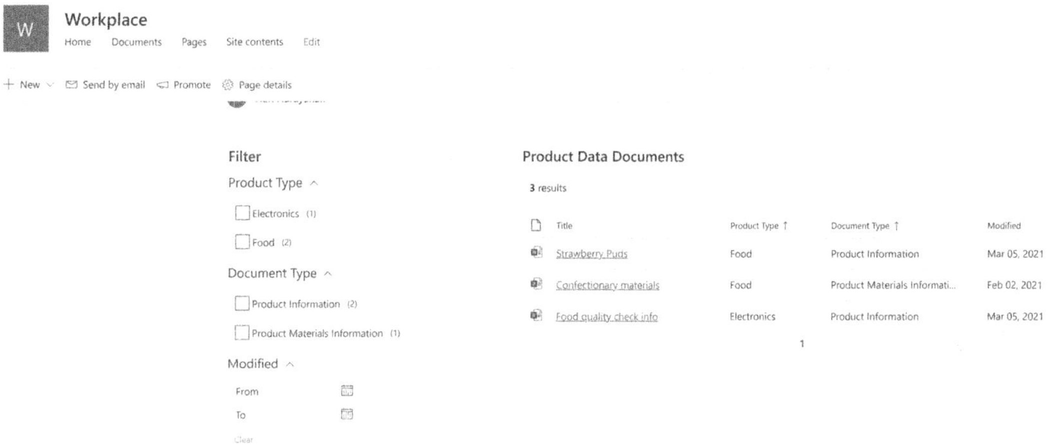

W **Workplace**
Home   Documents   Pages   Site contents   Edit

+ New ∨   ✉ Send by email   ⊲ Promote   ⚙ Page details

Filter

Product Type ∧
☐ Electronics (1)
☐ Food (2)

Document Type ∧
☐ Product Information (2)
☐ Product Materials Information (1)

Modified ∧
From   📅
To   📅
Clear

Product Data Documents

3 results

	Title	Product Type ↑	Document Type ↑	Modified
📄	Strawberry Pufs	Food	Product Information	Mar 05, 2021
📄	Confectionary materials	Food	Product Materials Informati...	Feb 02, 2021
📄	Food quality check info	Electronics	Product Information	Mar 05, 2021

1

Figure 7-21. *Modern Search results and filter*

At this point, you've successfully configured a search page and satisfied all the requirements for the Cloudhadi workplace search. Users can now search for product data documents, filter based on Product Type or Document Type, and sort the results.

We have Search Verticals and Search Box web parts as well in the Modern Search package. Search verticals allow you to browse data from multiple data sources. You can configure the verticals accordingly.

In the next section, we'll take a look at how we can send queries from the home page of the workplace site to the search results page.

Search Box

The search box is similar to the one we used for the OOB search box. You can enter free text queries that will be sent to the Search Results web parts. You can specify a page URL in the search box configuration, and the queries will be sent to that page as a query string parameter or URL fragments.

To add a Search Box, go to the workplace site home page and edit the page. Add a new section above the service portal. Search for PnP-Search Box and add it, as shown in Figure 7-22.

Figure 7-22. *Adding the PnP—Search Box web part*

Once the web part is added, configure it as shown in Figure 7-23. Switch on the toggle for Send the Query to a New Page, and provide modernsearch.aspx URL. Select Query String Parameter as the method and give a name to the parameter. Add placeholder text in the Search Box.

Figure 7-23. *Configuring the search box*

This will ensure that whenever a user enters a keyword and searches for it, they will be redirected to the search results page with the keyword passed as a query string parameter. For example, if you searched for "food," you would be redirected to {SiteURL}/ModernSearch.aspx?q=Food.

Next, we need to make sure that the Search Results web part can receive this query string. To do that, let's go to modernsearch.aspx and edit the page. Edit the Search Results web part. As shown in Figure 7-24, in the properties pane, set Use Input Query Text to On and configure.

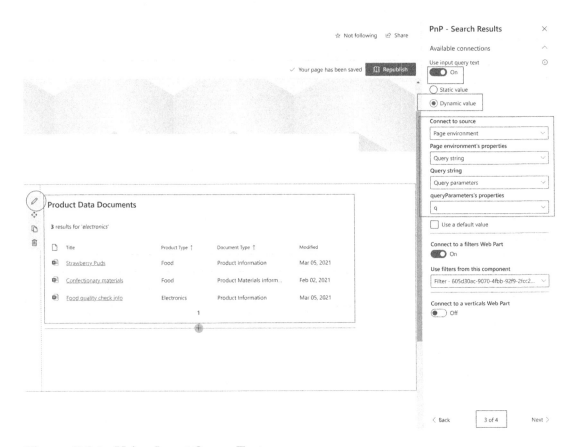

Figure 7-24. *Using Input Query Text*

Set Input Query Text as Dynamic Value. Under Connect to Source, choose "Page Environment." Select Query Parameters for the Query String, and choose *q* for the parameter's properties, which is the passed parameter from the home page search box. This can all be in done in Section 3 of properties pane under Available Connections.

The final step is to update the Query Template in the properties pane to filter based on the query string. Update the value to and(Path:"[*yourSiteURL*]/ProductData*", RefinableString01:{QueryString.q}).

The results will now be updated based on the search. If you search for "food" from the search box on the home page, you'll be taken to the results page for food. The results will look like those shown in Figure 7-25. I modified the Title web part and adjusted its headings, as well as the Search Results web part, to make it all look a little better.

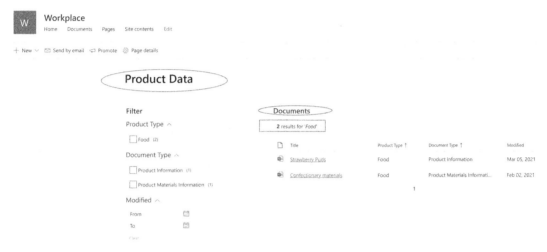

Figure 7-25. *Search results for the "food" keyword*

Note   To test out and debug search queries with the SharePoint Search Query Tool, there is a brilliant open-source tool made available by the PnP team that I suggest you explore. It will be a great help in building search solutions. You can find more information and download the tool at the GitHub repository: https://github.com/pnp/PnP-Tools/tree/master/Solutions/ SharePoint.Search.QueryTool.

Summary

The chapter has been about learning the fundamentals of modern searches using the PnP Modern Search web parts. We reviewed configuring Search Results and Filter web parts, as well as how to configure Search Box web parts. You learned about the search schema and how to configure managed properties.

SharePoint Search is quite powerful in terms of its features. You can explore more in this area by configuring the search with different result sources, queries, and so forth.

In the next chapter, we'll move on to Microsoft Teams development. We'll look at Power Virtual Agents and how to configure a chat bot. You'll learn about Microsoft Graph, as well.

CHAPTER 8

Teams and Power Virtual Agents

In this chapter, we'll be looking at Microsoft Teams. Teams is a collaboration platform with tremendous capabilities, including online meetings, document sharing, collaboration, live chat, and many more. Teams is very popular nowadays. Especially during the COVID-19 pandemic, Teams has played an essential role in making the virtual communication between real teams easier. In addition to the communication capabilities it offers, Teams is brilliant tool for collaboration. It is fully integrated with Microsoft 365 (M365) and has file storage, chat, and many more features.

The key focus of this chapter will be to introduce you to Teams, Power Virtual Agents (PVAs), and Microsoft Graph. To start the process of linking SharePoint Online with all of the above platforms, we'll link a SharePoint app to Teams using App Studio. Then, we'll move on to creating a chat bot in Teams using PVAs.

After that, we'll go over Microsoft Graph and how to add a team using PowerShell and Graph. The focus of this section will be on building a SharePoint Framework (SPFx) extension that sits in SharePoint and talks to Teams via Graph.

By the end of this chapter, you'll be familiar with the concept of Teams, PVAs, Microsoft Graph. You'll have learned how to link all these with SharePoint. In addition, you'll have created an SPFx Application Customizer extension. You'll have received a quick pass to PowerShell. We'll satisfy some of the requirements from our case study in the process.

What Are Team Apps?

As per Microsoft documentation, Teams apps are a combination of capabilities and entry points. People, for instance, have the capability of chatting with their app's bot in the entry point of a channel. We can build Tabs, Bots, Messaging extensions, and Webhooks with Teams.

© Harinarayanan V P 2021
Harinarayanan V P, *Building the Modern Workplace with SharePoint Online*,
https://doi.org/10.1007/978-1-4842-6945-9_8

Linking Workplace to Teams

Let's start by linking Workplace to Teams. This will give you an introduction to Teams apps and how to link a SharePoint site to Teams.

First, open Teams from your web browser using `https://teams.microsoft.com` and use the same SharePoint credentials. Alternatively, you can install and log into the Teams app. As shown in Figure 8-1, click the ... icon on the left navigation bar and then select App Studio. If you can't find the App Studio, you can access it by using the Find an App search box.

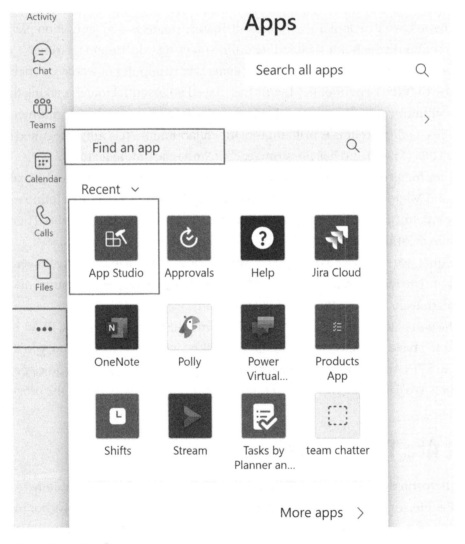

Figure 8-1. *App Studio*

The manifest details section will now be opened. Enter the App Details, as shown in Figures 8-2 and 8-3. For the Privacy Statement and Terms of Use, I just entered the home page URLs. You can leave other settings as is.

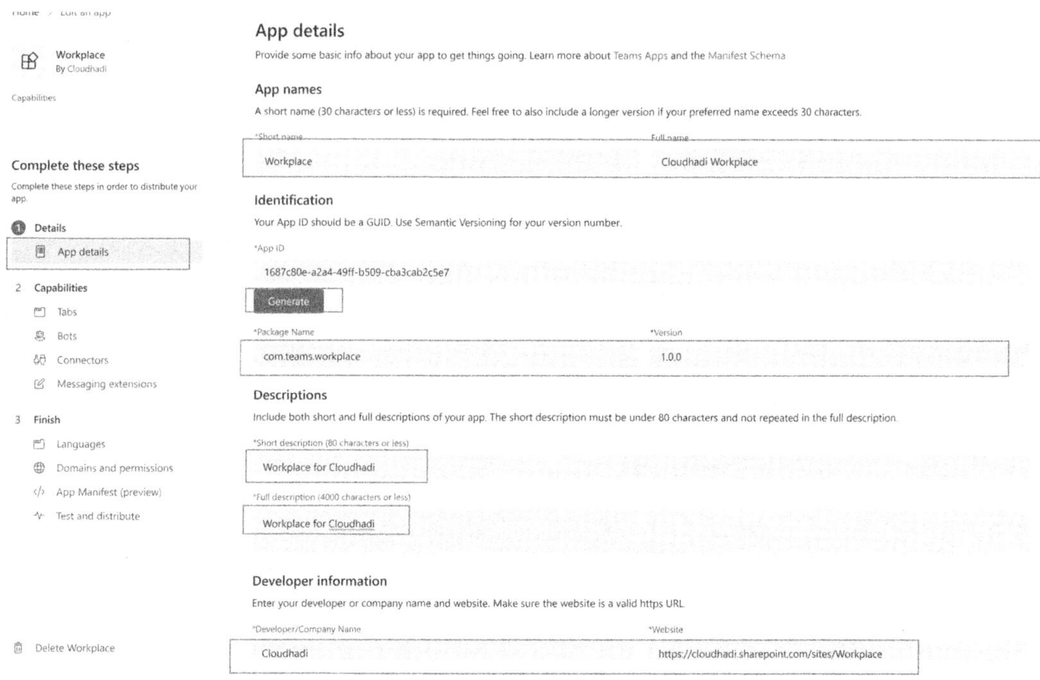

Figure 8-2. *App Details page (1)*

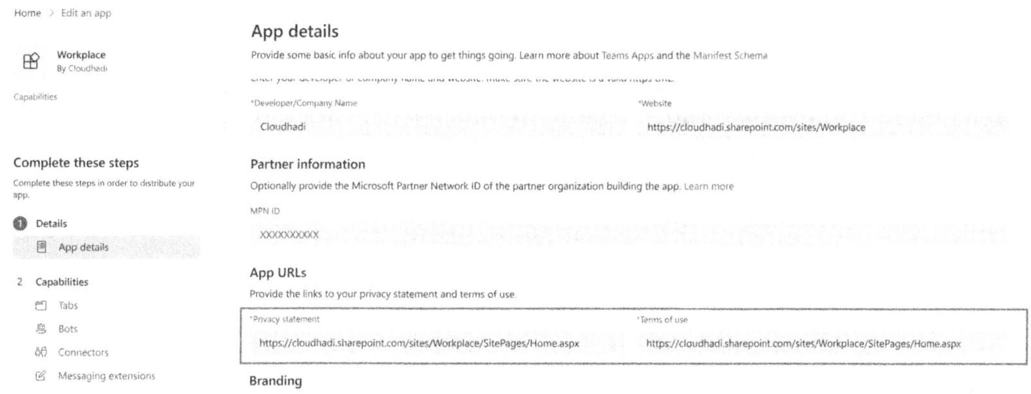

Figure 8-3. *App Details page (2)*

Under Capabilities, select Tabs and add a Personal Tab. In the pop-up, enter the details as shown in Figure 8-4. You can enter a random number for Entity ID and enter your Workplace site URL for Website URL. For Content URL, add [*YourSiteURL*]/_ `layouts/15/teamslogon.aspx?SPFx=true&dest="`[*YourHomePageRelativeURL*], replacing [*YourSiteURL*] with your Workplace site URL and [*YourHomePageRelativeURL*] with a relative link to the home page.

Figure 8-4. *Filling in the Personal Tab*

Now, as shown in Figure 8-5, go to Finish in the left navigation pane, then click Domains and Permissions, and add your domain if it isn't already there. For AAD App ID, enter a random GUID (globally unique identifier). You can generate a GUID online or use the Visual Studio Code extension that we installed in Chapter 2.

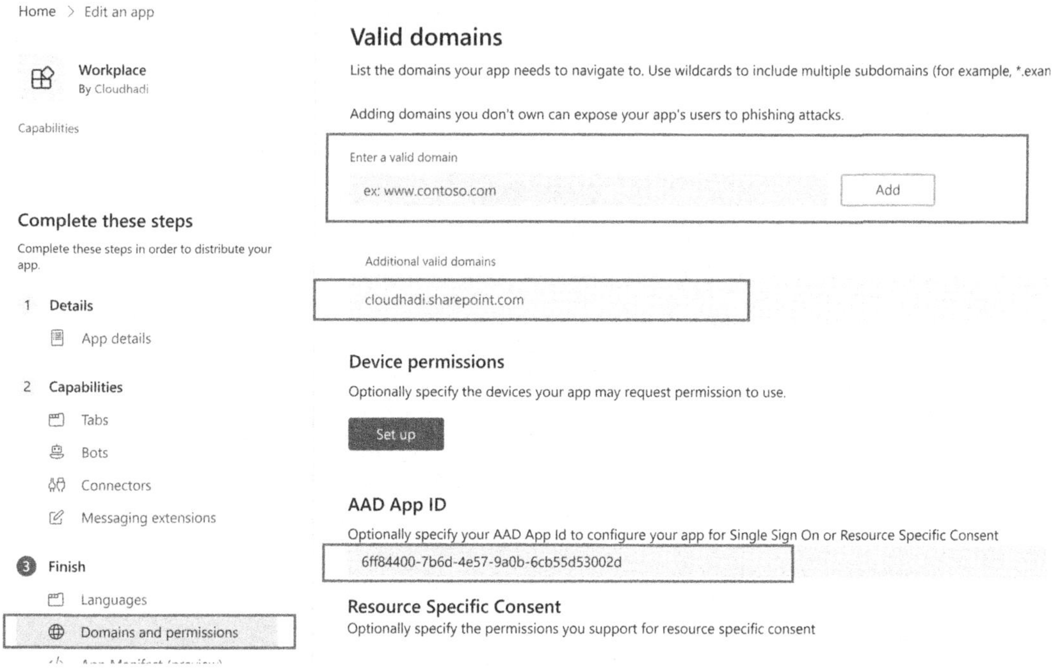

Home > Edit an app

Workplace
By Cloudhadi

Capabilities

Complete these steps

Complete these steps in order to distribute your app.

1 **Details**

   📄 App details

2 **Capabilities**

   📑 Tabs

   🖳 Bots

   🎛 Connectors

   🗒 Messaging extensions

3 **Finish**

   📑 Languages

   🌐 Domains and permissions

   </> App Manifest (preview)

Valid domains

List the domains your app needs to navigate to. Use wildcards to include multiple subdomains (for example, *.exan

Adding domains you don't own can expose your app's users to phishing attacks.

Enter a valid domain

ex: www.contoso.com   [Add]

Additional valid domains

cloudhadi.sharepoint.com

Device permissions

Optionally specify the devices your app may request permission to use.

[Set up]

AAD App ID

Optionally specify your AAD App Id to configure your app for Single Sign On or Resource Specific Consent

6ff84400-7b6d-4e57-9a0b-6cb55d53002d

Resource Specific Consent

Optionally specify the permissions you support for resource specific consent

Figure 8-5. *Adding a domain and AAD App ID*

Now, click and download the app under Test and Distribute section, as shown in Figure 8-6. The app will be downloaded as a ZIP file.

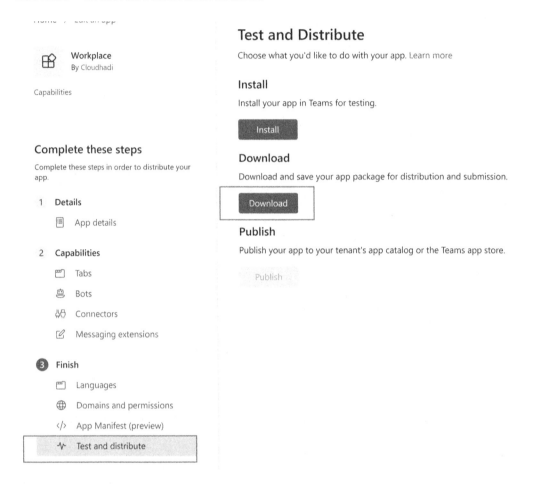

Figure 8-6. *Downloading the app*

Once the app is downloaded, click the ... icon in the left toolbar and then click More Apps. See Figure 8-7.

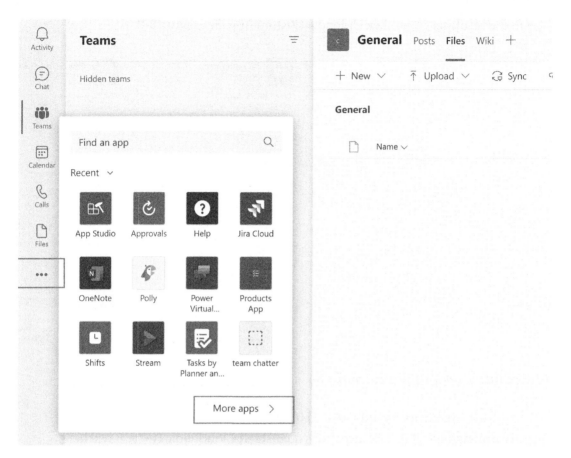

Figure 8-7. *Navigating to More Apps*

On the resulting page, click Upload a Custom App. See Figure 8-8.

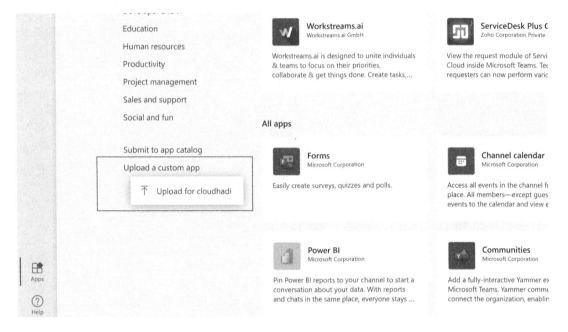

Figure 8-8. *Uploading a custom app*

Now click Upload for Cloudhadi and browse for the downloaded ZIP file. Your organisation name will be displayed for you instead Cloudhadi. The app will be uploaded. You can see the app Workplace under Apps. See Figure 8-9.

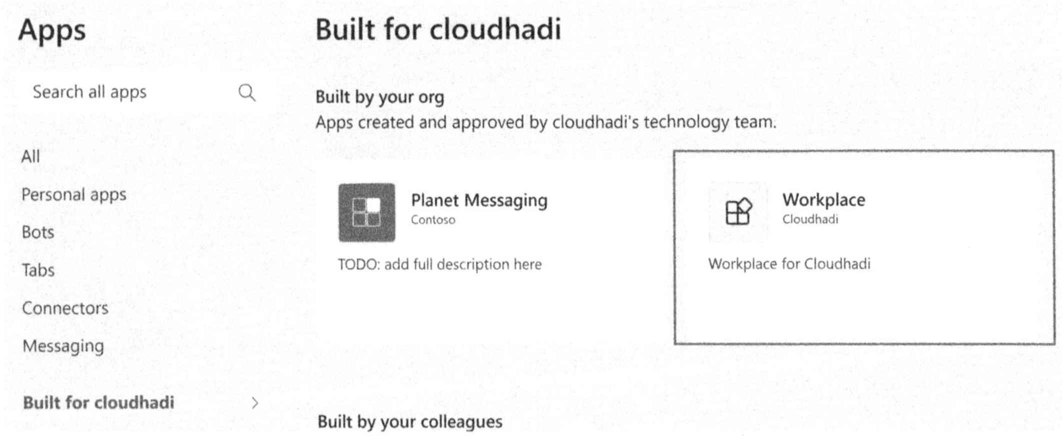

Figure 8-9. *Uploaded app*

In the pop-up, click Add, as shown in Figure 8-10.

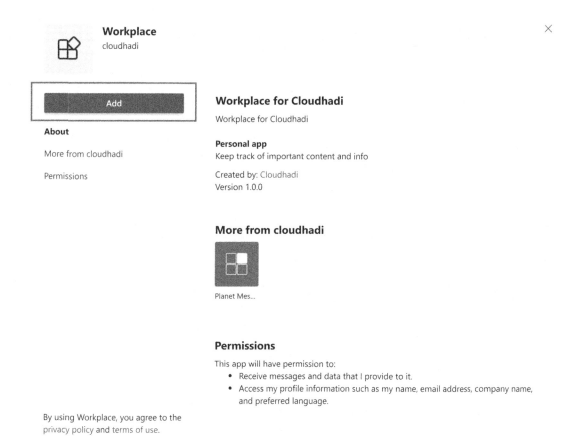

Workplace
cloudhadi

Add

About

More from cloudhadi

Permissions

Workplace for Cloudhadi

Workplace for Cloudhadi

Personal app
Keep track of important content and info

Created by: Cloudhadi
Version 1.0.0

More from cloudhadi

Planet Mes...

Permissions

This app will have permission to:
- Receive messages and data that I provide to it.
- Access my profile information such as my name, email address, company name, and preferred language.

By using Workplace, you agree to the privacy policy and terms of use.

Figure 8-10. *Adding Workplace app*

The app will now be pinned to your left navigation bar. By clicking on it, the app will be loaded with the SharePoint home page in it. As shown in Figure 8-11, you can now search for product data documents or submit a new service request within Teams itself.

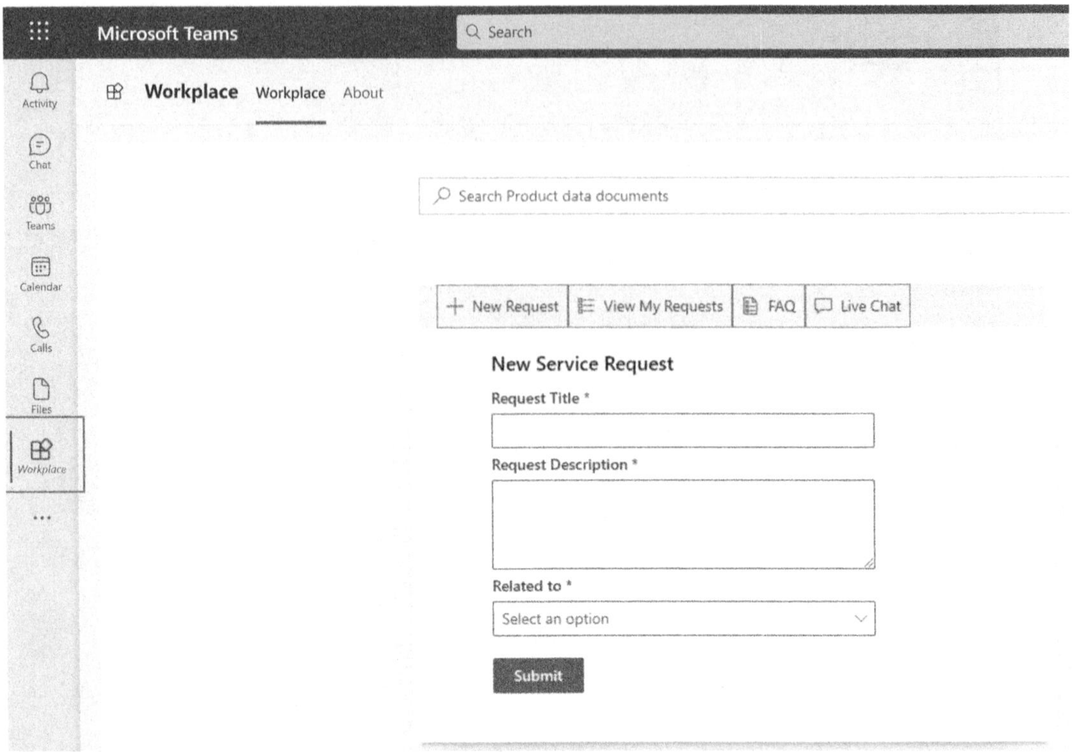

Figure 8-11. Workplace in Microsoft Teams

If you log in with your service account, you can't see that Workplace app is pinned to the left navigation bar, as the pinning happened only within the user context. So, what if you want to pin Workplace for all users? To do that, we need to make changes in the administration of Teams. Let's do that so that we can have hands-on Teams administration.

To access the administration for Teams, go to `https://admin.teams.microsoft.com/`. Choose Teams Apps, then click Setup Policies, and Global (Org-Wide Default), as shown in Figure 8-12.

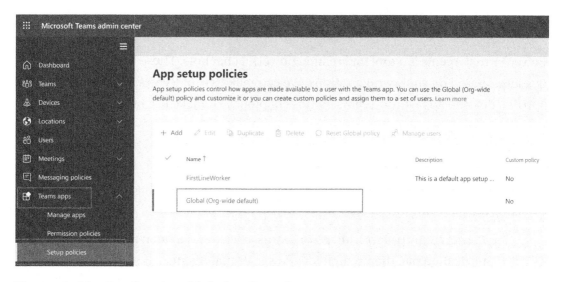

Figure 8-12. *Configuring Global policies for Teams apps*

Turn on Upload Custom Apps, so that users can upload apps. Under Pinned Apps, click Add Apps. Then, in Add Pinned Apps, search for Workplace and add it. See Figure 8-13.

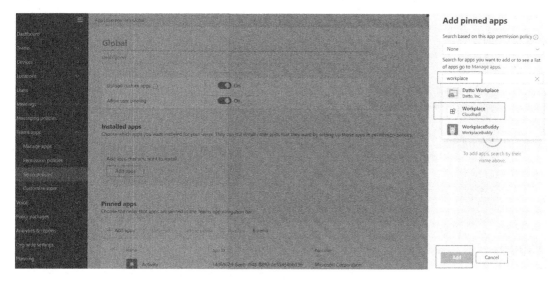

Figure 8-13. *Adding a pinned app - Workplace app*

The app will now be added to the Pinned Apps section. All users will be able to see Workplace in their Teams and browse the site.

In the next section, we'll build a bot using Power Virtual Agents and add it to Teams.

Power Virtual Agents

Power Virtual Agents is a tool for creating powerful chat bots. These bots can answer questions based on your configurations. We can make use of PVAs as a stand-alone web app or a discrete app within Teams. In this chapter, we'll make use of PVAs from Teams.

Creating a Chat Bot

Let's create a chat bot for the service portal by using PVAs within Teams. We can do that by taking the following ten steps:

1. *Locate PVA*: To start with, go to Teams, click the ... icon in the left navigation bar, then search for "Power Virtual Agents," as shown in Figure 8-14.

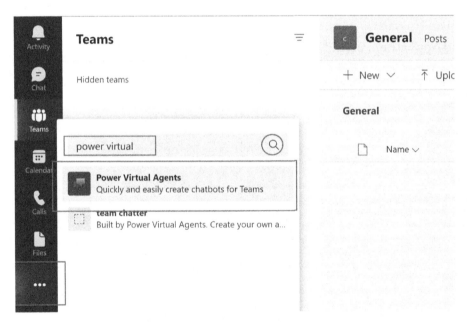

Figure 8-14. Navigating to Power Virtual Agents

2. *Select a team*: On the Power Virtual Agents screen, click Start Now. Select a team from the What Team Is Your Bot Joining? drop-down. Once you select the team, click Continue. See Figure 8-15. You can either choose the default team or you can go to Teams in the left navigation bar and create a new team from the Join or Create Team link at the bottom.

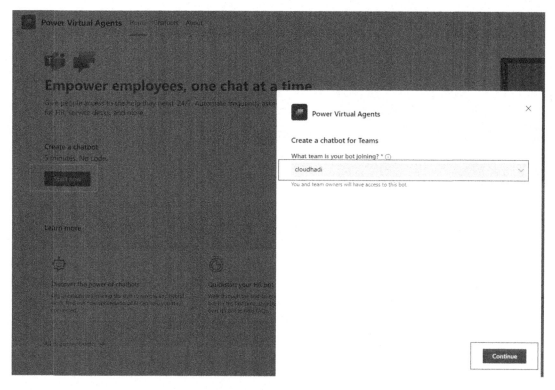

Figure 8-15. *Selecting a team for the chat bot*

3. *Create the bot*: Give the bot a name and click Create, as shown in Figure 8-16.

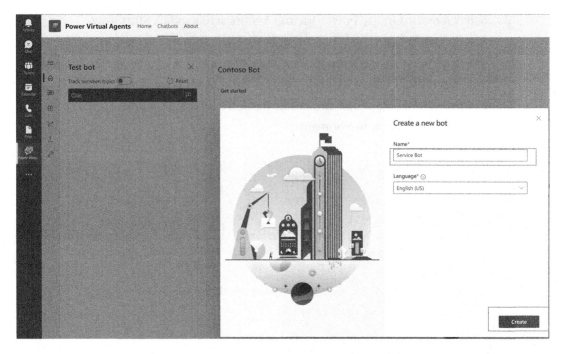

Figure 8-16. *Creating a chat bot*

Once your bot is created, you'll be given the options to author or automate topics, to edit and test the bot, and to publish the bot, as shown in Figure 8-17.

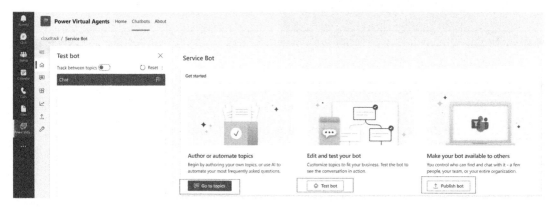

Figure 8-17. *Bot interface*

4. *Create a topic*: In order to define responses, we need to create a topic. Let's use two phases, "Service Request" and "Create Service Request," as triggers for the topic. If a user types in either phrase, the bot should start asking questions about creating a service request.

    To do this, first click Go to Topics. This will take you to the Service Bot page where you can create a topic, test a bot, publish, and more. See Figure 8-18.

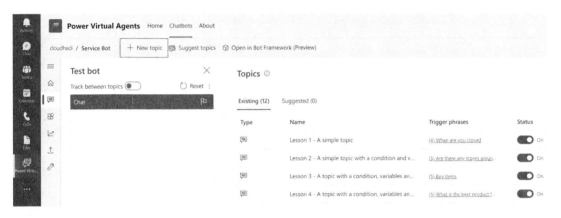

Figure 8-18. *Topics screen*

    Then, click New Topic, and provide a name for the topic. As mentioned earlier, add two triggers, as shown in Figure 8-19.

Figure 8-19. *Adding triggers for the topic*

5. *Configure authoring canvas*: If a user types any of these three phases, the bot will be triggered. We can configure the bot's response in the authoring canvas. Click Save Topic, then click Go to Authoring Canvas. See Figure 8-20.

Figure 8-20. *Configuration questions*

When you go to the authoring canvas shown in Figure 8-20, you can see that the triggers in Trigger Phrases highlighted. The Message box have already been created. Add a message in the Message box such as, "Hi, Thanks for contacting Service chat bot." Then, under Question, click + to add a node (which is not visible in the Figure, but you will find it below by moving the cursor), and in the Ask a Question box, type in, "Can you please provide details for this request?" In the Identify section, select User's Entire Response. For Save Response As, click the pencil icon and enter "varTitle" as the variable name.

What we've done so far is to ask the user a question if they type in any of the three defined triggers. The user's response will get saved as the varTitle variable. Next, we'll add a Condition that checks whether the user has provided a value. If they haven't, the bot won't proceed to the next step.

Let's configure the bot to ask the user for description details, as shown in Figure 8-20. Add the steps Question and Condition like we did for "varTitle".

6. *Configuring multiple options for the user*: Once the user enters the description, the bot should then ask, "Your request is related to?" and provide the user with the Access, Materials, Equipments, and General options. After the user responds, the bot should create a service request. See Figure 8-21.

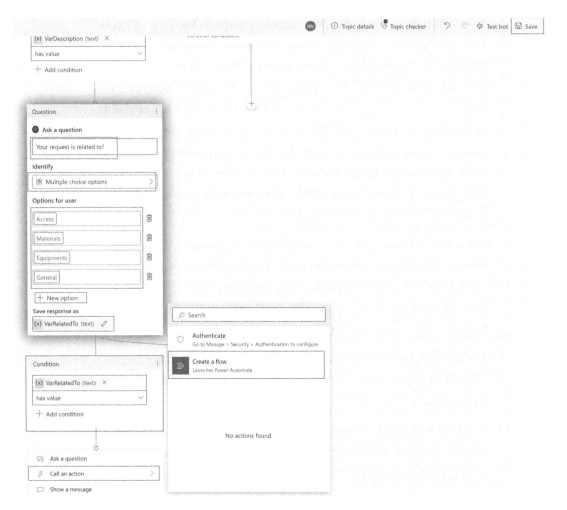

Figure 8-21. *Configuring multiple options and calling for an action*

To set this up, choose Multiple Choice Options under Identify, as
shown in Figure 8-21. To add options, click +New Option. Add all
four options and configure the variable for saving the response.
Add a Condition to check whether the variable has value. Select
Call an Action and Create Flow. Save your changes using the Save
button in the top left-hand corner. Ignore any errors for now.

7. *Create and configure a flow*: Power Automate will now open within
Teams. Select Power Virtual Agents Flow Template to create the
flow, as shown in Figure 8-22.

Figure 8-22. *Creating a Power Automate flow in the Power Virtual Agents template*

The flow designer will open. On the Power Virtual Agents screen, add the following three inputs: "title," "description," and "relatedTo," as shown in the first panel of Figure 8-23. On the Initialize Service Number screen, initialize a serviceNumber variable and add "CSR" plus the expression "rand(10000, 99999)" for the value. This will create a random number for the title.

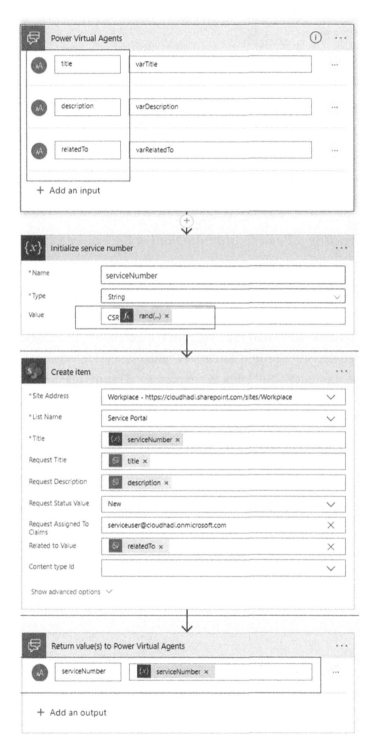

Figure 8-23. *Configuring the Service Request creation flow*

Then, enter the details for the Create Item screen, as shown in the third panel of Figure 8-23. Assign serviceNumber for the Title. Use the variables shown in the figure for Request Title, Request Description, and Related to Value. Set the Request Status Value to New, and provide your service user email ID for Request Assigned To Claims. On the Return Value(s) to Power Virtual Agents screen, add serviceNumber as the output variable, so that the service number will be returned. The flow will return this output to PVA once the execution is successful.

8. *Call the flow*: Save the flow and click the back arrow to go back to the authoring canvas. The flow will be available to select by clicking on Call an action. Refer Figure 8-24 for the Call an action link. You can click the flow details on renaming the flow. I renamed it "Bot Service Request Creation." Click the icon against Bot Service Request Creation to add the action to the canvas. See Figure 8-24.

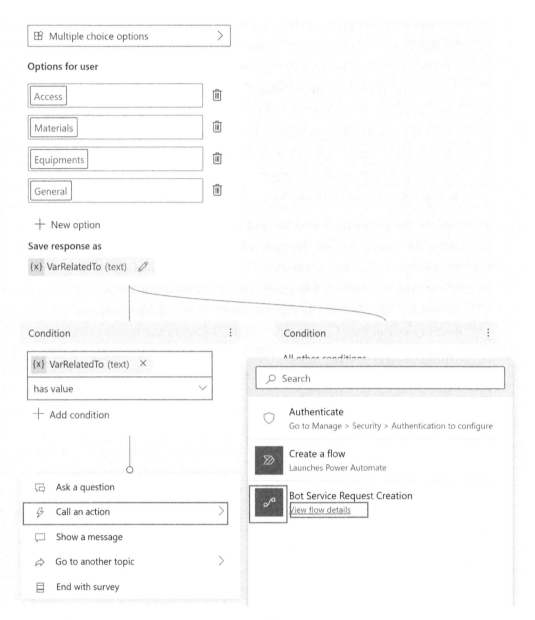

Figure 8-24. *Adding a flow action to the canvas*

9. *Pass inputs to the flow*: Once the flow action is added, provide variable values for the Power Automate Inputs by clicking each input and selecting the appropriate variable from the drop-down menu, as shown in Figure 8-25. Assign outputs to give value to serviceNumber.

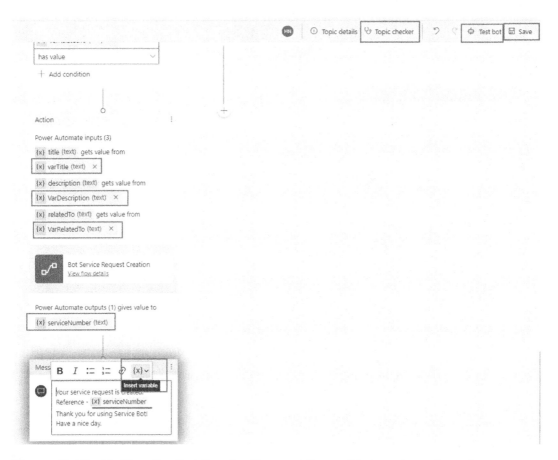

Figure 8-25. *Calling the Bot Service Request flow with inputs and receive output*

Next, add a message with the service number by clicking the Insert Variable drop-down, then clicking Topic Checker in the toolbar to check for any errors. If you get a response error, reselect Identify for the title and description questions.

Save the topic using the Save button in the upper right-hand corner.

10. *Test the bot*: Now it's time to test our bot! Open and close Test Bot by using the Test Bot button at the top. Test Bot button is highlighted in Figure 8-25. Figure 8-26 shows the test I ran.

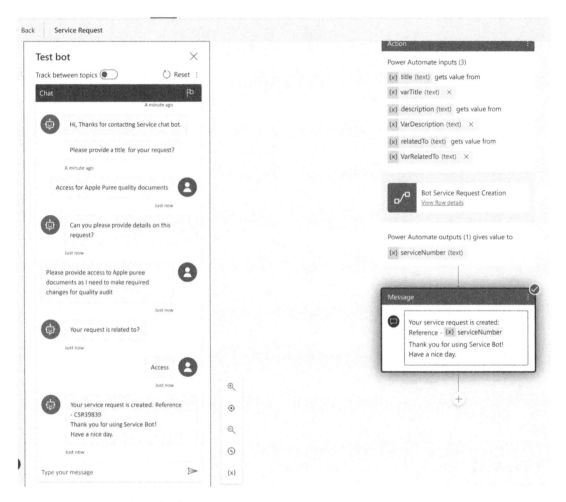

Figure 8-26. *Testing the bot*

As you can see in the figure, the bot is responding to my chat and asking questions. The bot also created a service request and provided me with a reference number. If I go to service portal list, I can see that my request has been created there.

Workplace

Home   Documents   Pages   Site contents   Edit

+ New ∨   ⊞ Edit in grid view   ⌁ Share   ⊞ Export to Excel   ◈ Power Apps ∨   ⚙ Automate ∨   ⋯

Service Portal

Title ∨	Request Title ∨	Request Descri... ∨	Request Status ∨	Request Assign... ∨	Related to ∨
CSR57247	Access for Documents	Please provide access to food quality document	Completed	service user	Materials
CSR1552	Procurement of MacBook	Please provide a macbook for operations team	New	service user	Equipments
CSR93162	Food processing machine request	Please provide a food processing machine for os jam maker team	Completed	service user	Equipments
CSR79959	Enquiry regarding new office site	Provide details on new office site for Strawberry processing team	New	service user	General
CSR9305	Material access for service users	please provide material access for service users	New		Access
CSR41093	Strawberry farm cleaning	Please arrange services for farm cleaning	New	service user	General
CSR39839	Access for Apple Puree quality documents	Please provide access to Apple puree documents as I need to make required changes for quality audit	New	service user	Access

Figure 8-27. *Verifying my request in the service portal list*

So, within a minute, the bot created a service request for me. Now it's time to publish and share the bot.

Publishing and Sharing the Bot

To publish the bot, click the back arrow in the top left corner. When you're on the bot page, click Publish on the top right corner. Click Publish, then confirm by clicking Publish again on the pop-up. See Figure 8-28.

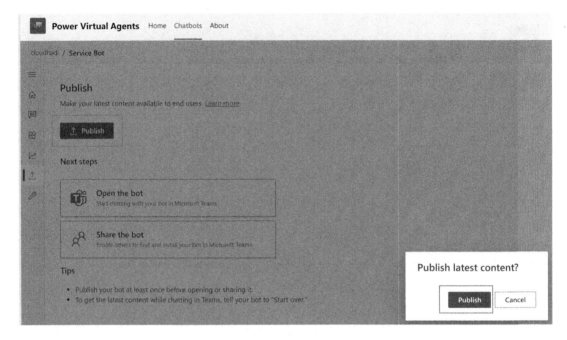

Figure 8-28. *Publishing a bot*

It will take a few seconds for the bot to publish. You should then share the bot with the organization so that everyone can access it. To so this, click Share the Bot, as shown in Figure 8-29. In the sliding window, click Submit for Admin Approval. The program will then wait for the approval.

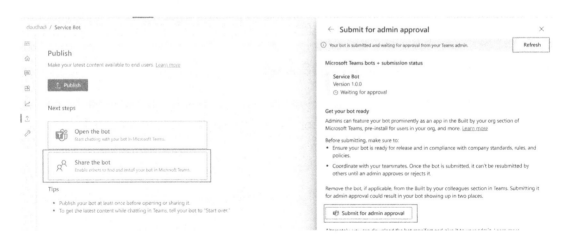

Figure 8-29. *Sharing the bot and submitting for admin approval*

To approve the app, you need to go to the Teams admin center at `https://admin.teams.microsoft.com/` and select Manage Apps under Teams Apps in the left navigation pane, as shown in Figure 8-30. You can see that one app is pending approval. If you look at Service Bot in the next section, you can see the app is submitted and the current status is Blocked.

Figure 8-30. *Managing apps in the Teams admin center*

If you click on Service Bot row, it will take you to the Details page for the app. Choose Publish on the Publishing Status drop-down. The app will then be published and the status will change from Blocked to Allowed. See Figure 8-31. The Figure shows the page after published.

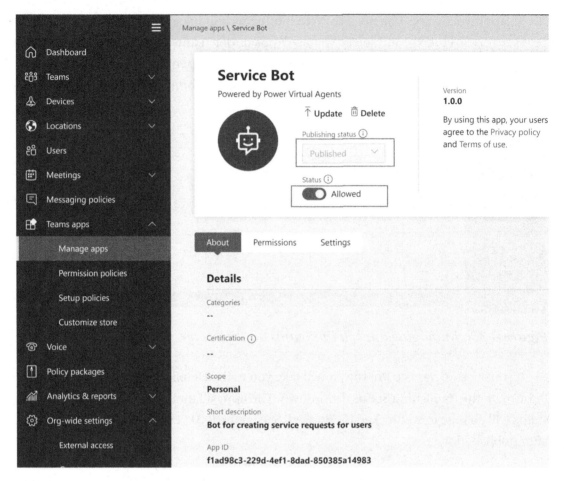

Figure 8-31. *Approving the app*

Now go back to the Publish page and click Refresh in the Submit for Admin Approval window. You can see that the Service Bot has been published by your organization, as shown in Figure 8-32. Click Open Bot.

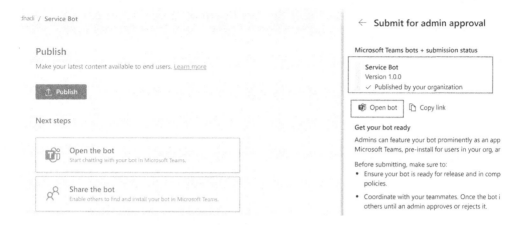

Figure 8-32. *Opening the published bot*

A pop-up will open up giving you the option to add the Service Bot. You can also see all the details we provided earlier about the app. Clicking Add will add the app to your Teams. See Figure 8-33.

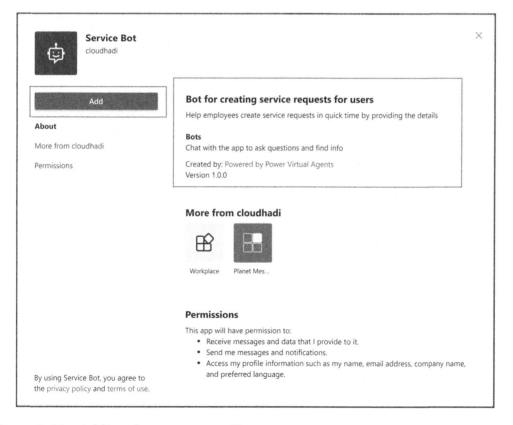

Figure 8-33. *Adding the app to your Teams*

Now if you go to Teams, you can see Service Bot in the top left corner of navigation pane. You can click Chat to create a service request for the bot. See Figure 8-34 for an example.

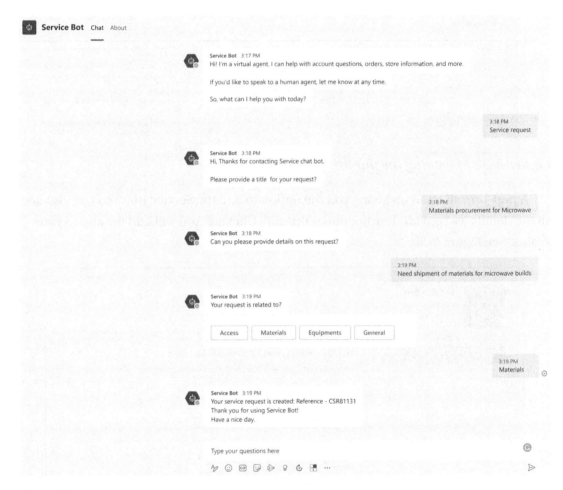

Figure 8-34. *Service Bot in operation*

Note   Each user needs to add the Service Bot app to their Teams to make use of Service Bot. You can add the app by clicking the ... icon in the left navigation bar. If you want to pin the app for all the users in your organization, you need to set up global policies in the Teams admin center and add Service Bot to pinned apps. We did this for the Workplace app earlier. See Figures 8-12 and 8-13.

Now you've successfully created your first bot. The bot can interact with Teams, SharePoint, and Power Automate. If you want, you can explore more about the Topics and you can create more intelligent chat bots. In the next section, we'll get introduced to Microsoft Graph and how we can use it to create Teams.

Creating Teams with Microsoft Graph

Using Microsoft Graph allows you to access huge amount of data in Microsoft 365. It provides you with a single end point: `https://graph.microsoft.com`. You can interact with SharePoint or Teams data using Graph. For example, if you want to get your calendar events, you can use the GET request at `https://graph.microsoft.com/v1.0/me/events`.

In the next section, we'll see how to create a team, add a team member, and post a message to Teams using Graph.

Let's now create a team for service executives with the help of Microsoft Graph and PowerShell. This will give you an idea of how to communicate with Teams using the application programming interfaces (APIs) provided by Graph.

I'm making use of the existing M365 group team1 here and adding a team to that. You can see all M365 groups in your tenant by going to `https://admin.microsoft.com` and selecting Groups ➤ Active Groups. Pick any of the groups and save a copy of the name. See Figure 8-35.

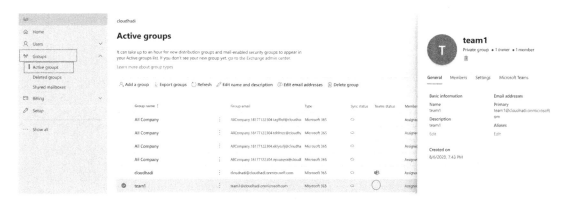

Figure 8-35. *Microsoft 365 group*

Notice that there is no Team Status for the group, whereas our default group Cloudhadi has a Team Status.

Now open a blank document in Notepad, copy the following code into it, and save it as "serviceTeamCreation.ps1."

```
# Connect to Microsoft 365
Connect-PnPOnline -Scopes "Group.ReadWrite.All"
# Get access token for Graph
$accessToken = Get-PnPGraphAccessToken

# Pass access token to headers
$headers = @{
"Content-Type" = "application/json"
Authorization = "Bearer $accessToken"
}
# Get list of M365 groups
$groupResponse = Invoke-RestMethod -Uri "https://graph.microsoft.com/v1.0/
groups" -Method Get -Headers $headers -UseBasicParsing
#filter Target group
$targetGroup = $groupResponse.value | Where-Object -FilterScript
{$_.DisplayName -EQ 'team1'}
#get group id
$groupId = $targetGroup.id
# Create team for service executives
$serviceTeam1 = @{
memberSettings = @{
allowCreateUpdateChannels = $true
}
messagingSettings = @{
allowUserEditMessages = $true
allowUserDeleteMessages = $true
}
funSettings = @{
allowGiphy = $true
giphyContentRating = "strict"
```

```
        allowStickersAndMemes= $true
        allowCustomMemes= $true
    }
}
$serviceTeamBody1 = ConvertTo-Json -InputObject $serviceTeam1
$newTeam = Invoke-RestMethod -Uri "https://graph.microsoft.com/v1.0/
groups/$groupId/team" -Method PUT -Headers $headers -Body $serviceTeam
Body1 -UseBasicParsing
Write-Host $newTeam
```

Let me explain the code. In the first line, we make a connection to M365. In the second line, we get an access token for Graph. Next, we declare a headers variable by passing the access token. Then, we query all M365 groups and filter the results by team1. From the filtered result, we get the groupId and store it into a variable.

After that, we define a team with settings like the member, messaging, and so forth. Then, we convert the team definition into the JSON format. Finally, we invoke another Graph API call by passing the team request body and groupId.

Then, we open the PowerShell script in Windows PowerShell Integrated Scripted Environment and execute. It will ask you to log in to M365 with the credentials. Once you complete the execution, the team details will be printed in the console.

Now, if you go back to Teams, you'll see that a new team, team1, has been created there, as shown in Figure 8-36. You can right-click team1, edit it, rename it "Service Executives Team," and provide a description.

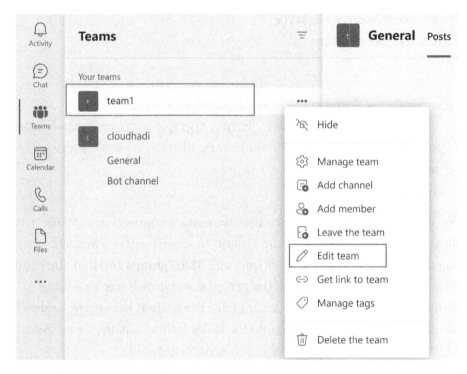

Figure 8-36. *New team created*

If you want to add a service executive to the team, right-click the team and click Add Member. In the pop-up, type in the service executive's name, select the name, and click Add. Then, close the pop-up. See Figure 8-37. You can also add more service executives to the team if you'd like.

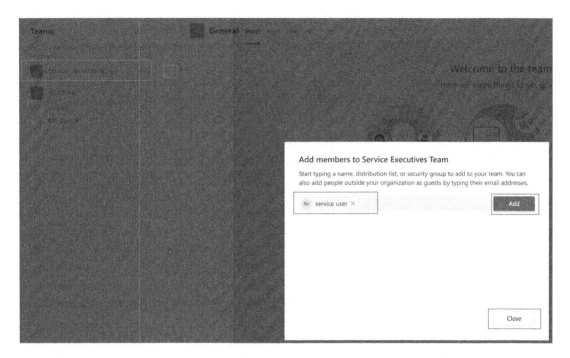

Figure 8-37. *Adding a team member*

This has been a small example to get you introduced to using Microsoft Graph and PowerShell with Teams. In the next section, we'll create an SPFx extension that creates an interaction between SharePoint and Teams with the help of Graph.

Posting a Message to Teams

During our Chapter 6, we didn't create an SPFx extension, so In this section, we're going to create a simple SPFx Application Customizer extension. This extension will sit on the footer of our Workplace site and interact with Teams with the help of Microsoft Graph. It will enable users to post a message to the General channel of the Service Executives Team.

To start, create an SPFx project like you did earlier. Give "service-extension" as the solution and extension name. Fill in the information and enter each line as shown in Figure 8-38.

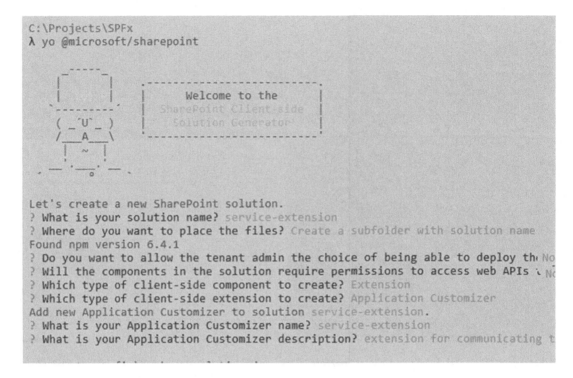

```
C:\Projects\SPFx
λ yo @microsoft/sharepoint


      _ _ _ _ _
     |         |        _ _ _ _ _ _ _ _ _ _ _ _ _ _ _ _ _ _ _
     |         |       |           Welcome to the           |
      _ _ _ _ _        |       SharePoint Client-side       |
     ( _'U'_ )         |        Solution Generator          |
     /_ _ A _ _\        _ _ _ _ _ _ _ _ _ _ _ _ _ _ _ _ _ _ _
      |   ~   |
    _  _ _ . _ _  _  _
   -              o    -

Let's create a new SharePoint solution.
? What is your solution name? service-extension
? Where do you want to place the files? Create a subfolder with solution name
Found npm version 6.4.1
? Do you want to allow the tenant admin the choice of being able to deploy th No
? Will the components in the solution require permissions to access web APIs  No
? Which type of client-side component to create? Extension
? Which type of client-side extension to create? Application Customizer
Add new Application Customizer to solution service-extension.
? What is your Application Customizer name? service-extension
? What is your Application Customizer description? extension for communicating t
```

Figure 8-38. *Creating an SPFx Application Customizer*

Note   The complete code for the SPFx extension is available in the Chapter 8 section of the GitHub repository: `https://github.com/Apress/building-modern-workplace-sharepoint-online/tree/main/Chapter%208`.

Once the project is created, open the solution in Visual Studio Code. Go to Src ➤ extensions ➤ serviceExtensions and update ServiceExtensionApplicationCustomizer.ts as follows. I'll provide an explanation after the code.

```
import { override } from '@microsoft/decorators';
import { Log } from '@microsoft/sp-core-library';
import {
  BaseApplicationCustomizer,
  PlaceholderContent,
  PlaceholderName
} from '@microsoft/sp-application-base';
import * as strings from 'ServiceExtensionApplicationCustomizerStrings';
```

```
import * as React from "react";
import * as ReactDOM from "react-dom";
import TeamsFooter, { ITeamsFooterProps } from "./TeamsFooter";
const LOG_SOURCE: string = 'ServiceExtensionApplicationCustomizer';
/**
 * If your command set uses the ClientSideComponentProperties JSON input,
 * it will be deserialized into the BaseExtension.properties object.
 * You can define an interface to describe it.
 */
export interface IServiceExtensionApplicationCustomizerProperties {
  // This is an example; replace with your own property
  Bottom: string;
}
/** A Custom Action that can be run during execution of a Client Side
Application */
export default class ServiceExtensionApplicationCustomizer
  extends BaseApplicationCustomizer<IServiceExtensionApplicationCustomizer
  Properties> {
  private _bottomPlaceHolder: PlaceholderContent | undefined;
  @override
  public onInit(): Promise<void> {
    Log.info(LOG_SOURCE, `Initialized ${strings.Title}`);

    // Added to handle possible changes in the existence of placeholders
    this.context.placeholderProvider.changedEvent.add(this, this._
    renderPlaceHolders);

    // Call render method for generating the HTML elements
    this._renderPlaceHolders();

    return Promise.resolve();
  }
  private _renderPlaceHolders(): void {

    // Handling the bottom placeholder
```

```
if (!this._bottomPlaceHolder) {
  this._bottomPlaceHolder =
    this.context.placeholderProvider.tryCreateContent(
      PlaceholderName.Bottom,
      { onDispose: this._onDispose });

  // The extension shouldn't assume that the expected placeholder is
     available
  if (!this._bottomPlaceHolder) {
    console.error('The expected placeholder was not found.');
    return;
  }

  const elem: React.ReactElement<ITeamsFooterProps> = React.
  createElement(
      TeamsFooter,
    {
      context:this.context
    }
  );
  ReactDOM.render(elem, this._bottomPlaceHolder.domElement);
  }
}
private _onDispose(): void {
  console.log('[ReactHeaderFooterApplicationCustomizer._onDispose]
  Disposed custom top and bottom placeholders.');
  }
}
```

In this set of code, we're accessing the placeholders on the page. We're importing all the necessary modules and updating the OnInit method by calling the renderPlaceHolders method. Inside renderPlaceHolders, we're creating a placeholder at the bottom using this.context.placeholderProvider.tryCreateContent. If you provide PlaceholderName.Top instead of PlaceholderName.Bottom, it will add the extension on the top.

Next, we will create a react element, TeamsFooter, by passing the context to it. The interface for the element is ITeamsFooterProps. Finally, we'll render the element in the bottom placeholder. So, we have the placeholder and will render the element on the placeholder set with this code.

Let's now create a react component, TeamFooter.tsx. To do so, right-click Extensions\ Service Extensions Folder, then select New File, and name it "TeamFooter.tsx." Let's define it as a functional component. Copy and paste the following code, after which I'll get into more detail about it.

```
import * as React from "react";
import { CommandBar } from 'office-ui-fabric-react/lib/CommandBar';
import { MSGraphClient } from '@microsoft/sp-http';
export interface ITeamsFooterProps {
    context: any;
}
function TeamsFooter(props: ITeamsFooterProps) {
    // Post message to Teams
    const postMessage = () => {
        const chatMessage = {
            body: {
                content: 'Hey Team, an urgent issue notified!
                Please look out in the service portal'
            }
        };
        props.context.msGraphClientFactory.getClient().
            then((client: MSGraphClient): void => {
                client.api('/teams/ed943053-550e-48d5-b679-
                a2e8af9820a4/channels/19:1740ec0332f24802b31a31538e
                7801d4@thread.tacv2/messages')
                    .post(chatMessage)
                    .then(success => {
                        alert("Message posted")
                    }, error => {
                        alert("failed")
                    });
            });
    }
```

```
    // Data for CommandBar
    const getItems = () => {
        return [
            {
                key: 'Teams',
                name: 'Notify Urgent Issue to Service Executives
                Channel',
                iconProps: {
                    iconName: 'TeamsLogo'
                },
                onClick: () => postMessage()
            }
        ];
    }
    // Command bar
    return (
        <div className={"ms-bgColor-themeDark ms-fontColor-white"} >
            <CommandBar
                items={getItems()}
            />
        </div>
    );
}
export default TeamsFooter
```

The previous code in the react component posts a message to the General channel of the Service Executives Team. We're importing React, MsGraphClient, and the Fluent user interface command bar. In the command bar, we have an item named Notify Urgent Issue to Service Executives channel that has the TeamsLogo icon.

When a user clicks on Notify Urgent Issue, it invokes the Graph API and posts a static message. We're making a post call with Graph here. To access the channel, we need to pass the teamId and ChannelId to the end point in the /teams/[teamid]/channels/[channelid]/messages format.

To find out the teamId, go to Teams, click the ... icon after Service Executives Team, and click Get Link to the Team. In the pop-up, copy the group ID GUID. See Figure 8-39.

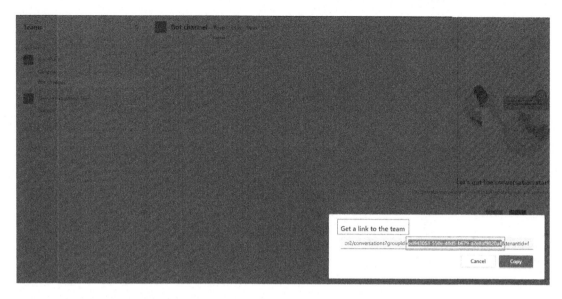

Figure 8-39. *Getting the teamId*

To get the ChannelId, click the ... icon after the General channel below the team. Click Get Link to Channel. Copy the GUID from channel/ until the next slash. See Figure 8-40.

Figure 8-40. *Getting the ChannelId*

Replace the characters 19%3a with : and %40 with @. For example, I replaced 19%3a1740ec0332f24802b31a31538e7801d4%40thread.tacv2 with 19:1740ec0332f24802b31a31538e7801d4@thread.tacv2 for the correct ChannelId.

So, now you have the teamId and ChannelId. Go ahead and put them in the respective places in the graph end point which is /teams/[*teamid*]/channels/[*channelid*]/.

Before packaging and deploying the extension to the App Catalog, we need to specify the permission requests in package-solution.json. Once we deploy this to the App Catalog, we need to go to the admin center and approve the requests.

Go to Config ➤ package-solution.json and put the following section of code into the solution object:

```
"webApiPermissionRequests": [
    {
      "resource": "Microsoft Graph",
      "scope": "User.Read.All"
    },
    {
      "resource": "Microsoft Graph",
      "scope": "User.ReadWrite.All"
    },
    {
      "resource": "Microsoft Graph",
      "scope": "User.ReadBasic.All"
    },
    {
      "resource": "Microsoft Graph",
      "scope": "Group.ReadWrite.All"
    },
    {
      "resource": "Microsoft Graph",
      "scope": "Directory.Read.All"
    },
    {
      "resource": "Microsoft Graph",
      "scope": "ChannelMessage.Send"
    } ,
```

```
{
    "resource": "Microsoft Graph",
    "scope": "Mail.ReadWrite"
}
]
```

Now go back to the project folder in the command prompt and execute `gulp build`. Once you've done that successfully, execute `gulp bundle –ship` and `gulp package-solution –ship` in that order. The solution will be packaged as the service-extension. sppkg file in the SharePoint ➤ solution folder.

Note   You can test the extension in Workbench like you did for the web part. But since we have Graph API calls in this extension, it won't work until the package-solution-json is deployed and the requests are approved in the Admin Center. After the initial deployment, you can always use Workbench for testing.

Now go to the App Catalog site ➤ Apps for SharePoint and upload the .sppkg file and deploy. Go back to the Workplace site ➤ Settings button ➤ Add an App, and select service-extension-client-side-solution. The extension will be installed and you can see the Notify Urgent Issue to Service Executives Channel command bar under the footer. But before you test that, you need to go to the admin center and approve the API access. We'll take a look at that next.

Note   The previously outlined steps for installing and deploying an SPFx extension are exactly like the one for installing and deploying an SPFx web part. In case you're unsure, you can refer back to the steps in Chapter 6 Developement Environment section.

Go to `https://admin.microsoft.com` and click SharePoint at the bottom to go to SharePoint admin page. Once there, click Advanced ➤ API access. Under Pending Requests, select each request one by one to approve it. Each of the requests will then go under Approved Requests, as shown in Figure 8-41.

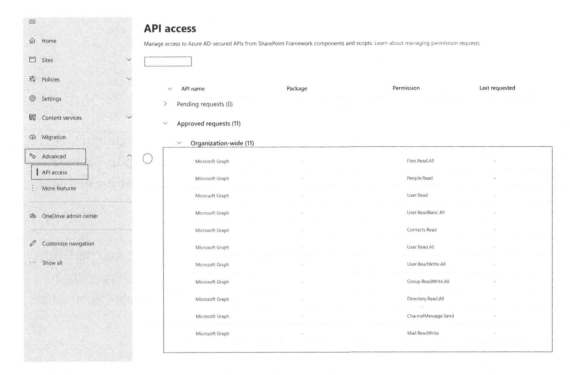

Figure 8-41. *Granting Graph API access for the package*

Now, go to the home page of the Workplace site, where you can see the Notify Urgent Issue to Service Executives Channel message in the footer of the screen, as shown in Figure 8-42. Click the command and you'll get an alert saying, "Message posted" in a few seconds.

Figure 8-42. *SPFx Application Customizer to communicate with Teams*

Next, go to Teams, Service Executives Team, then the General channel. You can see the message there! See Figure 8-43.

Figure 8-43. *Message posted to Teams*

Now you have successfully created an SPFx Application Customizer extension and used Graph to communicate with Teams. If a user wants to send an urgent message after raising a request to get an immediate attention, they can make use of this extension. You can make the message more dynamic by adding a text box, capturing its value by using state, and passing it on to the command. Also, you can make use of React toast notifications instead of alert.

Note   You can explore more about Microsoft Graph end points in Graph Explorer: `https://developer.microsoft.com/en-us/graph/graph-explorer`. Here, you'll get the whole set of end points Graph provides and an interface to test out queries.

Summary

In this chapter, you learned about Teams, Power Virtual Agents, and Microsoft Graph. We also discussed PowerShell and the SPFx Application Customizer extension on the path.

We started with an overview on Teams. You learned how to make use of App Studio to connect the SharePoint site to Teams. After that, you learned about Power virtual

Agents and how to create a chat bot and connect to Teams. We then went over Microsoft Graph and how to interact with Teams using Graph. You learned about how to create an SPFx extension and how to talk to Teams with the help of Graph. We satisfied some of the service portal business requirements in the process.

Throughout this book, our focus has mainly been on learning about SharePoint Online and different ways to develop using it. We learned about different customization and configuration options. We reviewed forms, workflows, and search. We learned about React, Power Platform, and Teams and how to make use of them for SharePoint development. We based our developments on a case study. Our approach to problem-solving focused more on the most modern and simple techniques. I hope you enjoyed the journey and please feel free to reach out to me if you have any questions. Thank you!

Index

© Harinarayanan V P 2021
Harinarayanan V P, *Building the Modern Workplace with SharePoint Online*,
https://doi.org/10.1007/978-1-4842-6945-9

Made in the USA
Coppell, TX
07 February 2022

73130733R00201